APPROPRIATE ENGLISH TEACHING FOR LATIN AMERICA

PAUL DAVIES

TESL-EJ Publications

ISBN: 978-0-9823724-3-2

CONTENTS

Preface   v
Introduction   vii

PART I
GENERAL ASPECTS OF ELT IN LATIN AMERICA
1. A Review of Two Surveys of ELT in Latin America   3
2. What's Special about English Language Teaching in Latin America?   13
3. The Most and the Least Successful ELT in Latin America   36
4. Affective Factors in Language Learning and Teaching   51
5. ELT Lessons from Europe   59
6. The Role of ELT Centres in Latin America   70
7. Teachers' Perceptions of ELT in Public Secondary Schools   78
8. What Should PRONI Teachers Really Do in Lower Secondary School?   94
9. Two Frameworks for ELT   103
10. ELT Futurology   139

PART II
SPECIFIC ASPECTS OF ELT IN LATIN AMERICA
COMMUNICATIVE SKILLS   151
11. Communicative Listening   153
12. Communicative Reading, and Language Learning Through Reading   160
13. Starting and Developing Communicative Speaking   167
14. Communicative Writing at Beginner-elementary Level   175
THE ENGLISH LANGUAGE   183
15. ELT as TEFL or TELF? Or Something Else?   184
16. Selecting Vocabulary   192
17. Exploiting Cognates   203

18. Teaching English Verb Patterns in Latin America   211
19. Working on the Pronunciation of English   220
20. Which English to Focus On?   232
     AIDS AND RESOURCES   239
21. Some Perspectives on EFL Textbooks   240
     TEACHER DEVELOPMENT   251
22. Actual ELT in Licenciaturas in ELT   252
23. Context and Learner-centred ELT Training   260
     ELT MANAGEMENT   267
24. ELT Coordination: Why and How   268
25. General Considerations for ELT Management   275
26. Management of ELT in Basic Education   283
27. Management of ELT in Higher Education   293
28. Management of ELT Centres   302

APPENDIX   313
About the Author   315

There are basic elements of ELT wherever it is practised around the world, but ELT should also vary significantly according to students' characteristics and needs, their learning contexts, their native language, and other factors, which may vary greatly from region to region and country to country.

All Latin American countries have most major factors related to ELT in common, but many are notably different from countries in Europe, Asia and Africa.

This book is about ELT specifically in Latin America, past, present and future.

INTRODUCTION

As its title states, this book is about English language teaching in Latin America, that is, *specifically* in Latin America—as opposed to ELT in Europe, the Middle East, Asia or elsewhere, or globalised ELT with little or no regional or local adaptation. Obviously, ELT almost everywhere has most ELT-related theory and ELT practice in common, but teaching English in Argentina, Brazil, Colombia, Mexico, Peru or any other Latin American country is significantly different from teaching English in The Netherlands, Germany, Egypt, Thailand or China, not to mention in an ELT centre in the UK or USA. For example, most of Latin America is distant from the USA, the UK, and indeed most of the rest of the world—even Mexico City is almost 1,000 kms from the nearest part of the US border (Texas) and almost 3,000 kms from the furthest part (California). Then there are socio-economic factors: an overwhelming majority of Latin Americans do not have the resources to travel or stay abroad, even just once in their lives. And there are linguistic factors: compared to Arabic and Japanese, and indeed most languages, Portuguese and Spanish have a lot in common with English, and both, especially Spanish, are widely used international languages, unlike Dutch and Japanese. All that, and more, affect the need most Latin Americans have of English (little or none for most Latin Americans, and more for use in the learner's own country than travelling and staying abroad for most of the important minority that do need English) as well as their motivation to learn English and their expectations of learning it successfully.

The articles on this topic area that are collected in this book are the product of a retirement project or hobby—an open-access online magazine for ELT professionals in Latin America called *English Language Teaching in Latin America*, and *ELTinLA* for short. Upon retirement, I kept myself happily busy for two years publishing 24 monthly numbers of *ELTinLA* between August 2018 and July 2020, with 38 of my own articles and 11 by other contributors, all with extensive ELT experience in Latin America. The magazine was perfect for me as my first retirement hobby and, I hope, was a useful last contribution of mine to a profession and a part of the world that have treated me extremely well. Note that the magazine was not intended to be mainly for ELT academics like most Applied Linguistics and ELT journals, but for classroom teachers, ELT coordinators and other practising ELT professionals of all kinds, up to and including ELT academics, and this book should reflect that broad, inclusive and essentially practical approach.

ELTinLA online magazine was itself the product of my 53 years of very varied ELT experience in Mexico (after an initial 2 years in Spain), with working trips to Guatemala, Costa Rica, Panama, Colombia, Ecuador, Peru, Uruguay and, above all, Brazil. In the decade or so before the end of my working (i.e., paid) ELT life, I wrote several articles on ELT issues specifically in Mexico and Latin America which were published in *MEXTESOL Journal* and one in *TESL-EJ*, and when full retirement finally came at the age of 79, ideas were still chattering away in my head, urging me to write them down. Those ideas were mainly about the long and continuing general failure of ELT in Mexico and other Latin American countries, especially, but not only, in public schools, but also about the satisfactory and even highly successful ELT in some places in Mexico and other countries, and about the reasons behind both the failure and the success.

Positive, negative, promising, disastrous, and yet-to-be-determined aspects of ELT in Latin America are presented and explored in this book. The real contexts, conditions and needs of the region, and the needs of its people, were always in my mind as I wrote the articles. The other contributors to *ELTinLA* online magazine also had Latin America and Latin Americans very much in mind, and their articles are referred to in this book where relevant.

As I've said, *ELTinLA* online magazine was published monthly from August 2018 to July 2020, which means that the last 6 numbers came out during the COVID-19 pandemic. My first response to that was in the editorial of the April number of the magazine, where I wrote, *"Happy Children's Day to the children in your life, and the child still playing in your heart! And, especially if you're 'getting on a bit' like me, may you get through this COVID-19 crisis fairly comfortably and come out of it ready to face whatever lies ahead"*. Three months later, in the editorial of the last number of the magazine in July, I referred to the pandemic again, mentioning that I was born in 1939, just before the beginning of *"the Second World War, the last massive global calamity before COVID-19. That's luck for you — global calamity at the beginning and at the end of a life! But I'm not complaining, only trying to make the most of it, just like you. That's life."* It is indeed life, and when my father came home from the War after my sixth birthday, life went on, but very differently from before the War and during the War. As I write this, eight months after lock-down was recommended for older people and people with health issues in Mexico, and elsewhere in Latin America, with almost 160,000 deaths in Brazil and 90,000 in Mexico and counting, and over 1,000 dead per 1 million population in Peru, the worst death rate in the world, the pandemic continues apace, with many serious issues related to it looming on the horizon. ELT is among the least of them, but it is one, and we should already be working on post-pandemic ELT.

I suggest we try to answer the following questions, and similar ones, with creative thinking, not just regurgitation of old, standard pre-pandemic answers:

1. *What proportion of all Latin Americans really need English and are prepared to put in the work usually required to learn it?* Note that most current (pre-pandemic) national English programmes in Latin America are based on the assumption that close to 100% do: that would include cleaning, construction, delivery, farm, home making, hospital, industrial, maintenance, restaurant, security, shop, traditional market, and all other workers, as well as professionals and skilled workers in certain industries like tourism.

2. *How can we best ensure that those Latin Americans who really do need English actually learn it?* Note that most current (pre-pandemic) national English programmes in Latin America seem to be based on the assumption that lots of classroom ELT for all school students is best (13 years in Mexico, starting in last year of pre-school), but after all those years of ELT most institutions of higher education start their students off at beginner level again. Many people who really need and want English turn to language centres, both in institutions of higher education and for the general public, and there's a plethora of online support for learners of English, most of it 'traditional' but some high quality, and this is sure to be even more important while the pandemic continues and after.

3. *How should ELT (and ELT materials) in Latin America differ from other parts of the world?* Note that most current

(pre-pandemic) ELT in Latin America follows 'international' models, especially based on the CEFR, and uses 'international' textbooks or local ones unthinkingly based on them. That ignores the similarities and differences between English and Spanish or Portuguese (lexis, grammar, pronunciation, usage) as opposed to German, Greek, Hungarian, Malay/Indonesian, Japanese, etc., and it also tends to ignore the real needs of Latin American learners of English (see 4 below).

4. *What English do most adult Latin Americans who need English actually need most?* Note that most current (pre-pandemic) national English programmes in Latin America seem to be based on the assumption that what is needed is English for social and transactional discourse like that in the USA and UK, and in international contexts, not English mostly for use in the learners' own countries, and for specific and occupational purposes, or for academic purposes, where reading is generally most important.

This book discusses and tries to answer those and other issues. I hope it will contribute something towards getting rid of most of the clearly inappropriate and downright bad (as well as extremely costly) pre-pandemic ELT in Latin America, and developing the more appropriate and better pre-pandemic ELT into English language teaching for a better future in Latin America as well as exploring new options.

PART I

GENERAL ASPECTS OF ELT IN LATIN AMERICA

"Presencia de América Latina" Mural by Jorge González Camarena

A REVIEW OF TWO SURVEYS OF ELT IN LATIN AMERICA

English in Mexico: An examination of policy, perceptions and influencing factors (British Council, 2015)

English Language Learning in Latin America (Cronquist & Fiszbein, The Dialogue, 2017)

Purpose and focus of the surveys

As stated in both surveys, after more than half a century of compulsory English classes in most lower and upper secondary education, two decades of expansion into higher education, and a decade or more of expansion into primary education, the results of ELT in Latin America are generally very poor, and quite inadequate for the aspirations of most countries. Both surveys presumably set out to identify key reasons for that, and present information and analysis to help Latin American countries make their national ELT plans and other English learning options more effective. Note that the British Council survey of English in Mexico is one of seven in *English in Latin America: an examination of policy and priorities*, which also has surveys of Argentine, Brazil, Chile, Colombia, Ecuador and Peru.

Both surveys present descriptions of government policies, plans and strategies (and some of the ideas behind them) as well as alternative ELT in the private sector, and large quantities of statistics and figures related to ELT in Latin America. The British Council (itself long engaged in ELT and ELT training and consultancy in Latin America) is more descriptive and informative, including a lot of information from original research, while Cronquist and Fiszbein (not themselves ELT experts, but well versed in national development issues, including education) enter more into evaluation and recommendations.

Information on English language teaching, learning and needs in Latin America

The two surveys contain much of the same (or very similar) information (with Cronquist & Fiszbein citing the British Council sixteen times). The surveys give information about:

- government ELT policies and plans (now covering 12 years for at least a few school students in most countries and for most school students in a few countries—from primary to upper secondary)
- the implementation, regulation, coherence and evaluation of ELT plans (mostly very deficient)
- the training, development and evaluation of teachers (mostly very inadequate for national ELT plans)
- the availability and uptake of private alternatives to public ELT (very significant for the middle classes but beyond the means of most of the population)
- ELT in higher education (improving, on paper at least, but not coherent or effective in many institutions)

- employers' demand for English-speaking employees (very high)

and so on.

Neither survey gives clear information about the level of functional English proficiency in the population, which is perhaps the best measure of national ELT success; the best available sources (e.g., Consulta Mitofsky in Mexico) suggest it's between 5% and 15%, depending on the country (about 10-12% in Mexico), compared with 22% in Spain, 27% in Portugal, 39% in France, 56% in Germany and 90% in the Netherlands (based on European Commission surveys), that is, very low and insufficient for most countries' needs. Cronquist and Fiszbein (p. 10), citing a source, say that "while 80% of job listings in Mexico require English proficiency, only 20% of professionals master the language"; that clearly refers to advertised professional and skilled work, so the percentage would be much less (10-12%?) if other work, informal sub-employment and unemployment were included to arrive at the national percentage.

Both surveys paint a generally unsatisfactory and costly picture, with some countries significantly better or worse than others, for example, Argentina and Honduras respectively, and a few areas of clear ELT success, for example, good private schools and good language centres. The picture shows virtually all Latin American countries trying to do roughly the same thing in their national ELT plans—provide all school students with English classes from the age of about 6 to 16 or above—with some providing additional English learning support through computers and online (e.g., CEIBAL Uruguay). Significantly better than past results have materialized in only a few countries, or places in countries, so far, for example, Argentina (not mentioned in Cronquist & Fiszbein is that Buenos Aires is treated separately in official statistics and, no surprise, it comes out far better than the rest of the country).

The British Council survey goes into things that Cronquist and Fiszbein don't consider or only touch on, for example, perceptions of the process of learning English, reasons for learning English, and reasons for not trying to learn English. An online survey of 1,000 Mexicans aged between 16 and 35 was used to get these data, but some of the data seems very odd. For example, answers to the question "Have you ever studied English?" (p. 30) come out at just under 80% for people in "healthcare support" (the highest percentage), just over 70% for those in "business and financial operations", just over 60% for "students" (haven't 99% of students over the age of 16 studied English at some time?), about 45% for the "unemployed" (doesn't English get you a good job?) and almost 0% for the "military". Perhaps the question was really "Have you ever paid to study English?" or something similar.

Looking behind, under and around the information

I said at the beginning of this review that the British Council survey is more descriptive and informative (though I've just questioned the validity of some of the information), while Cronquist and Fiszbein enter more into evaluation and recommendations. I'll go into that further here, with observations.

Both surveys present Latin American governments' typical reason for their massive and expensive national ELT plans, that is, that English is necessary in today's globalized world. The British Council quotes the Mexican educational authorities directly, without using their reasoning at all:

> '...contemporary society... demands citizens with the necessary competencies to face and incorporate into a globalized constantly-changing world. Basic education has the responsibility of providing students with the opportunity to develop these competencies. Thus, ... students need to acquire... at least one foreign language'. (p. 14)

Cronquist and Fiszbein echo that to some extent, but focusing on business and international communication rather than the whole population that goes through basic education:

> *English proficiency is increasingly necessary for business and international communication and... linked with prospects for economic competitiveness and growth in the global economy. Interest in learning the language continues to grow throughout Latin America... [which] has made considerable efforts to improve English language learning through policies and programs, resulting in more people in the region having access to English language learning.* (p. 3)

Both surveys seem to support universal English classes throughout basic education (and beyond), but the British Council perhaps more unquestioningly, or at least paying less attention to alternative and complementary ELT than Cronquist and Fiszbein (see below). It's up to me, then, to question universal English classes, from an early age and throughout basic education.

I strongly support Cronquist and Fiszbein's proposition of more "access to English language learning" (which means high quality ELT). However, I don't think compulsory English classes for everyone throughout basic education (much of it low quality ELT so far) is the best way to do it, and I don't think most Latin Americans actually need or want English. I also don't agree with some of the thinking (and perhaps lack of thinking) behind plans for universal English classes throughout basic education.

Successful additional language learning is dependent on need and motivation as well as good teaching. Almost all Dutch and Scandinavian people learn English because their languages are not spoken by the rest of the world, and most are rich enough to travel abroad frequently; they also have generally very good school ELT in good conditions. The French also have generally good ELT in fairly good conditions, and most can also travel abroad frequently, but only

39% learn English successfully: French is a major world language, and they simply don't need English so much as the Dutch and Scandinavians. Spanish is also a major international language, and only 22% of Spaniards learn English successfully. The percentage is lower still in Latin America: most Latin Americans don't have good English classes in good conditions, and most see English as hard to learn in their context and not necessary except for those aiming at fairly high level work, that is, the work that's available, or soon could be, for perhaps 25% of the population. The consequence is what we know, and what's reported in these two surveys: very poor ELT results.

However, 15-25% of Latin Americans, or more in some places (rather than the current 5-15%) really might benefit from knowing English, and their countries would benefit with them. The question, then, is how best to enable that 15-25+% to learn English, giving them access to high quality ELT and other learning support. The two surveys suggest that the main way is to continue to extend and improve national ELT plans, universal English classes throughout basic education (and beyond), which I've just argued against. Essentially, those plans imitate European ELT, but in very different and less favourable contexts, and they're based partly on two popular fallacies. One is "Everyone [in Latin America] needs English nowadays". That's not true at all. Everyone needs adequate nutrition, clothing, housing, health care, literacy and numeracy, and so forth, and everyone of working age and inclination needs a decent job, or at least one that pays essential living expenses; unfortunately, many people in Latin America don't have those things, over 40% of the population in some countries. Only 15-25% really need English and have employment opportunities that reward proficiency in English.

The other fallacy is "The earlier, the better [in second language learning]". That's only very partially true, so not really true at all. The earlier the better applies only in favourable language learning conditions, especially like in the Netherlands and Scandinavia, where everyone around the children can speak English and often does. Even then, it tends to improve native-like fluency and pronunciation, not general proficiency achieved as an older teenager or adult; many good non-native users of English didn't get beyond A1 level until they were older teenagers or young adults. In many Latin American contexts, early ELT can do more harm than good, turning many children off English for life.

While I welcome the ideas in both surveys to improve the quality of ELT in national plans (creating continuity in the ELT across levels of education, improving teacher competence, evaluating ELT practices and results, etc.), I don't agree with taking the extension of ELT to total coverage of all students in primary schools (or pre-primary). See my comments on "Everyone needs English nowadays" and "The earlier, the better". It would also mean investing precious and scarce resources in quantity rather than quality of ELT, and in ELT for the 70-80% of the population that doesn't and won't need English (as well as not wanting it). If 15-25% of primary school children will need English (and we don't know who will and who won't at that age), probably 20-30% of lower secondary school students, 30-50% of upper secondary school students, and 50+% of higher education students will need English: as young people advance towards work training, work and their adult lives, their need of English (or lack of need) becomes increasingly clear. ELT at older ages can target those who really need English and, given adequate quality and conditions, can be much more effective. It may produce fewer near-native speakers, but it can produce many more good speakers who actually need English with a similar investment to that in English classes for everyone from age 6 to 18.

Looking at alternatives and complements to ELT in basic education

Both surveys are devoted mostly to national ELT plans, that is, ELT in public basic education, but both do also look a little at ELT in higher education, in private education, and in language centres or academies. I was disappointed by the failure of the British Council to even mention public university (and other institutions of higher education) degrees in ELT and language centres; these are contributing more and more to ELT and to English learning, the language centres contributing significantly to the current 5-15% (future 15-25%?) of English speakers (mostly professionals, graduates from higher education). Cronquist and Fiszbein also fail to mention university and higher education language centres, but they do include university degrees in ELT among teacher preparation options. Good private schools also contribute significantly to the percentage of English speakers, of course, but they serve only, or mainly, the better-off middle classes, less than 10% of the total population in most countries.

Private language centres or academies are identified by both surveys as important ELT alternatives or complements to English in basic education and ELT options for adults: *Brazil trains millions of people annually in its private language institutions... 87% of middle class respondents stated that they had attended a private English institution... 400,000 Argentineans, or 40% of English language learners in the country..., study at private language institutes* (Cronquist & Fiszbein, pp. 18-19); *There are... upwards of 70 registered schools across the Mexican states, with a number of companies having multiple branches* (British Council, p. 26). Neither survey includes public university and other institution of higher education language centres, many of which serve the general public, including children and teenagers, as well as their own students. There's a public university in every Mexican state, most with language centres in every major city in the state.

Language centres, then, private (or commercial) and public, are an extremely important piece in the ELT jigsaw in most Latin American countries.

The British Council seldom goes beyond description and information, but Cronquist and Fiszbein often do. They see alternatives and complements to English in basic education as a possible way forwards: *While the focus of this report has been on ELL within the schooling system, it is imperative to look beyond formal education and consider ways of leveraging efforts at the school level with instruction in academies and independent training institutions, workplaces and households* (p. 59). I totally agree, and, moreover, I believe money for English classes for everyone in primary (and even pre-primary) education, would be much better spent on scholarships or coupons for classes in language centres—commercial, university, and Ministry of Education centres, for example, in schools outside school hours (Davies, 2009).

It would have been interesting and very useful if one or both of the surveys had researched how the current 5-15% of English speakers in Latin American countries started to be successful in learning English, but neither did. My bet would be that most started with classes in a private (or very exceptional public) school with good ELT, or in a language centre or academy, or with company classes and use of English, or with a bilingual childhood (bilingual family or residence in an English-speaking country), and only a very few with English classes in public basic education. Where would you put your money? The British Council and Cronquist and Fiszbein indicate where most Latin American governments are putting their money, and what the results are so far in very general terms. We need much more specific, detailed and reliable information about ELT in Latin America and about its results, good and bad (Davies 2020).

References

British Council Educational Intelligence. (2015). *English in Mexico: an examination of policy, perceptions and influencing factors*. In *English in Latin America: an examination of policy and priorities*. British Council. At www.teachingenglish.org.uk/article/english-latin-america-examination-policy-priorities-seven-countries.

Cronquist, K., & Fiszbein, A. (2017). *English Language Learning in Latin America*. The Dialogue. At www.thedialogue.org/wp-content/uploads/2017/09/English-Language-Learning-in-Latin-America-Final-1.pdf.

Davies, P. (2009). Strategic management of ELT in public educational systems. In *TESL-EJ*, vol.13, no.3. At http://www.tesl-ej.org/wordpress/issues/volume13/ej51/ej51a2/.

Davies, P. (2020). What do we know, not know and need to know about ELT in Mexico?. In *Revista Lengua y Cultura*, vol. 1, no. 2, Universidad Autónoma del Estado de Hidalgo. At https://repository.uaeh.edu.mx/revistas/index.php/lc/issue/archive

2

WHAT'S SPECIAL ABOUT ENGLISH LANGUAGE TEACHING IN LATIN AMERICA?

1. Latin America in a diverse world of ELT

Globalized ELT

English language teaching is a worldwide activity, from English language centres for foreign students and immigrants in English-speaking countries (Britain, the USA, Canada, Australia, Ireland) to primary and secondary schools in countries far away from where English is spoken as the national language, Argentina and Chile being almost as far away as you can get. Teaching English as an additional language (foreign, second, third or whatever) is always English language teaching, wherever and in whatever conditions it takes place, in spite of enormous differences in teaching-learning contexts.

In all cases, the students already have a first language, and sometimes a second one, that can both help and hinder them as they study English. In all cases, the English language has its particular characteristics, with variations of pronunciation, dialect and register, which students around the world, in different contexts, have to grasp, acquire and assimilate adequately if they're to be successful learners. All around the world, most of the literature on ELT methodology, widely used teaching-learning materials, and widely recognized proficiency tests come from the major English-speaking countries, mainly Britain and the United States, directly, or indirectly through imitation in different countries.

The historical reasons for the British and American dominance of ELT (with important contributions from Australia, Canada and elsewhere) began with English language teaching in British and American colonies (British in Africa and Asia, American in the Philippines and a few other places). Then came the spread of ELT beyond that, with many British and American teachers working abroad. In the USA and Australia ELT centres for immigrants were opened. Since the 1960s, there have been English language centres for foreign learners in Britain, the USA, Australia, and many people from abroad go to study English in them. All that produced a mass of English language teaching theory and methodology and materials development and textbook publication, and a lot of serious learning and teaching research. That historical and current thinking and activity is the bedrock of ELT around the world today.

Naturally, with British and American dominance of ELT, there's tended to be a one-size-fits-all character to much, if not most, ELT around the world, though not for all ELT methodologists and EL teachers, of course. Since the 1990s more and more theorists and methodologists have questioned the general uniformity, or conformity, of ELT and "native-speakerism", that is, the native-speaking teacher as the model for teaching and native-speaker English as the model of English to be taught and learned (Phillipson 1992, Holliday 1994, Pennycook 1994, Canagarajah 1999). All these people, and others with similar observations, had taught English or worked as ELT consultants in different countries and contexts around the world, Canagarajah in India at first.

Recognizing and responding to important differences in ELT contexts

Those theorists and methodologists (and, no doubt, many native-speaking EL teachers who had taught in two or more countries) recognized important differences that had been largely ignored. They included not only differences in ELT contexts, but also in the target English to be taught and learned. Why, they asked, should students around the world be expected to learn to speak and write like native Americans or Britons, when most of the English speakers they'll meet speak non-native English, with notable German, Japanese, Chinese, Scandinavian, Brazilian or other features? They saw English as an international language with many acceptable non-native variations (after all, there are many marked native varieties too—Irish, Scottish, London, New York, Mid-western, Texan, Australian, and so on).

But our focus here is on the very different contexts of ELT, in particular Latin American contexts. Obviously, teaching English to foreign students in Cambridge (England or Massachusetts) or to immigrants in New York or Sydney, is very different from teaching English in a technological institute in Rio de Janeiro or Lima, which again is very different from teaching English in a state secondary school in Beijing or Tokyo. Many differences have probably leaped immediately into your mind, perhaps including the following:

English language centre in Cambridge or Sydney: The students come from different countries and have different first languages, all their teachers are native-speakers of English who may not speak any of the students' native languages let alone all of them, the students have been placed in the course level they need, outside the classroom they're surrounded by English speakers.

Technological institute in Rio de Janeiro or Lima: The students are virtually all native speakers of Portuguese or Spanish, all or most of their teachers are Brazilian or Peruvian speakers of English, many students, if not most, are in a beginner or low elementary course for the third time in their lives, outside the classroom they have little contact with English unless they seek it out.

State secondary school in Beijing or Tokyo: The students are virtually all native speakers of Mandarin or Japanese, all or most of their teachers are Chinese or Japanese speakers of English, most students are in a beginner or elementary course for the first time, or, at most, the second time, outside the classroom they have little contact with English unless they seek it out.

Obviously, those different contexts call for marked differences in the English language teaching, apart from those inevitably imposed by the different contexts. Different approaches to ELT are required not only by the age of the students (young children, older children, teenagers or adults) and the type of teaching institution (basic education, higher education, language centre in an English-speaking country, language centre in the students' own country), but also by regions and individual countries. Spanish- or Portuguese-speaking Latin America is one such region, and the Arabic-speaking Islamic nations of North Africa and the Middle East constitute another, while another is Scandinavia (where 80+% of the population speak English, including virtually all the parents of the school children).

Responding to the different native language (or languages) of the students

The native language (or languages) of students is an important element in the learning of English, or any language. In one type of situation, English courses in English-speaking countries, there is little teachers can do about native languages (they usually have native speakers of many different languages in a group), and English is inevitably the language of communication in the classroom from the start, along with sign language and demonstration. Something similar occurs in many parts of Africa and Asia, where there are several local languages (in Nigeria or India the parents of some students may communicate in English because they have different mother tongues). That's not normally the case in Latin America, of course, where all the students and teachers usually have the same native language, Portuguese or Spanish. The temptation for students, and teachers, is to use the native language too much, and English not enough, especially for real communication. But there are other important considerations about native speakers of Portuguese or Spanish trying to learn English. Here's a question for you: Is it likely to be easier or more difficult for Latin Americans to learn English than for native speakers of German, or Russian, or Turkish, or Chinese? We'll look at the answer to that question, and others, next.

References

Canagarajah, S. (1999). *Resisting Linguistic Imperialism in English Teaching*. Oxford University Press.

Holliday, A. (1994). *Appropriate Methodology and Social Context*. Cambridge University Press.

Pennycook, A. (1994). *The Cultural Politics of English as an International Language*. Longman.

Phillipson, R. (1992). *Linguistic Imperialism*. Oxford University Press.

2. The students' native language: The gift of similar languages

Part 1 of this series of articles ended with the question: Is it likely to be easier or more difficult for Latin Americans to learn English than for native speakers of German, or Russian, or Turkish, or Chinese? The answer will obviously vary for specific learners (some people naturally find language learning easier than others), but consider where each group of speakers starts from—their native language:

- *The total energy of an isolated system remains constant.* (The Law of Conservation of Energy)
- In Portuguese and Spanish: *A energia total de um sistema isolado permanece constante.*

  La energía total de un sistema aislado permanece constante.

- In German: *Die Gesamtenergie eines isolierten Systems bleibt konstant.*
- In Russian: полная энергия изолированной системы остается постоянной. [Transcription: Polnay energiya izolirovannoy sistemy ostayetsya postoyannoy]
- In Turkish: *Yalıtılmış bir sistemin toplam enerjisi sabit kalır.*
- In Mandarin Chinese: 孤立系统的总能量保持不变 [Transcription: Gūlì xìtǒng de zǒng néngliàng bǎochí bù biàn]

Obviously, from this sentence (and most formal texts would show the same), the easiest additional language for native speakers of Portuguese is Spanish (which doesn't mean they won't have many challenges in pronunciation, grammar and vocabulary), and for native speakers of Spanish it's Portuguese (ditto, with an even greater challenge in pronunciation). Then, for both Portuguese and Spanish speakers, English is next, especially formal English, which tends to have many Latin- and Greek-derived cognates with Portuguese and Spanish. German, another European language, is probably next (but wait until you get into the grammatical inflections and the order of parts of the sentence!). The other languages are all far more difficult, including different script for Russian and Chinese. In principle at least, learning English, especially formal English, is distinctly easier for Portuguese and Spanish speakers than for Russian, Turkish or Chinese (and most other) language speakers because English, Portuguese and Spanish are relatively similar languages.

Views of language learning

There was a time when many of the leading applied linguists of the day thought that the successful learning of an additional language was largely a matter of recognizing the similarities and differences between the first and the target language and dealing with the differences (in pronunciation, grammar, vocabulary, etc.), that is, avoiding first language interference errors. This view was strong among behaviourist psychologists and structural linguists who saw language learning in terms of habit formation—learning new language as habits and modifying existing ones (Lado 1957, Skinner 1957). As structural linguists (before language was seen also in terms of conceptual notions and communicative functions), Lado, Fries and others related habits mainly to the handling of the forms and structures of language. They worked on the "contrastive analysis" of pairs of languages, one assumed to be the native language and the other the target language of learners. Most contrastive analysis was done on English and Spanish because those linguists were American, with English as their native language, and Spanish was the most widely spoken other language around them.

Contrastive analysis began to lose support (but has survived in different forms) when Noam Chomsky's (1959) postulation of a "language acquisition device" in humans, and new views of language learning, or acquisition, challenged the structural-behaviourist hypothesis. However, the interaction between the native and the target language in the learner's mind continued to be a theme in the new theories, particularly in error analysis and interlanguage theory (Pit Corder 1967, Selinker 1972). These theorists saw additional language acquisition as a gradual progress from a rudimentary version of the target language with a lot of first language interference to a developed version with little or, in exceptional cases, no first language interference. It's important to emphasize that interlanguage is evident when a learner is trying to communicate, but it may be suppressed in controlled classroom practice and exercises: remember how your students may get target grammar right in class, but when they come up to say something to you in English after class, they get the same grammar wrong!

So, for a time, most linguists said most errors were interference from the first language, then many said most errors were universal, irrespective of the learner's first language, and for a long time now, most say it's a mixture of both. In short, the similarities and differences between the first language and the target language aren't the only important factor in learning another language successfully, but they are certainly one of them. The many similarities between Portuguese or Spanish and English are highly significant. However, globalized English language teaching and teaching materials intended for worldwide use obviously can't attend to that factor: such materials are for native speakers of any language. Local course managers and teachers—you?—have to look after it.

How Latin American course managers and teachers can exploit language similarities

First, from the very start, they can give older children and, even more, teenagers and adults much more reading practice than most international textbooks contain, or than would be possible with most beginners around the world. A reasonably educated Mexican or Brazilian with almost no English can largely understand the following text, but Arabic, Russian, Turkish, Chinese or Japanese speaking beginners (and most beginners around the world) could not:

> In physics, the Law of Conservation of Energy states that the total energy of an isolated system remains constant, and its energy is conserved indefinitely over time. The implication of this law is that energy cannot be created or destroyed. It can only be transformed from one form to another.

So, the first special option for English courses in Latin America is much more reading from the very beginning (a special option, that is, in relation to English courses in most countries, like the countries with the languages mentioned above). More reading is especially appropriate in courses for older teenagers and adults, and in situations where students need formal English (and reading of formal English) more than everyday colloquial English, like in higher education and most professional or skilled work (there will be more on students' needs in the third article in this series).

Another area where English teachers and students in Latin America have special options or advantages (again, special in relation to English teachers and students in most other parts of the world) is work on the language itself, its lexis and grammar. A lot of English vocabulary is cognate with Portuguese and Spanish vocabulary, especially in formal discourse. Many teachers see false cognates as a big problem for students, but for every false cognate between English and Portuguese or Spanish there are many true or partial ones (partial in the sense of true in some contexts, but not in others). That's one thing that makes reading in English relatively easy for Portuguese and Spanish speaking beginners, and more difficult or impossible for speakers of other languages. Especially for academic, technical and professional vocabulary, Latin American learners have an enormous advantage over Arabic, Chinese, Russian and other language speaking learners. Teachers can point this out to their students, sometimes asking them to find all the cognate or possibly cognate words in a reading text.

The grammar of English is different from that of Portuguese or Spanish in many ways, but even there, the similarities are relatively great compared to German, and even more compared to Russian, Arabic or Chinese. Affirmative sentence structure (subject-verb-object) is usually similar, or can be (interrogative sentence structure is usually different, of course), which is not the case with many other languages.

Also, most compound verb phrases are similar, for example:

- *David is sleeping. Laura can come. Eric had arrived. This laptop was made in China.*
- *David está dormindo. Laura pode vir. Eric havia chegado. Este laptop foi feito na China.*
- *David está durmiendo. Laura puede venir. Eric había llegado. Esta laptop fue hecha en China.*

Note that the first example, the present continuous, does not exist in French or German, and the corresponding sentences would be in the present simple tense: *David dort. David schläft.*

These and other similarities between English and Portuguese or Spanish can be exploited when we focus on grammar and usage. When there is correspondence between English and native language structure and usage, we can prepare examples that clearly reflect that correspondence, and we can then ask our students if the English examples are similar to the corresponding sentences in their native language or different. We can do that also when there is no correspondence to native language structure and usage (to raise awareness of the difference), for example, the interrogative and negative of the simple tenses in English, with the *do-does-did* system, which is exclusive to English. Getting students to notice similarities and differences between English and their native language is common in "consciousness-raising", a technique used in Task-Based Learning. It's of little use when there are very few or no similarities, but when there are many similarities and also differences, as between English and Portuguese or Spanish, it can be very useful, particularly with older teenagers and adults.

So, in short, English language teaching in Latin America is special because of the similarities between English and Portuguese or Spanish (as opposed to English and most other languages), which can be exploited by teachers and learners, especially in reading, in vocabulary comprehension and development, and in grammar development.

But English language teaching in Latin America is special for other reasons also. In the third part of this article, we'll look at what's special about the learning context (or rather, contexts) in Latin America. Here's a question for you: In what ways, apart from native languages, is the context different for most English teachers and students in Latin America compared with the European Union (Portugal, Spain, France, Germany, etc.)?

References

Chomsky, N. (1959). *Review of Verbal Behavior by B. F. Skinner*. In *Language*.

Lado, R. (1957). *Linguistics Across Cultures*, University of Michigan Press.

Pit Corder, S. (1967). The Significance of Learners' Errors. In *International Review of Applied Linguistics*.

Selinker, L. (1972). Interlanguage. In *International Review of Applied Linguistics*.

Skinner, B.F. (1957). *Verbal Behavior*. Appleton-Century-Crofts.

3. Latin American teaching-learning contexts

ELT in Latin America and Europe: geographic, economic, and political differences

Part 2 of this series of articles ended with the question: In what ways, apart from native languages, is the context different for most English teachers and students in Latin America compared with The European Union (Portugal, Spain, France, Germany, etc.)? The answer depends on exactly which teachers and students we're talking about, of course (in state secondary schools, bilingual schools, higher education, etc.), but let's start with geography, economy and politics in general.

Parts of France, Belgium and the Netherlands are just two hours from London by direct train, and you can drive via a ferry in almost the same time, and London to Berlin or Prague by air is under two hours (like Mexico City to Monterrey or Sao Paulo to Brasilia). Europeans are, on average, three or four times better off than Latin Americans, so most of them can afford to travel and vacation abroad frequently, especially when "abroad" is very close. For the last quarter century, citizens of the European Union have been able to enter, live and work without a visa or permit in any of the member countries. Almost 3 million non-British European Union citizens were resident in Britain in 2017 (compare that with about 300,000 foreign residents, in total, in Mexico, which has double the population of Britain). That will change after Brexit, but massive travel between European countries will continue, for vacations, study, work, shopping and personal reasons. In 2017, around 20 million people from other European countries visited Britain, so you can imagine the number between all member countries of the European Union. And how do Germans communicate in Spain, Spaniards in Belgium, Belgians in Italy, Italians in Sweden? Most of them in English.

That European context for teaching and learning English (and other European languages) is very different from most of Latin America. Most Europeans have much more need and opportunity to learn— and use—English than most Latin Americans. How many of your Latin American students have been to an English-speaking country, even once? How many will ever go? The answer will probably be "Very few", perhaps even "Probably none". Unless, of course, you're teaching in a bilingual school, a top university, or similar. On the other hand, how many of your students may need English in their own country, for higher education, professional or skilled work, or communication with foreigners such as visiting experts, business people and tourists? Quite a lot, particularly if you're teaching in upper secondary school or above.

Obviously, not all English language teaching-learning contexts in Europe are favourable and not all in Latin America are unfavourable, nor is all ELT in Europe successful and all in Latin America unsuccessful. The best ELT in Latin America (in the best schools and language centres, and by the best individual teachers) is probably as good and, conditions permitting, as successful as that in Europe. And the worst ELT in Europe is probably not significantly better than the worst in Latin America.

However, the contrast in the general effectiveness of ELT in Latin America and Europe (and other parts of the world) is reflected in the proportion of the adult population with functional English. In Latin America the proportion of the adult population with functional English is not reliably known, but most estimates put it at between 5% and 15% of the adult population, depending on the country, with only Argentina probably above 15%. In Europe, the estimates, based on the Eurobarometer surveys of the European Commission, are much more reliable, and they give a very different picture: Spain 22%, Portugal 27%, France 39%, Germany 56%, Denmark and Sweden 86% and the Netherlands 90%.

Two important inferences, apart from what has previously been mentioned, can be made from the above statistics:

> Wealthier countries tend to do better than poorer ones; that's to be expected from their likely greater investment in education, better educational facilities, smaller maximum and average class size, ability of people to travel abroad, etc.

> Countries with important international languages tend to do worse than those with very "local" languages; again, that's to be expected, especially when added to wealth, because native speakers of Dutch and Scandinavian languages, for example, really need English for travel abroad, higher education, professional work, and so on, while speakers of Portuguese, French, German and, especially Spanish (with over 40 million speakers in the USA) need it less, or much less.

That means a lot of general motivation for learners of English in certain countries (e.g., the Netherlands and Scandinavia) and a lot less for most learners in other countries (e.g., Spain, Mexico and Colombia), and motivation is universally recognized as an absolutely key factor in successful language learning (and, therefore, teaching).

English in the "community", and learner expectations

The statistics on the percentage of the adult population that speaks English imply something extremely important in relation to motivation, and an associated factor, expectations about learning—or not learning—English. In many European countries, most school children expect to become functional in English, in virtually all Latin American countries most children don't.

In any school in the Netherlands or Scandinavia almost all the adults around the children speak English—their parents, relatives and neighbours, the school principal and all the academic staff, all the administrative staff, possibly even the maintenance and cleaning staff. Of course all the children are going to learn English! There's no question about it. Everybody learns English, period. It's similar, at least within the school itself, if not within all families and districts, for most schools in Germany, and then significantly less and less going south through France to Spain and Portugal. The students' expectations about learning English in any ordinary state school in the Netherlands and Scandinavia and most in Germany are like those of students in expensive bilingual schools elsewhere in the world.

Compare that with almost all schools in almost all cities and towns in Latin America (and other parts of the world, of course): few or hardly any of the adults around the children speak English—not even the school principal and the academic staff, even though they've been through basic education *and* higher education, with English courses all along the way. Of course, most children don't really expect to learn English! And most don't. And many, if not most, become confirmed in that expectation as they repeat beginner and elementary courses over and over, in each level of education, until they're eventually "pardoned" and start work without a functional command of English. Then, if a new job or a promotion in their current workplace later requires English, they may start once again, in an English language centre, paying this time, but now with strong instrumental motivation.

That repetition of beginner and elementary English courses happens (not just occasionally, but as a widespread pattern) for various reasons. One of them is that the established programs in primary, secondary, upper secondary and higher education actually repeat beginner and elementary levels, but that reflects the recognition that most students enter each level with little or almost no

English. Other factors may include very large groups, mixed level groups and little class time. But perhaps the most important factor is the lack of English in the school community, with few or none of the adults around the children and teenagers having a functional command of English even though they studied English at school when they were children and teenagers. Consciously or subconsciously, the children and teenagers are bound to expect the same to happen in their generation.

Creating positive teaching-learning contexts within existing contexts

Some schools and other institutions in Latin America (and in less favoured parts of Europe and elsewhere too) manage to avoid or get round the generally unfavourable ELT teaching-learning context around them. They set up as a bilingual or semi-bilingual school, or an English language centre (perhaps you're a teacher or manager in such a school or centre), with all or almost all the staff competent speakers of English, with students clearly progressing through the course levels, many up to upper intermediate or advanced levels and international proficiency tests, and with many English-speaking parents financing their children's path to English.

However, creating such an "ELT-L oasis" in unfavourable territory (e.g., most parts of Latin America, where almost all the children go to state schools) is difficult and/or expensive. But it isn't impossible. Imagine an English teacher in a public secondary school in a Latin American city (perhaps you can just think of yourself!), with a school principal or head teacher who doesn't speak English but would like to, and just one other person in the school who speaks English (the other English teacher). One day, the principal asks that first English teacher if she would give her private classes. The teacher agrees. The principal then suggests forming a group of school staff and parents interested in learning English, and involving the other English teacher. The principal and the two English teachers put their heads together, prepare a plan, and announce the English course, to be held in the school in the late afternoons. Now you continue the story, which I'll pick up in part 4, the last part of this article.

References

Consulta Mitofsky. (2013, January). *Mexicanos y los idiomas extranjeros.* Encuesta nacional en viviendas.

EF. (2017). *English Proficiency Index (Brazil).* At https://www.ef.edu/epi/regions/latin-america/brazil/.

European Commission, Eurobarometer. (2012).
Europeans and their languages. At http://ec.europa.eu/commfrontoffice/publicopinion/archives/ebs/ebs_386_en.pdf.

4. Conclusions

Concluding that story

Part 3 of this article ended with an unfinished story:

> *Imagine an English teacher in a public secondary school in a Latin American city (perhaps you can just think of yourself!), with a school principal or head teacher who doesn't speak English but would like to, and just one other person in the school who speaks English (the other English teacher). One day, the principal asks that first English teacher if she would give her classes. The teacher agrees. The principal then suggests forming a group of school staff and parents interested in learning English, and involving the other English teacher. The principal and the two English teachers put their heads together, prepare a plan, and announce the English course, to be held in the school in the late afternoons. Now*

you continue the story, which I'll pick up in the 4th, and last, part of this series.

If you read Part 3 and did your homework, you'll have your own continuation and conclusion of the story—it might even be a true story, about your school, and you. Different readers will have different versions, of course. Here's mine:

> *The course started with the school principal, her secretary, three subject teachers and four parents. That was three years ago. There are now three courses, at A1, A2 and B1 levels. Several people have passed Cambridge KET and two are about to take PET. Also, results in English for students in the school are notably better than three years ago and several have passed KET.*

That's a 'happy ending', but it really is possible in some parts of Latin America, especially where there's a lot of professional and skilled work available, some in international companies, and/or international travel and tourism. The authorities could help by giving preference or bonuses to teachers and school staff (especially school principals) who have passed recognized English proficiency tests.

However, that happy ending isn't so possible, or at all likely, in schools in most parts of Latin America, urban as well as rural. First, it requires one or more English teachers capable of getting students up to B1 level, and that isn't the case in many Latin American schools. Second, English is simply not needed by many people in many parts of Latin America because there are few or no jobs or opportunities there for people who speak English. That brings me to an important general matter, with political, educational, economic and human facets.

Latin American countries need more appropriate ELT plans and strategies

Many Latin American countries have embarked on and invested heavily in a national bilingual plan (national language + English), and some countries have made that explicit: Colombia Bilingüe, Panamá Bilingüe, etc. These are plans on the European model but without European economic and human resources or European contexts and school conditions, and with other more pressing needs crying out for more investment and more effective systems, like the reduction of poverty and the improvement of really key subject results in basic education. Compare these results in native language literacy, mathematics and science:

	Science	Reading	Mathematics
Germany	506	503	509
PISA average	493	493	490
Chile	447	459	423
Argentina	432	425	409
Colombia	416	425	390
Mexico	416	423	408
Brazil	401	407	377

Figure 1. Native language literacy, mathematics and science
(PISA 2015)

The fact is, English is not high priority for most people in Latin American countries, though it is, of course, for a very important minority. That's true also for many European countries: in France less than half the population speaks functional English (39%), in Portugal 27% and in Spain only 22%. Those statistics for France, Portugal and Spain come after over half a century of almost universal ELT in schools and almost three decades of the Common European Framework of Reference for Languages. But the fact is that most people in those countries simply don't need or want English. That's even truer for Latin America, though it does need many more people who speak English than at present—the 22% of Spain would be good, the 27% of Portugal even better.

Canada is an illuminating example of monolingualism vs bilingualism. It's a rich country with two official languages, English (the world's current lingua franca) and French (also internationally important, especially for Canada, which naturally has a special relationship with France). It may surprise you then to learn that only 17.9% of Canadians are English-French bilinguals (Statistics Canada, 2017). In dominantly English-speaking provinces the figure is lower (e.g., 11.2% in Ontario, 6.8% in British Columbia), though everyone has French classes at school. In dominantly French-speaking Quebec it is highest, but still below 50% (44.5%), even though everyone has English classes at school. Conclusion: when people really need a second language and have classes in it, they usually learn it, and when they don't really need it, most don't learn it, even with years of classes, even with the generally excellent school conditions of a country like Canada.

Latin America isn't Canada or Europe, yet most Latin American countries apply European-type foreign language teaching plans and strategies in basic public education, and seem to expect better results than those achieved in many European countries, for example, Portugal and Spain. There must be plans and strategies that are more appropriate for Latin America, which recognize Latin American socio-economic realities, including the reality that most Latin Americans don't and won't need English, while many that do need it or could benefit from it are not being taught English effectively during their school years.

If, for example, such unrealistic plans for universal bilingualism (6+ years of English classes for everyone in basic education) were not pursued and were cut back to 3 or 4 years, and much more were invested in high quality ELT for the 20-30% of the population that really needs or wants English, particularly through language centres with free classes for children and teenagers as well as paying classes for adults, the results might be a lot better, both for individual people and for the nation (Davies, 2009). In Latin America, language centre results tend to be much better than ordinary school English results because people themselves have chosen to study English, they are more motivated, and the conditions and atmosphere of language centres are usually more conducive to successful language learning.

Summing up

Over Parts 1, 2, 3 and now 4 of this series of articles, I've noted and discussed a number of special aspects of ELT in Latin America in some detail and made some suggestions for ELT plans, strategies and teaching, the last one immediately above this. They don't all apply to all ELT institutions and teachers in Latin America, but they do apply to most. Here's a summary:

While some English teaching-learning contexts in Latin America are suitable for globalized Anglo-American ELT or top European country ELT and excellent results are achieved (good bilingual schools, for example, get most of their students to B2 level or above and through international proficiency tests), *ELT in the vast majority of Latin American contexts can benefit enormously from the recognition of Latin American realities and the specific realities of each context, and the adaptation to them of ELT plans, strategies, materials and teaching.*

One important Latin American reality is that the native language of the students is Portuguese or Spanish, languages that are relatively similar to English, while the international or international-type textbooks they use don't (and can't) take the L1 of students into account. *ELT managers and teachers in Latin America should take L1 into account, giving teenagers and adults much more reading, especially fairly formal texts*, from beginner level than is usual in textbooks, and* *helping them notice and exploit similarities between L1 and English, in grammar and particularly in vocabulary.*

*The more formal and technical the texts, the greater the similarity between English and Portuguese or Spanish.

A second important Latin American reality is that, especially compared with European countries, very few Latin American students, or even successful learners, of English will travel and use English outside their own country, while the international or international-type textbooks they use tend to focus on everyday social and transactional communication in English-speaking countries or international travel. *ELT managers and teachers should make sure students also (or instead) get practice of communication in the situations they're really likely to encounter, from talking about their own city and country with foreign visitors (perhaps as a tourist guide) to talking business with foreign executives, experts and customers in their place of work, and reading for professional development. The English appropriate for such situations is likely to be more formal than the colloquial native-speaker English in some textbooks, and many foreigners will not be native speakers of English.*

A third important Latin American reality is that most schools and many institutions of higher education don't have 'an English speaking community' in and around them; often the English teacher or teachers are the only people who speak English in a school, and the students naturally expect *not* to learn English, just like the school principal, other subject teachers, administrative staff, parents and older siblings. This is a reflection of another, fundamental, reality: most Latin Americans simply don't and won't need or want English, and the 20-30% that do tend to be in contexts where there's work and opportunity for English speakers (international manufacturing and business, travel and tourism). *Where possible, educational authorities, ELT managers and teachers should try to create an English-speaking community in and around* schools. Where not possible, English probably doesn't matter, except to the few students with ambitions beyond their immediate environment, and special provisions should be made for such students, at least when they reach upper secondary education.

References

Davies, P. (2009). Strategic management of ELT in public educational systems. In *TESL-EJ*, vol.13, no.3. At http://www.tesl-ej.org/wordpress/issues/volume13/ej51/ej51a2/.

Organisation for Economic Co-operation and Development. (2015). *PISA 2015: Results in focus.* At https://www.oecd.org/pisa/pisa-2015-results-in-focus.pdf.

Statistics Canada / Statistique Canada. (2017). *English-French bilingualism reaches new heights. At* https://www12.statcan.gc.ca/census-recensement/2016/as-sa/98-200-x/2016009/98-200-x2016009-eng.cfm.

3

THE MOST AND THE LEAST SUCCESSFUL ELT IN LATIN AMERICA

The focus of this article is on ELT in institutions or systems such as schools, institutions of higher education, language centres and company courses, not on the ELT of individual teachers, though they're obviously an essential element in successful ELT in institutions and systems.

Successful ELT: What is it and where is it?

ELT is clearly successful where it consistently and continually helps most students in a system of English courses progress towards an adequate functional level of English. That level varies for different people: around B1 level may be adequate for people who need and want English only occasionally and for basic communication in international travel, brief encounters with foreigners and such, but those who use English a lot in their higher studies, their work and their lives in general need higher levels of proficiency.

Successful ELT, producing good learning results, starts by helping most beginners in English courses progress to low elementary level

(A1.2), then mid elementary (A2.1), then high elementary (A2.2), then low intermediate (B1.1) and intermediate (B1.2). Around then, where CEFR 'independent user' levels begin, and sometimes a bit earlier, many people develop their English further simply by using it, but others choose or have to take more courses to push their progress forwards. That kind of progress in English happens consistently in courses in some educational institutions or systems but not in others, which is the case in far too much ELT in Mexico and the rest of Latin America.

Assuming that the success of ELT is reflected in learning results, most ELT in Latin America hasn't been and isn't being successful. Although English has been a compulsory subject in all lower secondary and upper secondary schools in most Latin American countries for over 50 years, in many universities for 20 or 30 years, and now progressively in more and more public primary schools, the most reliable estimates of the percentage of adults with a functional command of English are very low. They vary greatly from country to country, of course, with Argentina almost certainly highest, possibly at around 20%. Below are examples of surveys for Mexico, Peru, Brazil and Chile. It isn't clear what "speak English", "know English", "have some knowledge of English" and "speak [English] with relative fluency" mean below, but we can assume it's around B1, where CEFR 'independent user' levels begin, or higher.

- 11.6% of the adult population of Mexico speaks English (Consulta Mitofsky 2013)
- In Peru, "only 8% of those surveyed declared that they knew [English]" (GfK Perú 2015)
- "In Brazil, 5.1% of the population aged over 16 state that they have some knowledge of the English language" (British Council 2013)
- "A study by the Universidad de Chile and Ministerio de Educación reveals that only 2% of over 15-year-olds has an

advanced level of English and 6% speaks with relative fluency" (Economía y Negocios Online 2008)

The above percentages, ranging between around 5 and 12%, are almost certainly below what can be considered the percentage of successful ELT in different countries because many people who eventually attain a functional level of English have a mixed experience along the way, at times stagnating or going backwards instead of forwards. For example, four siblings may learn quite a lot of English in a lower secondary school (successful ELT), stagnate in English in a different upper secondary school (unsuccessful ELT), forget much of their little English after leaving school, and then two of them eventually get to and beyond B1 level in a university language centre (successful ELT) while the other two don't and stay among the mass of Latin American adults without a functional level of English or with virtually no English at all.

Though it's very far from sufficient, successful ELT in Latin America is extremely important: with even less of it than now, the percentages of adults with a functional level of English would be even lower, with negative consequences for individual people and for countries.

Here are five types of place where ELT in Latin America is usually notably successful:

1. **Bilingual schools**, with several curricular subjects taught in English or partly in English.
2. **Schools with 'value-added' ELT**, with a team of competent and well-coordinated teachers, possibly more than the minimum of 3 hours (or three 50-minute classes) of English a week, and even a little CLIL (Content and Language Integrated Learning, i.e., subject teaching in English)
3. **Language centres**, in universities and other institutions of

higher education, bi-cultural centres, commercial language centres.

4. **Curricular English in higher education**, for example in degrees in Tourism, International Relations, International Commerce, and, of course, ELT, where students often start with very low level English.
5. **Company English courses**, in a company language centre or for different staff areas.

A degree of success in ELT is also achieved in other places, of course, both in some institutions, especially schools, and by good individual teachers. In fact, outstanding teachers may achieve some success even in quite unfavourable conditions such as schools with large groups in isolated towns or disadvantaged areas of large cities. However, their success is usually only with exceptional groups and with some highly motivated and linguistically gifted students in other groups, and if the other English teachers in the institution or system are doing bad and/or unsuccessful ELT, the ELT in the institution or system as a whole is unsuccessful.

The successful ELT in the five above-mentioned types of place almost certainly provides a major portion of the adult population in Latin American countries that 'speaks' or 'knows' English, though some get their English from other sources or experiences. These include temporary residence in the USA or elsewhere (particularly in the case of returnees to Mexico and Central America), an environment of English speaking parents, relatives and friends (like in my family and perhaps yours), informal work with foreigners (for example, in international tourist centres like Cancún, Cuzco/Machu Picchu and Rio de Janeiro), and, as mentioned above, classes with outstanding teachers in schools that aren't very favourable or are distinctly unfavourable for ELT.

Why is ELT in certain types of place generally successful, and in others not?

Good ELT depends on competent and diligent teachers and good coordination of courses, along with appropriate syllabuses, methodology and materials. When all those elements come together, successful ELT might be expected, with most students moving steadily ahead in their learning of English, course by course. However, that isn't always the case, as many a competent and diligent teacher knows well after working in difficult conditions, such as all the other English teachers not being competent and diligent and large groups of unmotivated students. Successful ELT depends on other things apart from good ELT, most of them related to context, and while very good teachers can improve on inappropriate syllabuses, methodology and materials by modifying them, they can't usually change the context within an institution much, and they can't change the wider context beyond the institution at all.

Consider first the very different contexts for ELT within two schools in Mexico, the first one generally positive for ELT and the learning of English and the second one generally negative:

INTERNAL CONTEXT 'P'

The school principal is fluent in English, and all academic and most administrative staff have at least B1 level English.

Most parents speak English, some very well, many being ex-students of the school.

There's a 50-minute English class daily, that is, 4 hrs10 mins a week, and three subject teachers are required to do a 15 to 20-minute activity in English each week.

Maximum group size is 30 students.

The principal and other staff often use English around the school, including with students.

Students in lower years see students in the years above them learning more and more English and leaving school fairly fluent in it.

Because of all that, almost all students' initial expectations and motivation about learning English well are high and increase continually.

————

INTERNAL CONTEXT 'N'

The school principal and the staff, apart from the English teachers, have no more than false-beginner English.

Almost no parents know English, though most had at least 3 years of English classes at school.

There's a 50-minute English class three days a week, that is, 2 hrs 30 mins a week, and virtually no English at all is used in the school outside the English classes.

Group size is often 40 or more students.

The principal and other staff are uncomfortable when English is spoken in their presence.

Students in lower years see students in the years above struggling with English, learning little, and most leaving school quite lost in English.

Because of all that, almost all students' initial expectations and motivation about learning English well are low and fall continually.

———

Now consider the wider context around those two schools, the first one again generally positive for ELT and the learning of English and the second one generally negative:

———

EXTERNAL CONTEXT 'P'

The school is in a historic metropolitan city with major industries, and there's an international airport not far away.

The city receives many foreign visitors and there are services and provisions for them.

The city has many institutions of higher education and vocational training.

There are many employment opportunities in the city that require English or could use it.

Because of all that, English is often heard in the city, quite a lot of local adults know English and use it in their studies, work and lives, and most older school students recognize its possible importance in their future lives, as in the lives of the parents and older siblings of some.

EXTERNAL CONTEXT 'N'

The school is in a fairly large but quite isolated town in a mainly agricultural area with a little domestic industry.

The town very rarely receives foreign visitors and there are no services or provisions for them.

There's only a regional technological institute a 2-hour bus ride from the town.

There are virtually no employment opportunities in the town or area that require English.

Because of all the above, English is very rarely heard in the town or area, very few local adults know English, those mostly returnees from the USA, and most school students, even older ones, see very little likelihood of English being important in their future lives.

Imagine for a moment that all the English teachers in both schools are very similar in terms of their command of English, their ELT competence, and their diligence. Even in that case, much better English learning results are to be expected in the school with Contexts P than in the school with Contexts N, not because of the ELT itself in each school but because of the contexts of the ELT, internal and external to each school.

But the above hypothetical similarity between the English teachers in both schools is very unlikely in reality, of course. The school with Contexts P is clearly Type 2 in the list of five types of place with successful ELT above—a school with 'value-added' ELT. As such, it almost certainly has English teachers with strong English and ELT competence, and also strong ELT coordination—otherwise the school wouldn't really have 'value-added' ELT. And the school with Contexts N, is very unlikely to be able to attract highly qualified and ambitious English teachers, so most are likely to have rather weak English and to be not very competent in ELT, or very motivated. Put those different teachers and the resulting different ELT together with the different contexts, internal and external, and you almost certainly have very successful ELT in one and generally unsuccessful ELT in the other.

Like the above example, a school with 'value-added' ELT, the other four types of place in my list of where ELT in Latin America is usually notably successful—bilingual schools, language centres, curricular English in higher education, and company English courses—also usually have the advantages of both fairly high quality ELT and contexts favourable for ELT and English language learning,.

Bilingual schools, for example, usually have all the advantages of that school with 'value-added' ELT, and more, especially more exposure to and focus on English through more hours of subject teaching in English and more extra-curricular activities and events.

Language centres usually have high quality ELT, an environment in which English is seen (in posters, notices, etc.) and heard (among staff and more advanced students), and most of the students are studying English voluntarily, motivated by need and/or high expectations of learning English well, like the more advanced students around them; the wider context, usually in a city, generally includes opportunities for higher education studies and then professional work that require English.

Curricular English in higher education degree programmes is even more firmly set within the context of higher education and then professional work requiring English, and usually has at least an element of English for Specific Purposes (ESP), responding to the students' needs in their present and future life contexts and ambitions.

Company English courses are usually carefully thought out to serve the needs of the company and its employees, and most employees are motivated to learn English not only because success will further their careers in the company but also because failure will jeopardise them.

All five types of place, then, usually have good ELT (and often more hours of ELT, perhaps including CLIL or ESP, than in regular schools) as well as favourable contexts for ELT and English learning, both within the institution or system and around it. In addition, many such places exploit the internal and external contexts in order to favour the success of the ELT. For example, bilingual schools usually have extra-curricular activities and events in English involving not only English teachers and students but also other English speaking staff and English speaking parents, and relationships with institutions of higher education and local employers where English is widely used, perhaps involving visits by students to those places and talks in the school by representatives of those places. English courses in universities, either in a language centre or curricular courses in degree programmes, may have a strong element of academic English (EAP), as opposed to purely English for general purposes, and/or ESP related to the degree studies and future professional work of the students.

Most successful ELT, then, is not only of good quality in itself and, ipso facto, appropriate for specific types of student, but it also usually benefits from a favourable context within the institution that's doing the ELT and a favourable wider context around it, and it exploits the potential synergy across the ELT, the internal context and the external context:

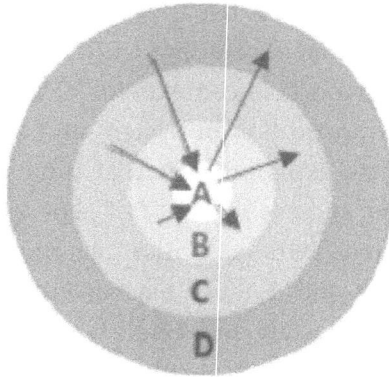

Figure 2. ELT Students and contexts

A—Students as individuals, groups, and populations (age, nationality, etc.)

B—English courses, in classrooms and beyond (homework, online, etc.)

C—Institutional context: school, higher education, language centre, etc.

D. Wider context, local, regional, national

↘ 'Messages' to students, positive and negative, from B, C, and D

↗ 'Reactions' from students, positive and negative, to 'messages' from B, C, and D

———

The 'messages' to students from B, C and D may include:

- "These English classes are for your real lives" OR "English is just another compulsory subject".
- "All the staff know English, it's important" OR "Only the

English teachers know English, it doesn't matter".
- "Students in higher courses know English well" OR "Students in higher courses don't know much English".
- "Most people in your family know English" OR "No one in your family knows English".
- "Most successful people around here know English" OR "Even successful people don't know English".
- "You'll need English in most jobs you aspire to" OR "There are no jobs requiring English around here".

The reactions of students to 'messages' from B, C and D may include positive or negative expectations and motivation, which are keys to successful learning of another language:

- "I see how English could be useful for me" OR "I don't see how English is likely to be useful for me".
- "It's normal for people to know English" OR "It's rare for people to know English, even professionals".
- "I expect to learn more and more English in higher courses" OR "I don't expect to advance in English".
- "English can help me be successful in life" OR "I can be successful or OK in life without English".
- "English will get me a much better job" OR "English won't get me a job around here".

What about all the ELT in Latin America that isn't notably successful?

I've focused so far mainly on five types of place where I believe ELT in Latin America is "notably successful" and which I believe "almost certainly provide a major portion of the adult population in Latin American countries that 'speaks' or 'knows' English", while also noting that some people get their English from other sources and experiences, including individual good English teachers, sometimes even in quite unfavourable contexts. That paints a picture something like this for ELT in Latin America:

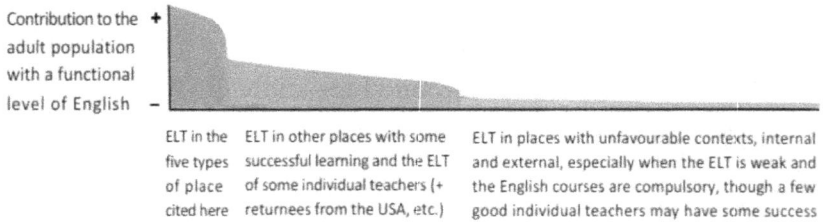

Figure 3. Contribution to the adult population and a functional level of English

In other words, most of the ELT in Latin America is largely or almost totally unsuccessful, even where some teachers are making a laudable effort and doing the best job possible under the circumstances, and it contributes little to the creation of adults with a functional level of English. Most of that unsuccessful ELT is in public schools and weaker private schools, especially in local and regional contexts where English is hardly ever used and there's very little higher education and work requiring English.

The results of ELT in less successful places can usually be improved a bit, sometimes substantially. ELT itself can be improved almost anywhere, though usually at some cost, and the contexts within institutions and systems can also be made more favourable for ELT and English learning. For example, that can be done where almost nobody except the English teachers have more than false beginner English by establishing a policy of giving bonuses to existing staff who go back to studying English and pass a recognised proficiency test at B1 level or higher, and giving preference to candidates to join the staff who have such a certificate. However, the context around the institution or system can't be changed much at all: if there are lots of higher education and work opportunities that require English in the local area or region, splendid, if there aren't, bad luck. In some contexts, ELT is simply doomed to general failure largely because, in those contexts, English is usually hardly used or needed at all.

Summing up and concluding

ELT in institutions and systems is clearly successful where it consistently and continually helps most students in English courses progress towards an adequate functional level of English, which for most people is at least B1, where CEFR 'independent user' levels begin. Assuming that success in ELT is reflected in the percentage of the adult population with a functional level of English, most ELT in Latin America hasn't been and isn't being successful since there's only between around 5 and 12% of adults at that level in most countries according to surveys and estimates, with Argentina a high outlier at around 20%.

Success in ELT depends on the quality of the ELT itself (competent and diligent teachers, good coordination of courses, appropriate syllabuses, methodology and materials) but also and very significantly on the contexts around the ELT and the students (as well as the language learning capacity and motivation of individual students, of course). The internal context within an institution can be very favourable (most staff members knowing English, English being used around the institution, students in higher level courses showing they've learnt a lot of English, etc.) or very unfavourable (only the English teachers knowing English and some not very confidently, no English being used in the institution outside the English classes, students in higher level courses showing they've learnt little English and don't like the 'subject', etc.). The wider context outside the institution can also be very favourable (many English speakers in the community and region, many opportunities in higher education and work requiring English, English used a lot with foreign visitors, international industry and business, etc.), or very unfavourable (very few English speakers in the community and region, almost no opportunities in higher education and work requiring English, very few, if any, foreign visitors, etc.). The internal context within an institution can sometimes be made a little more favourable by promoting English among all the staff or similar, but the wider context can't.

The internal and external contexts tend to have a great impact on the expectations of students about actually learning English and their motivation to work at it. That affects the results of ELT enormously, making some very successful and some very unsuccessful and hardly worthwhile at all. In the latter case, which is mostly but not only in schools, few students are likely to ever need English in their lives, because of the wider context in which they find themselves, and those that eventually find they do need English are far better served by language centres, which usually have generally successful ELT.

References

British Council. (2013). *Learning English in Brazil*. At https://www.britishcouncil.org.br/sites/default/files/learning_english_in_brazil.pdf

Consulta Mitofsky. (2013, January). *Mexicanos y los idiomas extranjeros*. Encuesta nacional en viviendas.

Economía y Negocios Online. (2008). Sólo 8% de los chilenos habla inglés. At http://www.economiaynegocios.cl/noticias/noticias.asp?id=49795

GfK Perú. (2015). Press release: Perú ¿país de bilíngües? At https://www.gfk.com/es-pe/insights/press-release/peru-pais-de-bilinguees/

4

AFFECTIVE FACTORS IN LANGUAGE LEARNING AND TEACHING

In another article (Davies 2019), I wrote about the potential impact of context on the results of ELT: where English is widely spoken in an institution and students in higher courses have clearly learnt a lot of English ELT results are likely to be much better than where English is known only by the English teachers and students in higher courses clearly haven't learnt much English, and also where English is widely used and needed in the community and region as opposed to where it isn't. In this article I focus on the potential impact of affective factors on the results of ELT. Putting contextual factors, affective factors and ELT together, we have something like this:

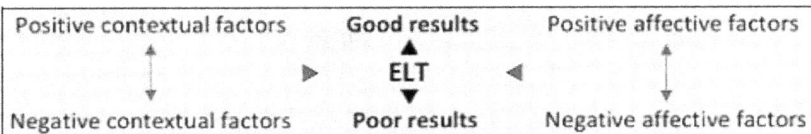

Positive contextual factors	Good results	Positive affective factors
▲	▲	▲
⋮ ▶	**ELT**	◀ ⋮
▼	▼	▼
Negative contextual factors	**Poor results**	Negative affective factors

Figure 4. Affective factors and ELT

In other words, while ELT may be considered of good or bad quality according to syllabuses, materials, methodology, teachers, etc., the effectiveness and the results of ELT depend significantly on other things also, including contextual factors and affective factors. The last two probably account to a considerable extent for the much greater general success of ELT and English language learning in Scandinavia and the Netherlands compared with France and Spain in Europe, and also Latin America, which in addition faces greater socio-economic challenges. In particular, contextual factors can have a significant impact on expectations of learning English (most Swedish and Dutch children expect to learn English successfully, most Spanish and Mexican children don't) and motivation to learn it. Expectations and motivation about learning English are, of course, among the affective factors in learning and teaching a foreign language, or almost anything.

Unfortunately, many ELT professionals largely ignore both contextual factors and affective factors and focus on the quality of ELT itself, and usually English for general purposes for any students anywhere (or English for no specific purposes for no specific students anywhere), with more learner-centred teaching only for children, who demand something more specific from teachers with any sensitivity at all, fun English at the very least.

Affective factors in language learning

Arnold (2011) writes that "basically affect is related to 'aspects of emotion, feeling, mood or attitude which condition behaviour'", and, in order to relate that more to language learning, she quotes Stevick (1980), who observed that "success [in language learning] depends less on materials, techniques and linguistic analysis and more on what goes on inside and between people in the class-room". She goes on to write that "positive affect can provide invaluable support for learning just as negative affect can close down the mind and prevent learning from occurring altogether". Referring to Krashen's (1985) metaphor of the affective filter, Arnold emphasizes that "just as important as avoiding negative affective reactions is finding ways to establish a positive affective climate.

To a large extent, a positive affective climate exists now (but not 50 years ago) in and around Scandinavian and Dutch schools, though it naturally varies for individual students of English. All the school staff speak English quite comfortably, as do almost all the parents, older siblings and relatives of the younger students, and almost everyone in the community, and indeed the whole country—of course the students are going to learn English fairly well. Children, teenagers and adults play games in English, listen to songs in English (including songs by ABBA, Ace of Base, A-ha, Anouk, Björk, Robyn, Roxette, etc., etc.), watch TV and films in English, and so on—of course the students are going to use English to participate in those activities. English is a national second language and learning it is almost like learning the first language, though we shouldn't forget that some people have more trouble than others articulating their thoughts in their first language, let alone their second language, especially in front of several or many other people, so teachers still have to work at maintaining a positive affective climate in their classrooms. Much of the above may apply in some other European countries, such as Germany and Greece, and in bilingual schools everywhere, including Latin America.

However, some European countries, or parts of them, and most of Latin America are very far from that, especially in isolated rural areas and in impoverished urban areas. Few people speak English there, and few learn it successfully in school, no matter how many years of classes they receive. Students' expectations of learning English and their motivation for learning it tend to be low from the start, and as the years of English classes pass, especially where the classes are compulsory, they find their self-esteem as learners of

English going down and their inhibition, anxiety, even fear, and negative attitudes in general towards their English classes and the English language going up.

Optimists and some ELT theorists assert that National English Programmes like those that have been spreading around Latin America for two or more decades now will eventually turn Latin America into an English-as-a-second-language zone like Scandinavia and the Netherlands, or at least an English-as-a-very-widely-spoken-foreign-language zone like Germany and Greece. However, realists tend to doubt that will ever happen, not because of the quality of the ELT, though socio-economic factors still hold that back in Latin America, but more because of contextual factors and affective factors.

Unfortunately, some contextual factors cannot be changed at will and are unlikely ever to change much: distances and some local isolation will always be great in much of Latin America and relatively small in Europe, and Spanish, and to a lesser extent Portuguese, are likely to continue as international languages indefinitely and most European languages as national languages only (Bulgarian, Czech, Danish, Dutch-Flemish, Estonian, Finnish, Greek, Hungarian, Italian, Latvian, Lithuanian, Norwegian, Polish, Romanian, Serbo-Croat, Slovak, Slovenian, Swedish). The same is true of affective factors, especially where they're related to contextual factors: English language learning expectations and motivation are likely to continue generally high in much of Europe and generally low in most of Latin America, and self-esteem, feelings and attitudes related to the study of English are likely to continue generally negative in most of Latin America and generally positive in much of Europe.

Even so, much can be done in Latin America to improve the affective climate in many schools and ELT contexts, as well as in individual classrooms, and something can be done in most, though far from all. I refer you to Arnold (2011) for a comprehensive discussion of affective (and cognitive) factors in foreign language learning, and continue below with a list of some of the many practical ideas for creating a more positive affective climate in classrooms and institutions and attending to individual students.

Attention to affective factors in language learning

Start lessons with activities that are virtually guaranteed to be successful, for example, chatting with the group in already familiar English about already familiar topics, getting students to respond physically to familiar instructions (TPR), repeating a familiar pair or group activity. In other words, start by focusing on what the students can already do successfully rather than on what they still have to learn to do.

Modify or substitute textbook activities to attend to what specific groups of students really need to do in English (if they actually need to anything at all in English outside the classroom) and/or what they seem to like and be good at doing. In other words, make English courses as relevant and satisfying as possible for students, not just a compulsory academic subject.

Be encouraging and sensitive in feedback on student production, spoken and written, responding to *what* students say in English not just *how* they say it. Both recognition of success (which is often partial, not total) and attention to problems (and correction as appropriate) should be seen as processes extending through the whole course, not one-off moments or actions in a specific lesson, and different students may require slightly different approaches, more or less sensitivity.

Work at creating a collaborative, supportive and tolerant atmosphere in your groups, with success in learning English perceived as something to be aimed at and achieved by all students in the group, to slightly varying degrees, not a notorious contrast between 'succeeding students' and 'failing students' with the rest struggling anxiously in between.

Err on the side of generosity rather than rigorousness when giving grades, though this must be balanced against providing students, other teachers and the institution with adequate information about real levels and progress in English. This starts with tests that give credit for success in communication, receptive and productive (like most international proficiency tests nowadays), and don't focus too heavily on linguistic accuracy.

Where only the English teachers in an institution know English above A1 level or so, encourage other members of staff to work on their English and use it around the institution: provide English courses for staff, organize English song festivals, English poster exhibitions, and other cultural and social events involving English, and so on. In other words, get the director and the staff of the institution to set an example for the students and make English 'present and normal' in the institution.

All the above ideas focus on creating a positive affective climate for groups and students in general. However, in the final analysis, language learning is a highly personal matter, with different learners affected to different degrees and in different ways by inhibition or self-assurance, anxiety or serenity, and other feelings, negative or positive, about learning English. It's important, then, for teachers to try to know their students not just as 'good', 'average' or 'bad' students of English, but also for their personalities and sensibilities, their ways of interacting with teachers and other students, and their apparent preferences in the English class (e.g., preferring some skills and activities over others).

Concluding observations

Apart from contextual and affective factors, cognitive and other differences among students should also be taken into account in ELT. Some students, and learners in immersion situations, are simply better equipped cognitively for language learning, though almost everyone can learn to communicate adequately for essential purposes in a second language, given the right conditions. Individual students may also vary in other ways, some perhaps having imperfect hearing, imperfect eyesight, or a condition such as a degree of autism, and many people stumble or choke up when required to speak before a crowd (and a class is a small crowd), even when they may be able to write with great proficiency. Teachers shouldn't demand or expect that all students behave and progress the same in English courses and achieve the same degree of proficiency in English any more than all students should be expected to behave, progress and achieve the same in a music course, a sports course, or, for that matter, a maths course. Contextual and some affective factors can affect almost all students in an institution or a group, and affective, cognitive and other factors can affect individual students.

General and individual success-or-failure in actually learning English in a course and an institution is a powerful force. When individual students, almost all students in a group, or almost all students in an institution continually succeed in learning and progressing in English courses, expectations, confidence and motivation grow along with competence in English. When individual students, almost all students in a group, or almost all students in an institution continually fail to learn and progress in English courses, expectations, confidence and motivation stagnate along with minimal competence in English, or even decline and turn strongly negative. Where students at the end of 2, 3 or more years of English courses are still struggling beginners, the game has already been lost. Only a completely new game, started from scratch, might be able to lead to a winning result.

Arnold (2011) sums it up as follows:

- Language learning should take place in a low-anxiety atmosphere.
- Opportunities for learners to succeed and thus raise their confidence should be built into classroom activities.
- The learner should be considered holistically: cognitive, emotional and physical aspects.
- Language learning should involve personally meaningful experience.
- Learner knowledge and resources should be drawn upon and autonomy is to be favoured and developed.

References

Arnold, J. (2011). Attention to affect in language learning. In *Anglistik. International Journal of English Studies*, 22/1. At https://files.eric.ed.gov/fulltext/ED532410.pdf

Davies, P. (2019). The most and the least successful ELT in Latin America. In *ELTinLA* and this book.

Krashen, S. (1985). *The Input Hypothesis: Issues and Implications*. Longman.

Stevick, E.W. (1980). *Memory, Meaning and Method*. Newbury House.

5

ELT LESSONS FROM EUROPE

Throughout the European Union, English language teaching in public schools has long been relatively similar in terms of syllabuses, methodology and materials, though it naturally varies from country to country, institution to institution, and teacher to teacher. The main guiding instrument for this degree of homogeneity has been the Common European Framework for Languages (CEF), with syllabuses, textbooks and proficiency tests based on it, but convergence has also come through meetings of ELT experts from different countries, the Open Method of Coordination (OMC) and other European organizations, processes and forums. In addition, socio-economic conditions and educational standards are relatively similar throughout the EU, again with variations due to socio-cultural traditions, national budgets (the poorest countries have a much lower per capita GDP than the richest ones) and other factors.

All that makes what I will call "The European ELT Experiment" (TEELTEX) extremely interesting for ELT specialists everywhere: When we compare, for example, Swedish, German, French and

Spanish school ELT, we are comparing similar ELT in similar school conditions, and the notable differences in results pose highly significant questions for ELT around the world.

By TEELTEX I mean the concerted effort to successfully teach English as the main lingua franca of Europe to all school students. It began around 1970, precisely when the first work was being done on what turned into the CEF. Before then, French, German and Russian were the main foreign languages taught in schools in many European countries and they, and English where it was the foreign language, were usually not taught in all schools, only in the 'academic' schools from which students might go on to higher education. Before 1970, only a small minority of people in each European country (with the obvious exception of the UK and Ireland) knew English. The enormous gap that exists today between English speakers in Sweden and in Spain, for example, has opened up over the past 40 or so years, that is, since TEELTEX began.

TEELTEX has been like an organized experimental project even more because a measurement system has accompanied it, Eurobarometer and Eurostat. We have been able to measure the results of school ELT in different EU countries from time to time, indirectly, at least. Eurobarometer is a series of surveys and reports that have been carried out for The European Commission since the 1970s. A number of these surveys and reports have been specifically on foreign language proficiency, which is especially important for the European Union as a multilingual union of countries. They look at the foreign language proficiency of the adult population (15 years old and above) of each country, which is obviously related to the effectiveness of foreign language teaching in schools. Eurostat draws on Eurobarometer and other data.

Eurostat 2019

The most recent data on languages in Europe, Eurostat 2019 (based on 2016 data), does not focus on individual languages, but on foreign languages in general (for data specifically on English as a foreign language in Europe we have to go back to the 2012 Eurobarometer report—see below). However, Eurostat 2019 notes that "English is by far the most widely spoken foreign language in the EU", and it is therefore now the first foreign language of almost all Europeans, certainly all young ones. The data in Eurostat 2019 shows that there was little increase between 2007 and 2016 in the percentage of people who knew only one foreign language (almost always English). That suggests that an increase in percentage of EFL speakers is hard to achieve, even in generally favourable circumstances like in the EU, after a country has notably improved foreign language proficiency over many preceding years, which most EU countries had indeed done over the two decades before 2007, the Netherlands and the Scandinavian countries to an impressive level. It is worth noting that much of that improvement was achieved before most countries had extended ELT to the early years of primary school, and many countries to primary school at all.

A few countries, however, did achieve a significant increase in the percentage of people with a functional command of just one foreign language (almost always English) from 2007 to 2016: +11% in Hungary, +10.1% in Czechia, +7.8% in Italy and +6.6% in Portugal —and that suggests that it might be possible to achieve significant, though small, improvements in some other countries. Of course, Russian was the main foreign language taught in schools in Hungary and Czechoslovakia until after 1989.

Eurobarometer 2012

The 2012 Eurobarometer Report, using 2012 data, is now rather old but it still came after 30 or more years of TEELTEX in most EU countries. Note that the development of the Common European Framework began in the early 1970s, *The Threshold Level for Modern Languages in Schools* was published in 1976, *Waystage English* in 1977, and other documents were published and discussed in meetings and congresses periodically after that, with the first full version of the CEF coming out in 2003. All that work on foreign language teaching, especially ELT, for The Council of Europe, and more work in different countries, is clearly reflected in Eurobarometer 2012. Here is a sample of data:

Percentage of Adult Population with a Functional Command of English (2012)

- Netherlands 90
- Denmark 86
- Sweden 86
- Austria 73
- Finland 70
- Germany 56
- Greece 51
- Estonia 50
- France 39
- Italy 34
- Portugal 27
- Spain 22

TEELTEX (that is, the CEF and all the work associated with it) was fully justified by Eurobarometer 2012. Only one country, Romania, came out lower than Spain, at 20%, and I'd guess that the improvement over the 20 to 40 years before 2012 in both Spain and Romania was around 100%, that is, from under 10% to 20-22%. In all the other countries, the improvement from a small minority of English speakers before 1970 was even more extraordinary, and from Estonia up it was absolutely phenomenal.

However, the range between the top countries and the bottom ones is enormous. I asserted above that it cannot be explained by very different ELT in very different conditions in different countries because ELT and conditions are relatively similar throughout the EU, and I will now argue that the above data, as well as other facts, support that assertion.

The range in the table above generally goes steeply downwards from north to south, and popular wisdom (often wrong and foolish, of course) may tend towards stereotypical North-South explanations such as that Scandinavians are innately better, brighter and more ambitious language learners (and, therefore, teachers) than Mediterraneans. That idea should be immediately rejected, noting that many less developed 'South' nations, particularly in Africa and Asia, have largely multilingual populations while many of the more developed 'North' nations have (or recently had) largely monolingual populations, and also that Greece in the south of Europe did almost as well in the Eurobarometer survey as Germany in the north, and far better than France.

Another North-South hypothesis might be that schools and education in the north are better than in the south, benefitting from more spending permitted by higher GDPs and larger government budgets. That might just be the case in the most extremely different countries, but there is far less difference within the EU than in the world in general, and the 50% of Estonia and the 51% of Greece (both among the lower per capita GDP countries of the EU) compared to the 39% of France (with around double their per capita GDP) do not fit with that hypothesis, which would predict that foreign language proficiency in France would be well above that in Estonia and Greece.

There are some other puzzles in the table above (and more in the complete table of the 25 EU countries where English was a foreign language in 2012—there are now 26 of them). For example, why does Austria have 73% of English speakers and Germany 56% when they are neighbouring countries with the same national language, and why does Finland have 70% of English speakers and Estonia, across just 70 kilometres of sea, 50%?

Anyway, I repeat that the percentage range of adult English speakers between the top countries and the bottom ones cannot be explained by very different ELT in very different conditions in different countries, or only perhaps in part in some cases. It must generally be the result of other variables.

Possible key factors in the different degrees of success of ELT in Europe

Assuming, then, that curricular factors (syllabuses, methodology, materials, etc.) and systemic factors (school and classroom conditions, teacher competence, etc.) are not the main causes of the enormous differences in the percentage of adult speakers of English, what are the main causes? Let's look outside or beyond curricular and systemic factors, that is, at extra-curricular contexts and the learners (as well as the students who are *not* learning much).

In the table above, the Netherlands, Denmark and Sweden are the countries with by far the highest percentage of English speakers, almost all the adult population, in fact. Also, Greece and Estonia are well above what might be expected of two of the poorer European countries. What do those countries (and Finland, also high-ranking) have in common? At the bottom of the table, far, far below, are Spain and Portugal. What do they have in common?

Well, one notable thing is that those six high-ranking countries have national languages that are very little used outside the country, on the Internet, in scientific and technical publications, and in international business and trade, and the lowest-ranking country, Spain, has a national language that is widely used outside the country (including the United States and most of Latin America), on the Internet and elsewhere, and Portuguese is also the national language of Brazil, Angola and Mozambique, and largely cognate with Spanish in its written form.

That takes us to learners (or students) of English. Learner motivation (and the lack of it in many people who are forced to study a foreign language) has long been considered a major factor in foreign language learning, and therefore teaching. That has been supported by a lot of research, and the data presented and discussed above also supports it. Dutch and Scandinavian students of English (among others) have much more need of English and therefore motivation to learn it than Portuguese and Spanish students of English. The result is 86-90% of English speakers versus 20-27%. French could be said to come after Spanish in international use (hence more English speakers in France than Spain, 39%), and German after French (hence even more English speakers in Germany, 56%).

No doubt there are many other factors apart from greater or lesser international use of a country's language that contribute to need/motivation and success in EFL learning. Perhaps, apart from the extremely low international use of Greek, Greece's dependence on shipping and international tourism has contributed to its surprisingly high 51% of English speakers. Perhaps the smaller and less industrialized economy of Austria, along with the many international organizations based in Vienna, has contributed to its 73% of English speakers compared to Germany's 56%, even though they are neighbours, both with German as their national language. The length, intensity and effectiveness of different countries' national ELT programmes may have contributed also. For example, where serious work was started in the 1960s or 70s and a high percentage of English speakers was achieved by 2000, as in the Netherlands, Scandinavia and even Germany, it becomes more and more embarrassing and career-inhibiting not to know English.

The future of ELT and English in Europe

The British Council recently published *The Future Demand for English in Europe: 2025 and Beyond* (2018). Among its key findings (or evidence-based predictions) are the following:

- English will continue to be the dominant lingua franca in Europe for the foreseeable future.
- There will be a fall in the number of people studying English in Europe. This will be due in part to demographics (declining birth rates) and in part to less study of English outside schools because school ELT will continue to improve, though only slowly.
- That slow improvement in school ELT will continue to be inadequate for the demands of 'requirers of English speakers' (institutions of higher educations and employers) and individuals' aspirations.
- There will be a small increase in older people studying English, especially those over 55 years old. This will be due in part to demographics (ageing populations), in part to inadequate English when leaving school, and in part to some people's need for higher level and/or specific purpose English later in life.
- The use of technology for teaching and learning English will continue to grow, mostly developing current services in more flexible, personalized, purpose-specific and time-effective ways, and trying to provide 'a smooth learning journey'.

Perhaps the most significant predictions are that school ELT will continue to improve, *but only slowly*, that there will be *an increase, albeit small, in older people studying English*, and that current ICT services will be developed in *more flexible, personalized, purpose-specific and time-effective ways*. Those last two predictions suggest that post-school or adult EFL learning options, especially learner-centred and specific purpose ones, will be important in Europe, perhaps as much as the improvement of English for general purposes in schools.

ELT lessons from Europe

There are possible lessons from the last 30 to 50 years of ELT in Europe (what I have called "The European ELT Experiment", TEEL-TEX) for ELT around the world, and certainly for ELT in Latin America, which is what interests me most. Here are the main lessons for national ELT programmes in Latin America that I have drawn from this exploration of TEELTEX.

EFL learning is highly dependent on real and perceived need of English and the motivation that usually arises from them. Many factors may affect real and perceived need of English and motivation, but they seem to be much lower in countries with strong international languages (e.g., Spain, Portugal and France) and much higher in those with languages that are little used internationally (e.g., the Netherlands, Scandinavian countries and Greece). Therefore, Latin American countries should look at Spain and Portugal as indicators of what they might achieve with their own national ELT programmes, that is, 20-30% of English speakers in the adult population. On the evidence of TEELTEX, aiming at the 80-90% of the Netherlands and Scandinavian countries, or even the 50-60% of countries like Germany, is probably a colossal error.

The level of English speakers in a country required to meet individual and national needs, whatever that level may be in each country, can be achieved without extending ELT to the early years of primary school, though that may improve results further where good results are already being achieved in the last years of primary school and in secondary school. That is the case in Sweden, where English is taught from first year (age 7) in some schools but not until third (age 9) in others, and in the Netherlands, where English is not a compulsory school subject until age 10. English is "in the family and the air" of most children in those countries, of course, but good results have been achieved by other European countries without taking English down to age 8, 7, or 6. Poor quality ELT in primary schools (especially when inserted before generally failing ELT in secondary schools as in most of Latin America) is most likely an enormous waste of time and money, and it may be counterproductive later, lowering expectations and motivation among older EFL learners.

In spite of the enormous success of school ELT in some European countries and considerable success in most others, many Europeans study English as adults, often to lift their 'fair' or 'good' English to higher levels, but sometimes to get from 'weak' or 'barely-existent' English to a level that serves their real needs. They may attend language centres in institutions of higher education or independent languages centres, including British Council ones, and some countries have government run or sponsored language centres, for example, Spain. The British Council predicts that the number of adults studying English will rise slightly over coming years. Most of the 20-30% of adults who really need English in most of Latin America do not realize that they need it until they are teenagers, many until they are young adults, and some until they are older adults. Latin American countries should look seriously at incorporating adult EFL (and other FL) centres into their national ELT programmes, shifting some of their investment in primary school ELT, especially early primary ELT, in that direction. Some of the adult ELT should be for specific purposes, especially in institutions of higher education.

References

British Council. (2018). *The future demand for English in Europe: 2025 and beyond (EU2025ENGLISH).* At https://www.britishcouncil.org/sites/default/files/future_demand_for_english_in_europe_2025_and_beyond_british_council_2018.pdf

European Commission / Eurobarometer. (2012). *Special Eurobarometer 386: Europeans and Their Languages.* At https://ec.europa.eu/commfrontoffice/publicopinion/archives/ebs/ebs_386_en.pdf

European Commission / Eurostat. (2019). *Foreign Language Skills Statistics: Number of foreign languages known.* At https://ec.europa.eu/eurostat/statistics-explained/index.php/Foreign_language_skills_statistics

6

THE ROLE OF ELT CENTRES IN LATIN AMERICA

The Latin American ELT scene

In most, perhaps all, Latin American countries, there are five main settings where teachers teach and students study English:

A 'Regular' primary and secondary schools (almost all public schools and many private ones)

B Bilingual primary and secondary schools and others with 'high quality ELT' (virtually all private)

C Curricular English courses in institutions of higher education (common core, etc.)

D Language centres with English courses (some within institutions, many for the general public)

E Private classes and specially provided classes (e.g., for companies)

The English language learning results in those different settings vary greatly, but are generally quite unsatisfactory for the needs and aspirations of people and nations. There are no very reliable estimates of the percentages of the population that can communicate effectively in English in different Latin American countries, but the best estimates available suggest that they range between 5% and 15%, with Argentina possibly at around 20%. One estimate for Mexico is 11.6% (Mitofsky 2013), which is probably a bit higher now. That compares with 22% for Spain, 27% for Portugal, 39% for France, 56% for Germany and 86% for Sweden according to fairly reliable estimates (Eurobarometer 2012).

By far the largest ELT operations in Latin America (and elsewhere) are in **A**, mainly public schools, which account for some 90% of all schools. In Mexico, almost all young people who complete upper secondary school now have had at least 6 years of English, and some, even in public schools, have had 12 years, starting in the first year of primary. Even with all those years of English, few students in regular schools (**A** above, including 'regular' private schools) learn much English. In contrast, most students in bilingual schools and schools with 'high quality ELT' (**B** above, representing perhaps 4 or 5% of the total school population) learn English quite well, many getting to B1+ level and some to B2+. Overall, however, according to Mexicanos Primero (2015), only 8% of school students reach A2+ level, and only 3% B1+.

The poor results of school ELT in Mexico (and most of Latin America) are reflected in the curricular English courses many institutions of higher education have for students in undergraduate degree programmes (**C** above): most students entering higher education go back into beginner or low elementary English courses. School ELT results are also reflected in the small percentage of adult Mexicans with functional English mentioned above, around 12% in Mexico. Where does that 12% or so learn English up to, say, B1+ level? In terms of numbers, probably mostly in **B** and **D** above, along with some from **C** and **E**—and returnee emigrants from the USA must contribute also.

ELT centres (**D** above) are very important for Mexico and Mexicans, then, as for other Latin American countries and Latin Americans. That importance can be summed up in a question: *Where would English in Mexico, and the rest of Latin America, be without ELT centres?* I can't give a firm figure for the student population in ELT centre courses (or foreign language centres with English courses), but I'd guess it's around one million for the whole of Mexico. That would be at any given time, and if a million students go through all the ELT centres in Mexico every 2 or 3 years, that would mean around 4 million new functional English speakers every 10 years. Of course, it doesn't work quite like that (a lot of students drop out and don't complete many courses), but it gives an idea of the important current role of ELT centres in the Mexican, and Latin America, ELT scene.

Teaching and learning English at school versus in an ELT centre

ELT in schools doesn't have to be the general failure it is currently in most of Latin America. The Latin American schools in **B** above demonstrate that, and in Scandinavia and other parts of Europe almost all children get to or beyond B1 level in regular public schools. How is that possible? Well, for a start, almost all the staff in Scandinavian schools and almost all the parents speak English, so of course the children are going to also (like in Mexican bilingual schools). And the English teachers have C1+ level English, the groups are usually well under 30 students, and so on. Success in ELT comes largely from a context of positive examples, positive expectations and positive conditions.

Compare that with most Latin American schools in **A** above. Few, if any, members of staff apart from the English teachers speak English (not even most school principals) and only the occasional parent; many English teachers barely have B1 level English, very few C1+; and the groups usually have 30+ students, often 40+, and sometimes 50+. The general failure of ELT is largely a consequence of negative examples, negative expectations and negative conditions —and, let's face it, also the fact that most Latin Americans simply don't need English (though some 20-30%, or perhaps more, do need it or could find it useful). While most schools continue with such contexts for English language learning, the results will continue to be poor, contributing very little to the percentage of adults who speak English, and requiring beginner's courses in higher education.

Other, better options than regular school ELT will continue to be sought by those who really need or want to learn English, and ELT centres will continue to be the main supply for that demand. The fact is that ELT centres are generally much more effective than school and other curricular ELT. Here's a list of some of the main reasons why:

- Almost all students in ELT centres take classes voluntarily because they like, want or need English. That translates into positive individual motivation (the generally recognised main key to success in foreign language learning) and positive group atmosphere. School ELT may also have those positive factors or some teachers create them, but there are almost always some, often many and sometimes a majority of students who don't like or want English or feel they need it for their life and ambitions.
- Most ELT centres employ only teachers with a high level of English and, nowadays, with solid ELT training. Also, if they're commercial or self-financing enterprises (as opposed, for example, to some subsidised university language centres), they quickly get rid of any teachers they

find unsatisfactory or that students complain about. None of that is the case in most regular schools.

- Most ELT centres have systems and norms for placement of students by level, for maximum group size (rarely over 25 nowadays and often under 15) and for certification (using international proficiency tests). None of that is the case in most regular schools.
- All the time, beginner and elementary students in most ELT centres see more advanced learners around them, often speaking English outside class with teachers and among themselves. They see and hear the good results of the centre's ELT. In most regular schools the younger students see very little or none of that, but rather older students, including siblings, struggling unhappily with the same beginner and elementary English year after year, educational cycle after educational cycle.

All the above (and often things like decoration with English language posters, a library of graded readers, a conversation club, events such as talks and sketches acted by teachers and higher level students) make most ELT centres much more successful than most schools (except bilingual ones, and those with 'high quality' ELT). Supply-demand ELT (for those who really like, want or need English) can generally be much more effective than compulsory-universal ELT (for everyone within 'the system').

The same is true for supply-demand vs. compulsory-universal music training, sports training, advanced computer training, etc. Every nation, every society, wants a lot of people (10, 20, 30%...?) who can play musical instruments, play sports and use computers at a high level, but not the whole population, and a supply-demand approach to training is much better than a compulsory-universal one. People with proficiency in Mandarin Chinese and AI management may soon be urgently needed, but should they be compulsory school subjects?

I've previously proposed 3 or 4 years of compulsory-universal ELT in schools (in the last 3 years of primary and first year of secondary, say) and, after that, free supply-demand ELT in language centres (Davies 2009). The courses in centres could be open to everyone between the age of, say, 13 and 19 or 20, but completely optional. It could be provided through free afternoon-evening courses in public schools (perhaps the only possibility in rural areas and small urban centres) and/or government language centres (which could offer other languages apart from English) in larger cities, and through government vouchers for courses in university, cultural foundation and commercial ELT centres. A decade after making that outside-the-box proposal, I still see it as a potentially better alternative to the 12+ years of compulsory-universal ELT (from primary to the end of upper secondary) that some Latin American countries started implementing years ago (at great and continuing cost, and with very disappointing results so far) and other countries are considering.

Summing up and concluding

So, do I see ELT centres not only as currently very important but also as the best solution to Latin American problems with English (too few English speakers, general failure of ELT in schools, etc.)? No, not alone. Bilingual schools and schools with 'high quality' ELT will obviously continue for children in well-off families, and more may be created, perhaps including some public schools in areas where English is important (e.g., big business centres, international tourist centres): they produce a significant number of the people who speak English proficiently in Latin America now. And it's worth investing in three or so years of curricular ELT for all students in all schools to give everyone a taste of what trying to learn English is like so that they can then decide whether or not to persevere. Obviously, though, the quality of those few years of school ELT must improve considerably in most schools to make it worthwhile. ELT centres become important, vital even, after all that school English has been provided and many people who like, want or need English still can't speak it, or not adequately.

At present, there are a lot of those people, and, consequently, there are a lot of ELT centres. In Puebla, Mexico, where I live there are at least 12 well-known organizations (including the Universidad Autónoma de Puebla, the Anglo Mexican Foundation, the Centro de Lenguas Volkswagen, Berlitz, International House, Angloamericano, Harmon Hall, Interlingua and Quick Learning) with over 25 centres/branches among them, plus many smaller ELT centres. I imagine it's similar where you live if that's a fairly large city. Currently, ELT centres are definitely a very big part of the alleviation, if not the solution for Latin American problems with English. That may not continue indefinitely into the future, or it may— perhaps until ELT is history and computer translation and interpretation have taken over. Meanwhile, here's a question about ELT in schools and in language centres: Assuming you're paid the same, would you prefer to teach a group of 40 students in the first year of a regular upper secondary school (mixed A1-A2 level, with a few A0 and B1 students) or a group of 20 teenagers in a Course 3 (A2.1) or 4 (A2.2) or 5 (B1.1) or 6 (B1.2) in an ELT centre? Or even a Course 1 in the ELT centre (A1.1) with students looking forward to a course that's much better than anything they've ever had at school?

References

Consulta Mitofsky. (2013, January). *Mexicanos y los idiomas extranjeros*. Encuesta nacional en viviendas.

Davies, P. (2009). Strategic management of ELT in public educational systems. In *TESL-EJ,* vol. 13, no. 3. At http://www.tesl-ej. org/wordpress/issues/volume13/ej51/ej51a2/.

European Commission/Eurobarometer. (2012). *Europeans and their languages.* At
http://ec.europa.eu/commfrontoffice/publicopinion/archives/ebs/ebs_386_en.pdf.

Mexicanos Primero. (2015). *Sorry. El aprendizaje del inglés en México.* At
http://www.mexicanosprimero.org/index.php/educacion-en-mexico/como-esta-la-educacion/estado-de-la-educacion-en-mexico/sorry-2015.

7

TEACHERS' PERCEPTIONS OF ELT IN PUBLIC SECONDARY SCHOOLS

The research reported in this article was designed in collaboration with Rosalina Domínguez of the Universidad Autónoma de Tlaxcala and organized by her. Then I wrote this article and Rosalina checked and approved it.

Background

It's generally recognised that the results of ELT in Mexican public secondary schools, and many private ones, are very poor. Evidence of poor results has long existed in estimates of adult Mexicans who speak English, and the level of English of students entering public universities, and some private ones. Most enter still at or little above beginner level, even with 6 years of English courses in lower and upper secondary schools, and increasingly more now with an additional 7 years of English in last year of pre-school and throughout primary school. Most universities have 'common core' English courses from beginner to A2 level (higher in some cases), and most students go into the beginner course—they start studying English from scratch again, for the third time, or even the fourth if they had English in primary school and their lower secondary school English was virtually false beginner level.

There are many possible negative factors that may contribute to these poor results in secondary schools (and other levels of schooling below higher education). They may include teachers without adequate English and/or training, inappropriate syllabuses and textbooks, excessively large groups, insufficient time for English courses, poor school conditions for learning English, and low expectations (e.g., because very few adults in the school and the children's environments have successfully learnt English at school).

We thought it would be interesting and useful to explore those and other factors as perceived by English teachers in their own schools, and we invited graduates from the 4-year degree course in ELT of the Universidad Autónoma de Tlaxcala, Mexico (where Rosalina works and Paul has worked) who are now teaching in a public secondary school to answer a questionnaire. As graduates from an ELT degree, the teachers could be discounted as one of the negative factors, more likely being an above-average positive factor. Thirty-three teachers responded. This article reports and discusses the data and indications in their answers.

The questionnaire, the answers, and some comments

We were very aware of the risk of personal feelings affecting the teachers' answers—the natural tendency to see things you like (or wish to feel good about) more positively than they are and to see things you don't like more negatively—and also of the risk that busy teachers might answer the questionnaire too hastily for accuracy. We tried to make the teachers also aware of these risks through this introductory comment: "The questions refer to 'your perception' of factors related to ELT in your school, but we need your answers to be as objective and true as possible, so please think carefully about each one. Thank you again." The generally high degree of agreement among the teachers suggests that they took the comment to heart, and real differences among the schools probably account for most of the markedly contrasting answers.

The questionnaire contained 16 questions, two of which were discounted in the analysis, leaving the 14 given below. Here they are, with the number of teachers for each option in **bold**, comments on the question, and comments on the answers.

1. *Approximately what percentage of students **enter** your school with some English (from primary school, etc.)?*

0% **x3** 10% **x17** 20% **x4** 30% **x2** 40% **x3** 50% **x1**
60% **x1** 70% **x2** 80% **x0** 90% **x0** 100% **x0**

Comments: Most public primary schools now have at least some curricular English courses, and where many students have had English in primary, results in secondary should be better. Among our 33 teachers, 20 have only 0-10% of students who've had English in primary, though 4 have over 50%.

2. *Do you have students in your classes who speak English quite well because they have lived in the USA or Canada?*

Always **x0** Often **x0** Sometimes **x2**
Very occasionally **x15** Never **x16**

Comments: There are many people in Tlaxcala State who've lived in the USA (usually 'undocumented') and have returned, speaking some English, sometimes quite good English. They include some children and teenagers. Where there are many in a school, it might help the English teachers' efforts. Among our 33 teachers, none usually have such students.

3. *How would you characterize the motivation for learning English of most **3rd year** students in your school?*

*Very high **x2** High **x3** Medium **x16** Low **x9** Very low **x3***

Comments: Motivation is generally considered an important or even essential factor in foreign language learning, and success or failure tend to have an impact on it, success in an endeavour lifting or sustaining motivation, and failure depressing it. Among our 33 teachers, most (16) feel that their students' experience of English classes in 1st and 2nd year hasn't impacted on their motivation much, either way. The other 17 teachers go in both directions, but more (12 against 5) feel their students have low motivation. It may be much the same with most school subjects, except when specific students are good at them, instinctively like them, or have very motivating teachers: all compulsory school subjects may be just that for many students—compulsory.

4. *What expectation of leaving school speaking English fairly well do you think most **1st year** students have?*

*Very low **x5** Low **x14** Medium **x11** High **x3** Very high **x0***

Comments: Expectation of success or failure often has an impact on motivation, and probably few students entering secondary school see many examples of success in learning English at school among their parents, older siblings, relatives, acquaintances, or school staff. That seems to be what most of our 33 teachers generally perceive, with most (19) answering low or very low, and only 3 above medium.

5. *What is student participation in your classes like in general?*

*Very good **x1** Good **x17** So-so **x12** Poor **x1** Very poor **x2***

Comments: Most of our 33 teachers consider participation to be good, and only 3 consider it to be poor or very poor. That generally positive perception may reflect the good work of the teachers (possibly in spite of the 'less good' work of other teachers in the school and the school environment) and the resilience of most Mexican teenagers!

6. *Approximately how many **effective** hours of English class do students receive per year?*

Under 80 **x1** *81-90* **x4** *91-100* **x11** *101-110* **x8** *111-120* **x3** *Over 120* **x6**

Comments: The norm here was set by the Secretaría de Educación Pública: "Given that a school term has 200 working days (40 weeks), the three weekly sessions (45-50 minutes each) make a total of 90 to 100 hours of study per grade" (SEP 2005). 28 of our 33 teachers estimate over 90 hours, with only 5 estimating under that.

7. *How many students are there in your English classes?*

Under 25 **x2** *25-30* **x8** *31-40* **x21** *41-50* **x2** *Over 50* **x0**

Comments: Group size in Mexican public secondary schools varies greatly and can be over well 50, especially in large cities, with smaller groups common in small towns and rural areas. In the schools of our 33 teachers, 31 have groups of under 41, and 10 of those groups are under 31. Note that Tlaxcala State is largely rural and has no large cities.

8. *How many English teachers are there in your school?*

Only you **x1** *2-3* **x18** *4-6* **x14** *Over 6* **x0**

(Comments below question 9)

9. *If there are 2+ English teachers, how much ELT coordination or collaboration is there among them?*

A lot **x4** *Some* **x14** *A little* **x10** *Virtually none* **x5**

Comments on 8 and 9: The lack of coordination among English teachers in a school, with different teachers doing different things (e.g., some establishing English as the main classroom language and others not), can have a negative impact on the courses and the overall results. Only one of our 33 teachers is working alone, and 14 are working with 3 or more other teachers. Only 4 report a lot of ELT coordination and 15 report little or none.

10. *In your opinion, how appropriate for the students in your school are the English syllabuses and textbooks?*

Not at all appropriate **x14** *Not very appropriate* **x9** *Fairly appropriate* **x8** *Perfectly appropriate* **x2**

Comments: The feeling of 23 of our 33 teachers is that the syllabuses and textbooks aren't really suitable for the students, with only 2 of them fully satisfied. Lines of thought and research leading out of that might be 'Why not?', and 'What kind of syllabuses and textbooks would be suitable for public secondary school students in small cities and rural Mexico?'.

11. *How well-supported is your ELT, for example, school CD player, computer projector, etc.?*

Not at all **x9** *So-so* **x18** *A lot* **x6**

Comments: Technology and aids for ELT, and other subjects, in Mexican public schools have been improving, but only 6 of our 33 teachers are happy with the situation in their schools, and 9 are very unhappy, presumably having to take their own CD player, etc., to their classes.

12. *To your knowledge, apart from English teachers, how many members of the school staff have B1+ level English?*

Over 10 **x1** *6-10* **x0** *3-5* **x4** *1-2* **x14** *None* **x14**

Comments: Where many members of staff in a school speak English, especially if the school principal is one of them, it's probable that students are more likely to learn the language, like in bilingual schools. Supposedly all the members of staff studied English at school, and if they didn't learn it they're poor examples for the students. Close to half our 33 teachers work in schools where only the English teachers know English, and most of the rest where only 1 or 2 other members of staff do.

13. *To your knowledge, how many students in your school have English speaking parents or relatives?*

Many **x0** *Some* **x3** *A few* **x19** *Almost none* **x7** *None* **x4**

Comments: This is yet another question related to environments with examples of successful learners of English, like questions 1, 2, and 12. A significant number of our 33 teachers (19) think a few students have English speaking parents or relatives, which isn't as good as we'd expected in a state like Tlaxcala, with a lot of emigration to the USA and re-immigration, but better than almost none or none.

14. *In your estimation, what percentage of students leave your school after 3 years at A2+ level in English (ready to pass the Cambridge A2 Key Test)?*

0-1% **x8** *2-10%* **x15** *11-20%* **x7** *21-30%* **x2** *31-50%* **x1**
51+% **x0**

Comments: This level was set by the Secretaría de Educación Pública as the goal for secondary school leavers: "[I]t is expected that by the end of basic education students should reach, as a minimum, a level equivalent to A2, Waystage" (SEP 2005). Having clearly failed to achieve that, the SEP is now aiming at B1+ in its latest plans, with ELT in public primary schools aiming at A2+. 23 of our 33 teachers consider that only between 0 and 10% of their students achieve A2+. They may consist at least partly of students who came to secondary school with some English from primary school (see Question 1), or from residence in the USA (see Question 2), or who have studied English outside school in a language centre.

General conclusions and reflections

The following conclusions apply directly to the 33 State of Tlaxcala teachers and schools in our survey, and by extension probably to most other public secondary schools in that small central Mexican state. While they may also apply to some, or even a large, extent to most schools in the rest of Mexico, there are almost certainly some very marked differences. Mexico stretches from the US to the Guatemalan border, from the Pacific to the Gulf coast, from wealthier states to much poorer ones, and from large cities to small towns and countryside, and many more surveys of this kind, and surveys going beyond this one, in different parts of Mexico are needed to discover the similarities and differences in ELT conditions and ELT results.

Our first general conclusion is that students entering secondary school with some English from public primary school (Question 1) and students with English from living in the USA (Question 2), even in a state like Tlaxcala with a lot of emigration/re-immigration across the US border, appear to be contributing little or nothing to the improvement of ELT results in secondary schools. There are very few of the latter (fewer than we anticipated), and very few schools have more than 20% of their new students entering with some English from primary school, either because they didn't have English classes there, or the classes were ineffective.

The expectation of students entering secondary that they'll actually learn English at school (Question 4) is medium to very low, with the largest number ranked as low. This almost endemic expectation of NOT being likely to learn English at school is probably linked to what they see around them: usually few or no members of staff, apart from English teachers, who speak English (Question 12), few relatives, etc., who speak English (Question 13), perhaps including older siblings, ahead of them at school. This negative expectation must impact on motivation, but the motivation of 3rd year students, as perceived by teachers, is not as bad as we'd anticipated (Question 3) and participation of students in general is quite good (Question 5). That may be credited to the teachers and the resilience and/or conformity of the students.

However, the results are still poor, and we consider that a vicious circle (in the diagram below) needs to be attacked, for example, by requiring all secondary school staff, or at least all new staff, to have, B1+ English (see the comment on Question 12 above). More effective ways to achieve better results also need to be explored, perhaps experimenting in some schools. As popular wisdom has it, "Nothing succeeds like success" and "Lead by example, not by force".

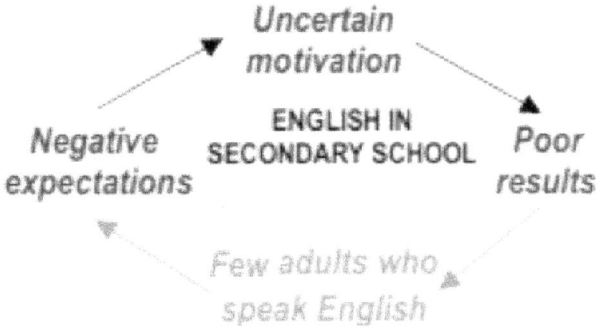

Figure 5. Expectations and results in English in secondary school

Teaching-learning conditions in the secondary schools in the survey are not as bad as we've experienced personally and have observed in the past. Most teachers reported 90 to over 120 hours of effective class time (Question 6), which is at or above the SEP norm, and groups of under 40 students (Question 7), which is well below the 50 students Paul once taught for two years and the 60+ he observed on several occasions many years ago. Support for ELT, that is, basic technology and aids like CD players and a computer projector (Question 11), varies enormously, with 18 schools indicating some, and 6 a lot, but 9 none at all. Overall, the conditions are not always very good (groups of under 30 and basic modern technology would be nice in all schools), but usually not very bad either.

In terms of methodology and materials used by all the teachers in a school, the general picture isn't very bright. All but 1 of the 33 teachers work with other teachers, some with more than 3 others (Question 8), but in 5 schools there's virtually no coordination of ELT, so different teachers may be doing very different things, in another 10 schools there's little coordination, and there's a lot of coordination in only 4 schools. Coordination of teaching in a school is very important because otherwise students may be confused and disconcerted by very different approaches in their 3 years of secondary school. On top of that, 14 of the 33 teachers consider the syllabuses and textbooks not at all appropriate and another 9 consider them not very appropriate, while only 2 teachers consider them perfectly appropriate. A big question here is: What syllabuses and materials *would* be largely appropriate for teenagers in public secondary schools in small cities, towns and the countryside of central Mexico, 1,000 kilometres from the nearest US border, and very unlikely ever to travel or stay outside Mexico except to join a largely Spanish-speaking family and community in the USA? Note (as 23 of our 33 teachers may have) that Tlaxcala is very different from a large, industrial, financial and business centre like Monterrey, or a large international vacation and convention centre like Cancún.

What matters most in ELT, of course, is results, and 23 of our 33 teachers estimate that under 10% of students leave their school with A2+ English, the SEP target until recently, but now actually being put higher (Question 14). Another 7 teachers estimate between 11 and 21%, and, surprisingly, 2 estimate between 21 and 30%, and 1 between 31 and 50%. These are estimations, of course, and the students would have to be reliably tested for us to be sure, but the difference between 8 schools estimated at under 1% and 1 school at over 31% is striking and possibly extremely significant.

Specific cases

Each of the 33 teachers who answered the questionnaire describes a specific situation and tells a specific story, but, as was to be expected, most situations and stories are very similar, hence the general conclusions above. However, some situations and stories are notably different. Here's data for three of them, with strikingly different levels of English for students leaving the school (remember, these are the teachers' estimates and they might not correspond to results in the Cambridge A2 Key Test).

	Teacher A	Teacher B	Teacher C
Students leaving school with A2+ English	*0-1%*	*11-20%*	*31-50%*
Students entering school with English from primary	70%	0%	40%
Students with English from residence in USA	Never	Never	Very occasionally
Expectations of learning English of 1st year students	Low	Very low	Medium
Motivation for learning English of 3rd year students	Medium	Medium	Medium
Participation in classes of students in general	Good	Good	Good
Effective hours of English class	Over 120	111-120	91-100
Number of students in groups	31-40	31-40	41-50
Support with basic technology and aids	Some	Some	None
Amount of ELT coordination and collaboration	Some	Some	A lot
Appropriateness of syllabuses and textbooks	Fairly appropriate	Not at all appropriate	Fairly appropriate
Members of school staff with B1+ English	3-5	None	Over 10
Students with English speaking parents or relatives	A few	A few	Almost none

Figure 6. Students leaving school with A2+ level English

We'll leave you to examine that data and form your own ideas, but note that the best results here (as estimated by the teacher) go together with over 10 members of school staff with B1+ English and a lot of ELT coordination and collaboration in the school, as well as groups of over 41 students and no support with technology and aids (teachers presumably take in their own CD players, etc.). That leaves many questions, which could lead to more research.

Matha Lengeling and Amanda Wilson, of the University of Guanajuato, later contributed an article to *ELTinLA* online magazine which reports on a replication of the research reported and discussed in the above article. In it, they give the same questionnaire to 9 public secondary school teachers in the state of Guanajuato, which takes the total number of teachers up to 42, in two different states, 33 in Tlaxcala and 9 in Guanajuato. The results for Tlaxcala (T) and for Guanajuato (G) are presented below with the top answers for each in bold.

1. *Approximately what percentage of students **enter** your school with some English (from primary school, etc.)?*

T 0% x3 **10% x17** 20% x4 30% x2 40% x3 50% x1 60% x1
70% x2 80% x0 90% x0 100% x0
G 0% x2 **10% x3** 20% x1 30% x2 40% x0 50% x0 60% x0
70% x0 80% x0 90% x1 100% x0

2. *Do you have students in your classes who speak English quite well because they have lived in the USA or Canada?*

T Always x0 Often x0 Sometimes x2 Very occasionally x15
Never x16
G Always x0 Often x0 Sometimes x1 **Very occasionally x6**
Never x2

3. *How would you characterize the motivation for learning English of most **3rd year** students in your school?*

T Very high x2 High x3 **Medium x16** Low x9 Very low x3
G Very high x0 High x0 **Medium x7** Low x1 Very low x1

4. *What expectation of leaving school speaking English fairly well do you think most **1st year** students have?*

T Very low x5 **Low x14** Medium x11 High x3 Very high x0
G **Very low x3** Low x1 **Medium x3** High x2 Very high x0

5. *What is student participation in your classes like in general?*

T Very good x1 **Good x17** So-so x12 Poor x1 Very poor x2
G Very good x1 **Good x6** So-so x2 Poor x0 Very poor x0

6. *Approximately how many **effective** hours of English class do students receive per year?*

T Under 80 x1 81-90 x4 **91-100 x11** 101-110 x8 111-120 x3
Over 120 x6
G Under 80 x1 81-90 x1 91-100 x2 **101-110 x3** 111-120 x1
Over 120 x1

7. *How many students are there in your English classes?*

T Under 25 x2 25-30 x8 **31-40 x21** 41-50 x2 Over 50 x0
G Under 25 x0 25-30 x2 **31-40 x5** 41-50 x2 Over 50 x0

8. *How many English teachers are there in your school?*

T Only you x1 **2-3 x18** 4-6 x14 Over 6 x0
G Only you x1 **2-3 x5** 4-6 x3 Over 6 x0

9. *If there are 2+ English teachers, how much ELT coordination or collabo-ration is there among them?*

T A lot x4 **Some x14** A little x10 Virtually none x5
G A lot x1 Some x0 **A little x4 Virtually none x4**

10. *In your opinion, how appropriate for the students in your school are the English syllabuses and textbooks?*

T **Not at all appropriate x14** Not very appropriate x9 Fairly
appropriate x8 Perfectly appropriate x2
G Not at all appropriate x3 **Not very appropriate x5** Fairly
appropriate x1 Perfectly appropriate x0

11. *How well-supported is your ELT, for example, school CD player, computer projector, etc.?*

T Not at all x9 **So-so x18** A lot x6
G **Not at all x4 So-so x4** A lot x1

12. *To your knowledge, apart from English teachers, how many members of the school staff have B1+ level English?*

T Over 10 x1 6-10 x0 3-5 x4 **1-2 x14 None x14**
G Over 10 x0 6-10 x0 3-5 x2 1-2 x1 **None x6**

13. *To your knowledge, how many students in your school have English speaking parents or relatives?*

T Many x0 Some x3 **A few x19** Almost none x7 None x4
G Many x0 Some x1 **A few x4** Almost none x2 None x2

14. *In your estimation, what percentage of students leave your school after 3 years at A2+ level in English (ready to pass the Cambridge A2 Key Test)?*

T 0-1% x8 **2-10% x15** 11-20% x7 21-30% x2 31-50% x1
51+% x0
G 0-1% x2 **2-10% x5** 11-20% x1 21-30% x1 31-50% x0
51+% x0

9 of the 14 top answers are the same for Tlaxcala and Guanajuato and 5 are 'next door', indicating a very similar situation in the two states and fair reliability of the answers. The most significant answers are probably 1 (overwhelmingly, most students enter public secondary school with virtually no English in spite of 6 years of English in public primary school), 4 (expectations of learning English at the beginning of public secondary school is low to medium), 3 (at the end of public secondary school motivation to learn English is medium to low—some credit to the teachers), 5 (student participation is good to so-so— again some credit to the teachers), 9 (ELT coordination and collaboration ranges from some to none), 10 (overwhelmingly, most teachers consider the syllabuses and textbooks not at all appropriate or not very appropriate), 11 (support

for ELT in the school is so-so to none), 12 (no staff, or just 1-2, in the school apart from English teachers have B1+ English), 14 (over-whelmingly, most students leave public secondary school with less than A2 English—the target is B1). On that combined evidence from the states of Tlaxcala and Guanajuato, public secondary school ELT in Mexico appears to be continuing to fail very badly.

8

WHAT SHOULD PRONI TEACHERS REALLY DO IN LOWER SECONDARY SCHOOL?

The lower secondary school syllabuses of PRONI (the Mexican Programa Nacional de Inglés en Educación Básica) start at A2 level (supposedly achieved by the end of primary school) and go up to B1 level, and the approved textbooks generally follow those syllabuses. The Third Year syllabus includes examples like the following, quoted from the syllabus, with a few slips or typos corrected (SEP 2017):

- I don't know what it is called. It is this kind of wheel that pushes water out of a river.
- Well, after listening to you, maybe you're right; it seems that your proposal is better.
- I felt overjoyed because that description moved me so much.
- I rather think that the wind made the bottle fall.
- It may have been a cat that broke the bottle.
- While living conditions worldwide have improved, there are some who do not agree.

With such challenging syllabuses and textbooks and the difficult ELT conditions in most public lower secondary schools, what do teachers actually do in class? Some probably try to follow the syllabuses and work through their textbooks no matter how lost their students may be, while others adapt their teaching to the reality of their situation and do A1-2 stuff instead of B1. In either case, the results are generally very poor, far below what's proposed in the syllabuses and textbooks.

Those results can be seen in the level of English of students entering institutions of higher education (most still go into beginner or elementary common core English—see *ELT in a Mexican university's language centres*, in this section of the ELTinLA Library, February, 2019), and in estimates of the adult population that knows some English (which range between 5% and 15%, with Consulta Mitofsky giving 11.6% in 2013). Aquino, Núñez and Corona (2017) tested a sample of 629 3rd year Secundaria students and found that 97.3% were at starter level, 1.1% at A1 level, 0.3% at A2 level, and 1.3% at B1 level. They also referred to another study (Székely et al 2015) that found only 3% of their sample of students finishing lower secondary to be at B1 level (most almost certainly got there through special circumstances, for example, time in the USA or extra-curricular classes, not through PRONI school English classes). So, with those syllabuses and textbooks up so high and those results down so low, what **should** PRONI teachers **really** do in their lower secondary school English lessons?

A way forward (or out) is briefly indicated in the PRONI syllabuses cited above, which contain a few recognitions that classroom realities vary, and authorize schools and teachers to depart from or modify the syllabuses, for example (my emphasis):

> Un currículo que aspire a *responder a la diversidad de expectativas y necesidades de todos los educandos* debe reconocer *los distintos contextos en que operará dicho currículo*, así como admitir *la*

heterogeneidad de capacidades de las escuelas para responder a *las demandas globales del currículo y a las específicas de su situación local.* De ahí que el currículo deba *ofrecer espacios de flexibilidad a las escuelas para que estas hagan adaptaciones en contenidos que convengan específicamente a su situación local.* (p. 96)

Estas orientaciones y sugerencias específicas son indicativas más que prescriptivas. Su propósito es ofrecer al profesor diversas formas de abordar los contenidos de acuerdo al enfoque pedagógico. *Cada profesor podrá adaptarlas a su contexto o desarrollar las propias.* (p. 153)

I doubt that the SEP is authorizing there what I'm about to propose, that is, to completely ignore the PRONI syllabuses in most schools, but I'm fairly sure many teachers are already doing that, so I'll try to help those teachers as well as others that are suffering, along with their students, from not doing so.

Context 1: Public schools with the best conditions for ELT

In the very best public schools for ELT, teachers may be able to work close to the syllabuses and textbooks. There are very few such schools, however, because, for a start, they have to receive students from primary school who are at or close to A2 level in English. That may be the case, for example, in a higher than average socio-economic area of a city, or in a Centro Escolar 'of excellence' with ELT (and education in general) coordinated from pre-school through to upper secondary. Normally, to continue from A2 or near-A2 level English achieved in primary school to B1 or near-B1 level English by the end of the 3 years of lower secondary school, all the English teachers have to have fairly good and confident English themselves (usually B2+), they have to work as a team, the students have to 'buy into' English language learning, and so on. Clearly, such schools are special cases, far from the norm.

Ironically, the teachers in such schools tend to be better able than most teachers to take advantage of the official (though muted) encouragement to adapt the syllabuses to local situations and develop their own contents and approaches. That's ironic because the 'Common European/Uncommon Latin American' syllabuses need least adaptation in such schools and contexts. However, even there, some adaptation may be appropriate:

> ELT in even the best public schools can be enriched and made more appropriate for the students by responding to and exploiting the local and regional context, for example:

- Schools near the US border can exploit students' cross-border experiences and possibilities, and cross-border projects may be possible. The situations and language in the courses can (and really should) reflect that aspect of the local/regional context.
- Schools in international tourism/vacation areas can exploit students' experiences with foreign visitors and the experiences of relatives/acquaintances that work in travel and hospitality services, and visits to international hotels, etc., may be possible. The situations and language in the courses can (and really should) reflect that aspect of the local/regional context.
- Schools in a major financial/industrial centre can exploit the experiences of students' relatives and acquaintances who work in jobs where they or colleagues use English a lot, and visits to some such workplaces may be possible. The situations and language in the courses can (and really should) reflect that aspect of the local/regional context.
- Schools in areas with a lot of emigration to and returnees from the USA can exploit the experiences of students' relatives and acquaintances. There may be English speaking returnee students in most classes, who can help teachers,

and adult English-speaking returnees can be invited to classes and school events. The situations and language in the courses can (and really should) reflect that aspect of the local/regional context.

Context 2: Public schools with rather better than average conditions for ELT

These are schools that have mostly competent English teachers, and that receive some students from primary school with A2 or near-A2 level English, some with A1 or near-A1 level English, some with around middle of A1 level English (A1.1, halfway towards full A1), and a few with virtually no English at all. Of course, the mix may vary, but it often ranges from A0 to A2, with the bulk a bit below or a bit above A1. The first issue and challenge here is the mixed level in English of the students in each year.

Based on the PRONI curriculum's suggestion that schools can, and indeed should, adapt contents to their local situation, I suggest that they can also adapt the format and type of courses. Some schools have the following option for dealing with the mixed level in English of the students in each year:

Large schools with students at different levels in English and mostly well below PRONI Secundaria syllabuses, can create two or more levels of course for students in each year, for example:

First Year

– Course A for students below A1 level

– Course B for students at or above A1 level

Second Year

– Course A for students below A2.1 level (halfway through A2)

– Course B for students at or above A2.1 level

Third Year

– Course A for students at or below A2 level

– Course B for students well above A2 level

Obviously, with this option, all the course syllabuses would have to be very different from the PRONI ones (but the PRONI ones can't realistically be followed in the classroom, anyway). One option is to go back to the Primaria A1-A2 syllabuses, but that's not really appropriate with the students who are now teenagers, not children. Another is to go back to the old Secundaria syllabuses and textbooks, which used to start at beginner level, perhaps beginning in the middle of textbook 1 in Course A and in the middle of textbook 2 in Course B in First Year, and so on. The strongest and most experienced teachers will be able to gather and organize appropriate material for themselves, which they could share with less experienced colleagues.

Teachers in schools in this 'rather better than average' category that can't do the above (because they don't have enough students for more than one group in every year, the principal rejects the idea, etc.), have to face the challenge of very mixed level groups realistically and pragmatically. Here are three ideas:

CLASSROOM ENGLISH: Stronger students will probably be used to English as the main classroom language from Primary School, but weaker students probably won't. All the English teachers in the school should agree to establish, maintain and develop English as the main classroom language.

ROUTINE ACTIVITIES: Routines initially taught through model dialogues, some done every week, others periodically, can consolidate basic English, and also allow stronger students to do more. Conversations: *What do you/does your mother/father do on Weekdays/Saturdays/Sundays/ vacations? What did you do last night/Saturday/Sunday/vacation? What are you going to do tonight/next Saturday/Sunday/vacation?* Roleplays: *Meeting a foreigner at a party. Checking a foreigner into a hotel where you're a receptionist. Telling an exchange student about your school.*

PAIRING STUDENTS: In mixed level groups, students can be paired 1. to have pairs work at different levels, some pairs on a lower level, others on a higher level, and 2. to have stronger students help weaker ones. The first type of pairing (stronger students together and weaker students together) is particular useful with communicative tasks, and the second type with tasks focused on language.

Context 3: Public schools with rather worse than average conditions for ELT

These are schools that have some inexperienced or improvised English teachers as well as competent ones, and, above all, schools that receive almost all students from primary school with less than A1 level English, most just false beginners or with virtually no English at all, heading almost inevitably towards joining the 90+% of students that leave most public (and many private) lower secondary schools with sub-A1 level English (Aquino et al 2017, Székely et al 2015). Attempting much above A1 level here is a ludicrous and demoralizing farce, for the students and the teachers. The PRONI Secundaria syllabuses and the corresponding textbooks should be totally ignored and the reality looked at with open, honest, intelligent eyes.

Yes, that's a brutally frank analysis, but I give it because I'm quite sure it's generally accurate and that it's potentially extremely useful to put it out there, in case someone in a position to radically modify PRONI is reading this.

What more can I say about Context 3? Well, obviously, when a lower secondary school and the English teachers in it know that almost all students enter First Year with less than A1 level English, most just false beginners or with virtually no English at all, they should put their heads together and agree to start with false beginner courses and aim at, say, A2 by the end of Third Year. In doing so, some of the ideas for Context 3 (above) may be viable and useful.

Context 4: Public schools with improvised, only sporadic or no ELT

These are almost always rural schools in remote areas, but there may be some in marginalized and neglected urban areas. What can I say? Nothing, except that, mercifully or cruelly, very few of the students in such schools will ever need English in their lives, and those that do will find ways of acquiring it after lower secondary school. The SEP could provide more help for those people who need or want to learn English from scratch as young adults, or older adults.

In Conclusion

This article has tried to address honestly and helpfully the extremely serious problems with PRONI (the Mexican Programa Nacional de Inglés en Educación Básica) at lower secondary school (Secundaria) level, and the question "What should PRONI teachers really do in lower secondary school?". It has offered suggestions for schools where the B1 level objectives of the PRONI lower secondary syllabuses, reflected in the corresponding textbooks, can be partially achieved but not with all students, where they cannot be achieved but A2 level or fairly solid A1 level can, and where only flimsy or almost no ELT is done.

The experience of writing this article drives me, yet again, to repeat loud and clear that PRONI urgently needs radical modification, or complete replacement. Its failure to produce anything near the intended results after more than 10 years of PNIEB-PRONI hits lower secondary school ELT particularly hard, and then ELT in upper secondary school (Prepa), and then ELT in higher education.

While nothing significant changes, I express my admiration for all the responsible and hard-working PRONI English teachers in public schools who are doing their very best under difficult, sometimes almost impossible, circumstances, trying to make their English classes as enjoyable and profitable as possible for their students.

References

Aquino, M. D., Núñez, D. M., & Corona, E. (2017). Competencia Lingüística y Estándares de Desempeño en Estudiantes al Terminar la Educación Básica. In XIV Congreso Nacional de Investigación Educativa, COMIE. At http://www.comie.org.mx/congreso/memoriaelectronica/v14/doc/1419.pdf

Secretaría de Educación Pública. (2017). *APRENDIZAJES CLAVE Lengua Extranjera. Inglés.* Secretaría de Educación Pública, México. At http://www.planyprogramasdestudio.sep.gob.mx/descargables/biblioteca/basica-ingles/1LpM-Ingles_Digital.pdf

9

TWO FRAMEWORKS FOR ELT

AND ONE NATIONAL ENGLISH PROGRAMME IN LATIN AMERICA

1. Introduction

Contexts and aims

There is just one framework for teaching languages, including English, that's known around the world—the Common European Framework of Reference for Languages. It was born in Europe, but has travelled around the globe, partly transported by textbooks and proficiency tests, and has had offspring in many parts of the world, especially in the form of national English programmes.

While virtually all ELT professionals around the world must be familiar with the A1-2, B1-2, C1-2 levels of language proficiency of the CEF, many, perhaps most, are probably not familiar with the CEF as a whole. That's unfortunate because it has a strong, and sometimes inappropriate, influence on most ELT in most countries, including those in Latin America, even though they are markedly different from European countries in important respects for ELT.

Below are three short excerpts from the CEF, the last two of which indicate how different Europe and Latin America are in ways that have, or should have, an impact on ELT:

> *The Common European Framework provides a common basis for the elaboration of language syllabuses, curriculum guidelines, examinations, textbooks, etc., across Europe.*

> *…..it is only through a better knowledge of European modern Languages that it will be possible to facilitate communication and interaction among Europeans of different mother tongues in order to promote European mobility, mutual understanding and coopera-tion, and overcome prejudice and discrimination.*

> *…..[the CEF aims] to ensure, as far as possible, that all sections of [European countries'] populations have access to effective means of acquiring a knowledge of the languages of other member states (or of other communities within their own country) as well as the skills in the use of those languages that will enable them to satisfy their communicative needs and in particular:*

> 1. *to deal with the business of everyday life in another country, and to help foreigners staying in their own country to do so:*
> 2. *to exchange information and ideas with young people and adults who speak a different language and communicate their thoughts and feelings to them;*
> 3. *to achieve a wider and deeper understanding of the way of life and forms of thought of other peoples and of their cultural heritage.*

As those excerpts show, the CEF was conceived specifically for the European Union (and neighbouring countries) to "facilitate communication and interaction among Europeans of different mother tongues in order to promote European mobility, mutual understanding and cooperation, and overcome prejudice and discrimination". Europe has a very different context and very different needs from Latin America. For a start, the EU has 23 different official languages, so multilingualism and lingua francas are extremely important, with English by far the most important lingua franca, though some other languages are also widely used across borders in Europe, especially French and German. In contrast, Latin America doesn't need a regional lingua franca because Spanish is the official language in almost all Latin American countries, and Portuguese, very closely related to Spanish, in Brazil. In addition, within the EU there is freedom of movement and citizens of EU member states can enter and reside in other member countries without visas or permits, so inter-country mobility is very high. English serves well as a lingua franca for tourism, business and some other purposes, but when Europeans wish to study or work in another country they need to know that country's main language, and it helps for retirement and extended vacationing also. In contrast, Latin Americans often need visas for travel abroad, and certainly for extended stays or residence: legal study and work abroad, especially outside Latin America itself, are for a small number of Latin Americans only, mostly privileged or fortunate ones.

Though not intended for use outside Europe the CEF mentions use of the framework in situations where adaptation may be necessary. Here are two excerpts possibly relevant for some ELT in Latin America:

> *The Framework includes the description of 'partial' qualifications, appropriate when only a more restricted knowledge of a language is required (e.g., for understanding rather than speaking), or when a limited amount of time is available for the learning of a third or fourth language and more useful results can perhaps be attained by aiming at, say, recognition rather than recall skills.*

...the framework should be open and flexible, so that it can be applied, with such adaptations as prove necessary, to particular situations.

The first excerpt refers to learning a third or fourth language, which many people do in Europe, with the assumption that the second language (English in most cases) will be learnt for full general use and to the highest possible level of proficiency. In Latin America, and elsewhere, the idea of 'partial' learning of a language could be applied to English, usually the first and only foreign language learnt: Many Latin Americans learn English only or mainly for occupation-related reading, and university English courses for undergraduates that focus mainly on ESP reading might achieve much more useful learning than typical university English for General Purposes courses do. Other skills may follow from fairly proficient reading if the need and opportunity arise for individual people.

The second excerpt refers to different situations within Europe: There should obviously be significant differences in the teaching-learning of a language, not necessarily English, in primary school, secondary school and higher education, in Sweden, Germany and Bulgaria, and so on. In Latin America, different ELT is also appropriate in different levels and types of education and different countries, but there are other situations and contexts that are common in Latin America and rare in Europe, for example, areas with endemic poverty and areas of rural isolation.

To sum up, the EU is very different from Latin America, geographically, demographically, politically, economically and linguistically: 27 countries in a close economic-political union, with a combined population of around 450 million and 23 official languages, occupying an area about half the size of Brazil, with citizens of EU countries able to enter, reside and work freely in any EU country. The CEF is designed to facilitate the teaching, learning and certification of all European languages, not just English, in order for EU citizens to move around the EU, collaborate and live in harmony, which they have not always done in the past. How, then, could it be appropriate for ELT in most of Latin America without considerable definition and adaptation? Significantly, the CEF recognises differences within Europe and within European countries, and aims to be an open and flexible framework that can be adapted to particular situations and circumstances. Though the CEF is not a framework for ELT in Latin America, some of it can be applied fairly directly, and more of it can be adapted, but even so, more than that is needed. This article explores the CEF, its influence on ELT in Latin America, and appropriate ELT for the different roles of English and different ELT contexts in Latin America.

2. The foundations and aims of frameworks for ELT

For this exploration of frameworks for ELT in Latin America, the Common European Framework of Reference for Languages (CEF) obviously has to be looked at, a postulated Common Latin American Framework for English Teaching (CLAFET) will also be presented, and Mexico's Programa Nacional de Inglés (PRONI) will be related to both. PRONI unquestionably owes a large debt to the CEF, but it should be well aligned with CLAFET if CLAFET is an appropriate framework for ELT specifically in Latin America. Note that CLAFET is directed only towards ELT in public education and private education that follows public guidelines: ELT in privileged schools and other privileged institutions in Latin America would naturally follow other guidelines, perhaps the CEF if many students in the school or institution travel, stay and study abroad like well-off Europeans, or perhaps the institution's own guidelines.

Table 1. ELT contexts considered in 2 frameworks and 1 national English programme

CEF (actual framework)

- Mainly the 27 countries in the European Union, but also some neighbouring European countries.
- There are 23 official languages in the EU, plus some regional or minority languages.
- Travel to European countries with different languages is generally quite fast and affordable, and all EU citizens can freely enter, reside, study and work in any EU country. Many Europeans also travel around the world for business or pleasure.
- Fairly high quality ELT in fairly favourable conditions is possible in all basic education and other education in all EU countries.

PRONI (national programme)

- Mexico only.
- Spanish is the national language (and about 5% of the population speak an indigenous language).
- Except for Mexicans in US border states, international travel is generally too time-consuming and expensive for most, but a growing minority does travel for business or pleasure, and some study or work in another country, which requires a visa or permit.
- Only low quality ELT in not very favourable conditions is possible or available in much basic and other education in Mexico.

CLAFET (postulated framework)

- All of Latin America.
- Spanish is the/a national language of 18 countries and Portuguese of Brazil (and an indigenous language is spoken by some of the population, over 40% in Guatemala).
- International travel is generally too time-consuming and expensive for most people, especially travel outside Latin America, but a growing minority does travel for business or pleasure, and some study or work in another country, which requires a visa or permit.
- Only low quality ELT in not very favourable conditions is possible in much basic education and other education in Latin America.

————

Table 2: Aims of the frameworks and the programme

CEF (actual framework)

- To provide a common basis for the elaboration of language syllabuses, curriculum guide-lines, examinations, textbooks, etc., across Europe, for preschool, for adult evening classes, and for the other scenarios in between.
- To promote European mobility, mutual understanding and cooperation, and overcome prejudice and discrimination.
- To ensure, as far as possible, that all Europeans can learn the foreign language or languages they need or want, including English, for effective communication, especially to deal with the business of everyday life and exchange information, ideas, thoughts and feelings with people who speak a different language, and to achieve a wider and

deeper understanding of the ways of life and forms of thought of other peoples and of their

cultural heritage.

PRONI (national programme)

- To provide syllabuses and guidelines for ELT in all Mexican public basic education from last year of preschool (taking advantage of the fact that young children "are known to have plasticity and understanding in the learning of languages") to last year of lower secondary school (10 years in all).
- To ensure that students leave lower secondary school "with the necessary multilingual and multi-cultural competencies to face the communicative challenges of a globalized world successfully".

NOTE: 11 years after the launch of PRONI in 2009, most public upper secondary schools still start ELT from beginner level as if the 10 years of PRONI didn't exist.

CLAFET (postulated framework)

- To provide a common basis for Latin American EFL syllabuses, materials, etc., in public education, taking into account national languages (Spanish or Portuguese) and the most common needs (study, work, etc., not residence in an English-speaking country) of Latin American learners of English.
- To ensure, as far as possible, that all Latin Americans training for or working in a profession or skilled job requiring English (perhaps some 25% of the adult population) know English for their studies, work, and

professional development, and can develop other domains of communication in English if needed or wanted.

- To ensure, as far as possible, that all school students have several years of fairly good quality ELT in fairly favourable conditions, preferably starting in late childhood or early adolescence, as a basis for more intensive ELT prior to and beginning higher education or occupational training.

———

Observations on Table 1

The ELT contexts of PRONI are very similar to those of CLAFET and very different from the CEF. Of course, Mexico is a bit different from the rest of Latin America in that it has a very long border with the USA, English-speaking and the most powerful country in the world. However, Mexico City is 1,200 kms from Houston and 2,500 kms from Los Angeles, and Spanish is widely spoken on the US side of the border and beyond, so Spanish-English bilingualism isn't needed by most Mexicans. By comparison, Paris (French) is 340 kms from London (English), 360 kms from Frankfurt (German), 430 kms from Amsterdam (Dutch), 640 kms from Milan (Italian), and 790 kms from Madrid (Spanish), so L1-English bilingualism (and multilingualism when possible) is much more important in Europe than in Mexico or the rest of Latin America. Add to that the fact that European countries are much wealthier per capita than Latin American countries, so they have more to spend on ELT in basic education, and individuals have more to spend on travel, vacationing and study in other countries. It would be expected, therefore, that the aims and contents of PRONI would be much more in line with CLAFET than with the CEF.

Observations on Table 2

In spite of the above observations, the aims and scope of PRONI are actually more similar to the CEF than to CLAFET, though they also differ from the CEF in some ways.

Both the CEF and PRONI aim at universal bilingualism (and the CEF at widespread multilingualism) in their zones, while CLAFET aims at bilingualism for all Latin Americans who really need English (perhaps around 25% of adults in most countries) but for most others just a good introduction to English at school that could be a springboard for later learning of English if needed or wanted. The much more limited and targeted approach of CLAFET is based on two perceptions: First, most Latin Americans (perhaps around 75%) don't and won't really need English, and, second, the capacity of Latin American countries to provide good quality ELT in fairly favourable conditions (the only really worthwhile ELT) is very limited; therefore, CLAFET aims at the necessary and possible (ensuring most people who really need English learn it well) and not at the unnecessary and impossible (trying to ensure that everyone learns English well, though most don't need it and only poor quality ELT can be provided to most).

The CEF aims mainly at full general bilingualism, that is, a second language for daily life in another European country, for multicultural communication and understanding in Europe, and for lingua franca communication for any purposes in Europe and beyond (mainly English). PRONI is roughly on that same wavelength but with slightly different tuning: English as the lingua franca in a multilingual, multicultural, globalized world in which all Mexicans, through English, will "face the communicative challenges... successfully". CLAFET, as noted above, is much more limited and targeted. It assumes that for the foreseeable future the vast majority of Latin Americans will continue to be monolingual users of Spanish or Portuguese, which (especially Spanish, and supported by technology) serve them for a lot of international communication, that only a minority really need English, and that most of that minority don't need English for daily life in another country but for use in their own country. CLAFET considers that most really need English mainly for higher education and occupational training, then for professional or skilled work, and for continual professional development. That suggests less full and general bilingualism than the CEF and PRONI aim at, a bilingualism more targeted towards study, work, professional development, and associated activities, and perhaps focused heavily, for example, on ESP reading (as suggested above for higher education English courses) or on routine exchanges in a specific context, such as an airport information desk.

The CEF has been applied in Europe to all modes of ELT, basic education, higher education, language centres, and so on. In order to better achieve the aim of universal bilingualism or multilingualism, ELT in Europe has increasingly been taken down into early primary school, but even countries with notably high success in school ELT have not gone down to first year primary or below (e.g., the Netherlands starts ELT at age 10), which PRONI has (starting in last year of preschool, age 5-6). CLAFET, in contrast, doesn't aim at universal bilingualism, and suggests late childhood or early adolescence as the starting point, which could be the last year or years of primary school or the first year of lower secondary school. At the other end of basic education, PRONI stops at the end of lower secondary school, pouring students down into beginner English courses in most public upper secondary schools, while CLAFET, like the CEF, considers ELT beyond that and outside basic education, especially ELT focused on higher studies, work, and professional development. That could cover ELT in upper secondary schools, in higher education and higher level vocational training, in language centres, and in companies.

Finally, note that CLAFET mentions EFL syllabuses, materials, etc., that take into account national languages (Spanish or Portuguese) and the most common needs of Latin American learners of English (study and work, more than everyday life in an English-speaking country). The attention to needs has already been discussed in these observations, but the dominant tongues in Latin America is another consideration, which PRONi doesn't appear to take into account, and the CEF can't because of the range of different languages in the EU: ELT for native speakers of Portuguese and of Spanish can be generally the same, though it must deal with different pronunciation and some other issues, but ELT for native speakers of Spanish/Portuguese, German, Polish, Hungarian, Greek, etc., as in the EU, should be more differentiated, not to mention ELT for native speakers of Russian, Arabic, Thai, Mandarin Chinese, Japanese and so on, to which the CEF is also applied.

Using essentially the same syllabuses and textbooks with students with very different mother tongues, with very different needs, in very different countries and regions goes against the strong theoretical tide of context-aware and learner-centred ELT. The CEF can usefully be referred to all around the world, but considerable adaptation is needed for effective ELT in many contexts. CLAFET is a hypothetical framework for Latin America, or a blueprint for a framework, which itself would need further adaptation or definition for the different contexts within Latin America.

References

Council of Europe. (2009). *Common European Framework of Reference for Languages.* At https://www.coe.int/en/web/common-european-framework-reference-languages

Secretaría de Educación Pública. (2017). *Aprendizajes Clave: Lengua*

Extranjera. Inglés. Educación Básica. Secretaría de Educación Pública, SEP, Mexico. At https://www.planyprogramasdestudio.sep.gob.mx/descargables/biblioteca/basica-ingles/1LpM-Ingles_Digital.pdf

2. Orientations, approaches, and adaptability

A framework for ELT in a region (the two examples in this article are the CEF for Europe and CLAFET for Latin America, a postulated or hypothetical framework) may propose a general approach to ELT, but different specific approaches are required for different contexts (e.g., for a national English programme, and, perhaps within that, for early primary school, late primary school, secondary school and higher education). That means flexibility in the framework and recommended adaptation and suggestions for different contexts. Below, Table 3 presents general orientations and approaches, and Table 4 presents more specific approaches or recommendations.

———

Table 3: General orientations and approaches

CEF (actual framework)

The CEF aims to be:

- flexible: adaptable for use in different circumstances.
- open: capable of further extension and refinement.
- non-dogmatic: not irrevocably and exclusively attached to any of the competing linguistic or educational theories or practices.

In general terms, CEF has an action-oriented approach. Language use and language learning are seen to involve actions, in social contexts, that employ and develop a range of communicative competencies. Engagement in language activities, using language processes to produce and receive texts on specific themes in specific domains, and using strategies for specific tasks, allows participants to monitor the actions taken, and competences are thus reinforced or modified.

PRONI (national programme)

PRONI is less open and flexible than the CEF, partly because it is not a general framework but a national English programme for public schools from end of pre-school to end of lower secondary school only, with free textbooks provided (a range from commercial publishers to choose from)

PRONI embraces the CEF approach, with little adaptation to Mexican public school contexts and students' needs (e.g., few Mexicans ever need English in a range of social contexts, or at all). PRONI takes an action-centred approach focused on social practices of language. These are oriented towards the process and integration of learning and offer students opportunities to participate in different communicative exchanges that require the appropriate use of knowledge, abilities, attitudes and strategies, and to reflect on different aspects of language, linguistic expression and culture.

CLAFET (postulated framework)

CLAFET aims to be flexible, open and non-dogmatic, but taking the specific EFL teaching-learning contexts, conditions and needs of Latin America into account.

In general terms, CLAFET has an approach close to CEF. In ELT methodology, all variants of CLT (Communicative Language Teaching) are accepted, from CLT-PPP (Presentation-Practice-Production of language items in an environment of communication and communicative activities) to CLT-TBL (Task-Based Learning, working through graded communicative tasks, preferably related to learner needs, and focusing on language as required through consciousness raising tasks and focused practice). Handling of language form/use should take the students' L1—Spanish or Portuguese—into account.

———

Table 4: More specific approaches and/or suggestions for adaptation

CEF (actual framework)

The CEF is designed as the basis for quite distinct curriculums, syllabuses, materials, etc., to be developed in reference to it, so it aims to be open and flexible.

Each of the components of the CEF may, if selected as a main learning objective, offer choices in content and approaches to the facilitation of learning. For some situations, the objectives might be broad and for general competences and skills in the public domain, with some attention to intercultural communication; in other situations, the objectives might be narrow and, for example, for specific competences and skills in the occupational domain, or even just for occupational reading comprehension or for routine information exchanges.

The CEF has examples of different curriculums based on it: Primary School, with the focus on language awareness, general competences, comprehension, sound, rhythm, etc.; Lower Secondary School, with more attention to the linguistic, socio-linguistic and pragmatic dimensions of communicative competence; and Upper Secondary School, with a shift from formal ELT towards subject teaching in English (and the option of classes in another foreign language).

PRONI (national programme)

PRONI is essentially a single 10-year English curriculum covering A0 to B1 CEF levels to be applied from the US border to the Guatemala border, from large cosmopolitan cities to isolated towns, and from industrial areas to international tourism centres. The only indication that goals and approaches should be varied according to contexts is in a few statements in SEP documents like this: "These orientations and suggestions are indicative more than prescriptive. Their purpose is to offer the teacher various ways to handle the contents within the [PRONI] teaching approach. Each teacher can adapt them to their context or develop their own."

CLAFET (postulated framework)

CLAFET is intended for ELT mainly in Latin American public education, and that includes very different contexts and situations, in some countries starting from some level of primary school, in lower secondary and upper secondary school, through to higher education and language centres in public institutions; all that in large cosmopolitan cities, small provincial cities, and isolated and under-resourced towns and rural areas. CLAFET actually recommends that ELT should *not* be attempted where it is almost certain to fail nor be continued where it has clearly been failing for some time (at least some of PRONI would be cut back applying this recommendation). On the other hand, CLAFET recommends public language centres and online learning resources for older teenagers and adults who did not learn enough English at school and find they need or want it.

In some respects, CLAFET itself can be seen as an adaptation of the CEF for ELT in Latin American public education, and any private education that chooses to follow CLAFET guidelines. Naturally, it is more limited and focused than the CEF, aiming rather less at highly fluent English and more at English for specific purposes of some kind.

———

Observations on Table 3

While PRONI generally follows the CEF approach, it doesn't do so in a "flexible, open and non-dogmatic" way, adapting the CEF specifically for Mexico and offering variations or suggestions for use in the markedly different regional and local contexts that Mexico has. CLAFET, however, does aim to do something on those lines and be a framework specifically for Latin America, taking the region's EFL teaching-learning contexts, conditions and needs into account, including the students' L1, Spanish or Portuguese. CLAFET also roughly translates the CEF's rather theoretical description of its approach to ELT into the wide range of communicative ELT methodology that most professional EFL teachers in Latin America are now usually familiar with.

Observations on Table 4

The CEF and CLAFET both consider different circumstances for ELT, within Europe (and now the world, which wasn't the intention of the CEF) and within Latin America respectively, and both aim at encouraging and facilitating the appropriate adaptation for those different circumstances of ELT based on the frameworks. PRONI doesn't do that, except for briefly mentioning adaptation: "Each teacher can adapt [the ways of handling the contents within the PRONI teaching approach] to their context or develop their own."

The impression given is that adaptation is for teachers who fancy doing some, and for different socio-economic circumstances (which it may be, e.g., in relatively well-off areas with some English in the environment and students' home, and in impoverished areas with little or none), and not that ELT should be a bit different along the US border (especially where there's a lot of border traffic), in cosmopolitan cities, in isolated towns and rural areas, in heavily industrialized areas, in international tourism and vacation centres, and so on.

General observations

The CEF arose as part—a political and educational part—of 'The European project' (or, to be more precise, the Council of Europe's 'Language Learning and European Citizenship' project), intended "to promote European mobility, mutual understanding and cooperation, and overcome prejudice and discrimination". That accounts to some extent for the approach of the CEF: It aims at universal bilingualism or multilingualism, and that for all normal communicative purposes in the first foreign language, including, even especially, everyday life in another country (remember that the first foreign language isn't necessarily English, though ELT is by far the largest CEF-based activity). Another factor that accounts in part for the approach of the CEF is the general development and wealth of European countries: They have the resources to realistically aspire to provide universal foreign language teaching of generally high quality. ELT, and other foreign language teaching, in Europe has become much more widespread and successful than 30, 40 or more years ago, and some of that is surely due to the CEF.

Though PRONI is a very different matter in a very different context, it's modelled closely on the CEF, far too closely. That happened for a number of reasons, no doubt, probably including: The global influence of the CEF (which the CEF didn't seek), incomplete understanding of the CEF (largely ignoring that it should be adapted to different circumstances), ill-considered acceptance of clichés like "Everyone needs English in today's globalised world" and "The earlier children start learning a second language, the better" (on that, see Rixon, 2000), and, of course, politics (promising social equity, though it can't be delivered). For a start, Mexico doesn't have the resources to realistically aspire to provide universal foreign language teaching of generally high quality, partly because Mexico isn't yet as developed and wealthy as Europe, and partly because even more resources may be needed in Mexico because of the size and varied conditions (one country in almost half the area of the EU, which contains 27 countries). Also, Mexico doesn't need bilingualism or multilingualism the way European countries do, especially those with notably non-international languages like Dutch, Swedish, Finnish, Polish, Czech, Hungarian, etc. If those and other considerations had been noted and acted upon, PRONI would have been a radical adaptation of the CEF, not only in its aims, but also in its general orientation and approach. Something on the lines of CLAFET, which itself could be considered an adaptation of the CEF, would surely have been a much better starting point for PRONI, but even then, variations in the programme and in the teaching approach are really needed for at least some of the very different contexts and circumstances in Mexico.

What is taught and how it is taught in ELT should be very different for young children (5-6 years old in PRONI), older children and young teenagers, young adults and adults (not covered in PRONI, but they really should be because they're the most likely users of English outside classrooms, in the working world), for students in places where some English is in the environment and the need of English is a more real possibility (US border areas, international vacation and tourist areas, industry and business areas) and in remote towns and rural areas where the need of English is just a remote possibility, for ESP in higher education (English for medicine, engineering, business, etc.) and specific domains and skills, as in company courses (technical reading, business correspondence, routine hotel and restaurant exchanges, etc.).

References

Council of Europe. (2009). *Common European Framework of Reference for Languages.* At https://www.coe.int/en/web/common-european-framework-reference-languages

Rixon, S. (2000). Optimum age or optimum conditions? Issues related to the teaching of languages to primary age children. British Council.

Secretaría de Educación Pública. (2017). *Aprendizajes Clave: Lengua Extranjera. Inglés. Educación Básica.* Secretaría de Educación Pública, SEP, Mexico. At https://www.planyprogramasdestudio.sep.gob.mx/descargables/biblioteca/basica-ingles/1LpM-Ingles_Digital.pdf

3. The content, methodology, and levels of ELT

The contents of ELT in a framework or programme, overall and by level, with implied or specified methodology, may be very complex and analysed down to considerable detail. The CEF identifies domains, themes, situations, communicative tasks and purposes, communicative activities and strategies, communicative language processes, texts and text types, competences, and, of course, can-do statements. And that's just the surface of the CEF analysis, which has sub-categories and discussion of all the above. Syllabus designers, textbook writers and teachers of specific student populations—for example, young children, older children, teenagers, adults, students in higher education, working professionals, in general and in a given area, etc.—tend to operate much more synthetically or holistically, perhaps with student motivation (or lack of), appropriate situations, appropriate communicative purposes, appropriate linguistic competence, and appropriate can-dos most in mind. They tend to think more in terms of "This is what these students need/want (or can be brought round to), this is what should work for them best". As an ex-teacher, syllabus designer and textbook writer myself, I can't help taking that approach to some extent below.

————

Table 5: Content in terms of domains and situations

CEF (actual framework)

- The CEF, a basis for all language syllabuses, curriculum guide-lines, examinations, textbooks, etc., in Europe, naturally covers all major general domains of language use (personal, public, educational and occupational), specific domains within them, and all common situations of use within them.
- These domains and situations are conceived almost entirely in adult terms, hardly at all in terms of young children or even older ones, probably looking intently towards tests and certification that will serve (young) adults in higher education and work, and towards their independent movement around Europe and beyond.

PRONI (national programme)

- PRONI, for public education from last year of preschool to last year of lower secondary school only, starts with a 3-year introductory cycle for children aged 5-6 to 7-8, aimed at "raising awareness of the existence of foreign languages and cultures", "basic communication in English, especially receptive, in personal and routine contexts", and "the exploration of texts, especially of an imaginative character".

- After those 3 introductory years, starting with students aged 8-9, the last 7 years of PRONI follow the CEF fairly closely, from A1 level (years 3-4 of primary school), through A2 level (years 5-6 of primary school), up to B1 level (by the end of lower secondary school).

CLAFET (postulated framework)

- CLAFET is intended as a basis for ELT in Latin America, especially in public education. It aims at ensuring that all those training for or in jobs requiring English have the English they need and can develop professionally and learn other domains of use if needed or wanted. As such, it focuses rather more on the educational and occupational domains and rather less on the personal and public domains as they relate to living in English-speaking countries, close relationships with English-speaking people, etc. It also pays close attention to partial bilingualism, such as study and occupational reading proficiency.

————

Table 6: Content in terms of can-do, communicative activities and language, and levels

CEF (actual framework)

- The CEF levels work their way up through general language proficiency in all skills, domains, themes, situations, etc. They're good for learners progressing through a foreign language almost as if it were their mother tongue, from simple and common communication and language in the everyday personal and public domains to become totally proficient users of the language: that, of course, is just what many Europeans do, especially in the north of Europe.
- The CEF global scale goes from *"Can understand and use familiar everyday expressions and very basic phrases aimed at the satisfaction of needs of a concrete type, ...introduce him/herself and others, ...ask and answer questions about personal details, ... interact in a simple way provided the other person talks slowly and clearly and is prepared to help"* [A1] to *"Can understand with ease virtually everything heard or read,...summarize information from different spoken and written sources, reconstructting arguments and accounts in a coherent presentation, ...express him/herself spontaneously, very fluently and precisely, differentiating finer shades of meaning even in complex situations"* [C2].
- Other scales deal with listening, speaking, reading and writing separately and in more detail, and partial proficiency is considered.

PRONI (national programme)

Here's the target learner profile for end of lower secondary school, which is end of PRONI, at B1 level:

- Understands and exchanges opinions about the general meaning, main ideas and some details of different clear spoken and written texts in standard language about familiar topics (work, study, leisure, etc.) and current events. Knows how to interpret and act in many community situations, and in those that might occur during a journey in an area where English is spoken, and even in some unexpected situations. Describes and justifies, in a basic way, experiences, events, wishes and aspirations, understands and expresses directions, explains briefly plans and points of view. Develops empathy for other cultures through games and literary activities.

And here are the intended learning outcomes from communicative activities in that last year of PRONI:

- Can negotiate topics of conversation, develop conversations, and end them.
- Can get the gist of TV programmes, write notes about emotions and reactions, and share them with others.
- Can grasp spoken accounts of unexpected situations, react to them, and give accounts of similar situations.
- Can present initial ideas about topics like young people's rights, take a position and anticipate others, and offer counter-arguments and defend own position.
- Can get the gist, main ideas and details of fantasy or suspense stories, describe the characters, and write about them and their actions.
- Can understand instructions and how they are structured, plan and write instructions (e.g., for a simple experiment), and check and edit them.
- Can understand accounts of historical events, plan and write account of historical event, and check and edit them.

CLAFET (postulated framework)

- CLAFET roughly follows the CEF levels, but brings certain things down to lower levels of teaching-learning (e.g., reading of simple, then not so simple, formal texts that tend to have many Portuguese/Spanish-English cognates, and, in higher education English courses, simple or routine educational and, occupational communication) and pushes certain things up to higher levels (e.g., describing and discussing personal feelings and emotions, colloquial language, and everyday life communication). That responds to the needs of most Latin American learners of English: Use in their own country mainly for study, training, work and continuous occupational development, not for living in an English-speaking country or frequent travel outside their country, or Latin America. However, learner expectations and motivations may call for more everyday English than they need or are ever likely to need.

- CLAFET gives even more attention to partial proficiency than the CEF: Reading, mentioned above, is one obvious area, and reading courses and certification could be important for both employers and employees, where other skills in English are hardly required; ESP courses in higher education and companies could also focus on partial proficiency of different kinds.

———

Observations on Table 5

The CEF was not designed specifically for English, but with European ELT largely based on it and its forerunners, English learning in schools and elsewhere in Europe has generally improved significantly over recent decades, and in some countries extremely impressively. Even so, most adults in the southern half and the east of Europe don't have a functional command of English; for example, in 2012 Eurobarometer estimated 22% for Spain and 27% for Portugal, which would probably be a little higher now. Beyond the home area of the CEF—Europe—the framework has been used, and misused, for ELT around the world, Mexico and PRONI being but one example.

PRONI took the CEF as its main basis, adapting it little for Mexico. What it did adapt was often inappropriate or unrealistic; for example, ELT in Mexican public schools from last year of preschool on, and B1 as the end-of-lower secondary school target (the most successful European countries in English learning, in Scandinavia and the Netherlands, start ELT from age 8, 9 or 10, and B1 for everyone leaving lower secondary school would be astounding for most European countries). Note that CLAFET (just a hypothetical framework, of course) is partly a product of PRONI and its generally infelicitous 11 years of existence, with mostly negative evaluations and reviews (Davies & Dominguez, 2020), and with lower secondary sent back down to beginner English courses in most public upper secondary schools.

As has been stated previously in this 4-part article, CLAFET suggests that ELT in most Latin American public education should normally start no earlier than the middle of primary school, with students usually aged between 8 and 11. That's because CLAFET doesn't aim at creating universally L1-English bilingual countries in Latin America (which is unrealistic, probably impossible, and quite unnecessary), but at ensuring that all those training for or in jobs requiring English have the English they need and can develop professionally and learn to use English in other domains if needed or wanted. That means English for use *in* one's own Latin American country much, much more than for use *outside* it. With that aim, ELT should intensify as people approach decision-taking on their adult working lives (upper secondary) and actually take decisions (higher education or occupational training), and the ELT should be largely directed towards English for higher study and work. The motivation of older learners receiving good quality ELT relevant for their studies or work can more than make up for the natural language learning ability of most young children, especially if the ELT they're receiving is poor quality and in poor conditions.

Observations on Table 6

The CEF covers almost everything that European foreign language curriculum and course designers, and textbook writers, might need to consider for a given ELT situation, from children to adults and from regular school to language centre courses, etc. It has established well-founded levels for general language proficiency, and also for proficiency in separate skill. However, ELT curriculum and course designers, textbook writers and so on should select from the CEF, adapt and perhaps add.

PRONI could have selected from the CEF, adapted and added what was likely to be most appropriate for Mexican public schools. It didn't. The vast majority of Mexican school graduates, or Mexicans in general, will never have an everyday conversation with a foreigner in English, nor travel in a country where English is spoken and Spanish hardly at all, nor talk in English about experiences, events, wishes, aspirations and opinions, nor watch and talk about TV programmes in English, nor play games in English, nor read and talk about literature in English (at least, not outside a classroom). What some certainly will need to do is use English for study, work and professional development, with reading especially important for many, in ways dependent on their occupational and other choices and fortune in life. That study and work related use of English may require travel and stays abroad and the use of English there. Also, with the English for basic social and transactional situations that they should learn at school, they can usually develop that as they go, perhaps becoming fluent conversationalists in English through use, not classes.

What was really needed instead of PRONI as it is, was a CLAFET-like selection from the CEF, plus adaptation and additions, and running from late primary school to the end of upper secondary school, and provision for upper secondary school graduates who need more English, perhaps through a system of public language centres. The vast majority of Mexicans and other Latin Americans working in shops, stores and markets, building and maintenance, transportation, agriculture, factories, vehicle maintenance, restaurants, cafés and bars, hairdressing, offices and public services, etc., simply don't need to know English. A few do even in those areas, of course, and many, but not all, professionals and skilled workers certainly do: A national English programme should aim to ensure that those people, specifically, can learn the English they need, and other public provision of ELT should fill any voids left by the national English programme, which commercial ELT will probably do otherwise.

References

Council of Europe. (2009). *Common European Framework of Reference for Languages*. At https://www.coe.int/en/web/common-european-framework-reference-languages

Davies, P., & Domínguez, R. (2020). Teachers' perceptions of ELT in public secondary schools. In ELTinLA and this book.

European Commission, Eurobarometer. (2012). *Europeans and their languages.*
At http://ec.europa.eu/commfrontoffice/publicopinion/archives/ebs/ebs_386_en.pdf.

Secretaría de Educación Pública. (2017). *Aprendizajes Clave: Lengua Extranjera. Inglés. Educación Básica.* Secretaría de Educación Pública, SEP, Mexico. At https://www.planyprogramasdestudio.sep.gob.

mx/descargables/biblioteca/basica-ingles/1LpM-Ingles_Digital.pdf

4. Blueprint for CLAFET

CLAFET, Common Latin American Framework for English Teaching, doesn't exist but is a hypothetical document postulated for this article. What does exist and has strongly influenced ELT in Latin America is the Common European Framework of Reference for Languages, CEF. That influence has been positive to some extent, and potentially entirely positive, but only if Latin American curriculum and course designers select from it, adapt what they select and possibly add things appropriately for the Latin American ELT situation or situations they're addressing.

Those Latin American curriculum and course designers, especially national English programme designers, should always bear in mind that Latin America isn't Europe, Brazil isn't Germany and Mexico isn't Sweden, and, indeed, Mexico City isn't Mexicali or Oaxaca City or Santa María Tlahuitoltepec (Oaxaca) or Cancún. They should try to keep politics (e.g., "Every child has the right to learn English from preschool on, not just the privileged few") and heavily flawed clichés (e.g., "Everyone needs English in today's globalised world", "The earlier children start to learn a second language, the better") out of ELT. They should be realistic about who really needs English, might need English, and doesn't need English, and how to best provide good ELT to those who really need or might need English, and keep plans within available budgets and human resources.

The blueprint for CLAFET that follows aims at helping them do that. Perhaps other, much younger, Latin American ELT experts will come along and develop this blueprint into a fuller framework, much indebted to the CEF, no doubt, but valuable in its own right as a more specific framework for ELT in Latin America, especially in the public sector. I do hope so.

Target zone and ELT contexts in CLAFET

CLAFET is for all ELT contexts in Latin America with the exception of highly privileged ones like bilingual and similar private schools and top private universities, where, like many Europeans, many students travel, study and live for periods abroad. CLAFET, then, is particularly for ELT in the public sector, which accounts for around 90% of all education in Latin America, and elsewhere.

Latin America is distinguished from other parts of the world by having Spanish or Portuguese as the or a national language of all the countries in an extremely large region (except for a few very small ones. e.g., Guyana, Haiti). Spanish and Portuguese are closely related international languages, Spanish with particularly wide-spread use around the world, and that gives Latin Americans access to much international and digital communication in their native language, unlike, for example, northern and eastern Europeans. That has implications for ELT in Latin America: ELT should be especially for those who really need English, not universally or extensively for everyone, including all those who will never need English. The relative similarity of Spanish and Portuguese to English, especially in more formal written texts, where cognates often abound, also has implications for ELT in Latin America, as opposed, for example, to ELT in Greece, Hungary, Poland and Finland, not to mention Russia, Iran, China and Japan: More 'comparative linguistics' can usefully underly ELT in Latin America, and more early reading, especially of formal texts (especialmente de textos formales / formais).

The geographic location and socio-economic conditions of most of Latin America mean that international travel is generally too time-consuming and expensive for most Latin Americans, including most of the 90% or so that go through public education, to travel outside Latin America. That has implications for ELT in Latin America: Most of the professionals and skilled workers that need English use it entirely or almost entirely in their own country, not frequently travelling, or studying or working abroad, let alone globe-trotting and frequently vacationing abroad.

Aims of CLAFET

CLAFET aims to provide a common basis for Latin American EFL syllabuses, materials, etc. (except in highly privileged contexts), taking into account Latin Americans' national languages (Spanish or Portuguese) and Latin Americans' needs (mostly English for study, work and associated activities, and mostly in the learner/user's own country, but sometimes travelling abroad, or studying/working in an English-speaking country).

CLAFET does not aim, like some current national English programmes in Latin America, to make Latin American countries universally L1-English bilingual, but rather to ensure, as far as possible, that all Latin Americans training for or working in a profession or skilled job requiring English (probably around 20-25% of the adult population) know English for their studies, work, and professional development, and can develop other domains of communication in English if needed or wanted. Towards that aim, CLAFET suggests that all school students should have several years of fairly *good quality* ELT in fairly favourable conditions, preferably starting in late childhood or early adolescence, as a basis for more intensive ELT prior to and beginning higher education or occupational training; language centres can provide *good quality* ELT for people who find they need English or more English after their school years. The quality and conditions of ELT are vital for good results, and resources should not be squandered on poor quality ELT, probably in poor conditions, for all children from a very early age as in some current national English programmes.

General orientation and approach of CLAFET

CLAFET aims to be flexible, open and non-dogmatic, but taking the specific EFL teaching-learning contexts, conditions and needs of Latin America into account. It accepts all variants of CLT (Communicative Language Teaching), from CLT-PPP (Presentation-Practice-Production of language items in an environment of communication and communicative activities) to CLT-TBL (Task-Based Learning, working through graded communicative tasks, preferably related to learner needs, and focusing on language as required through consciousness raising tasks and focused practice). Handling of language form/use should take the students' L1 (Spanish or Portuguese) into account.

More specific approaches and/or suggestions for adaptation of CLAFET

CLAFET considers the very different contexts and situations of ELT in Latin America, especially in public education, from primary school (with CLAFET suggesting it should *not* start before the middle of primary unless resources and conditions for successful ELT are definitely available), lower secondary and upper secondary school, through to higher education (where EAP, English for Academic Purposes, and/or ESP, English for Specific Purposes, is most appropriate, often with an emphasis on reading), language centres, and perhaps other provision of ELT; all that in large cosmopolitan cities, small provincial cities, and isolated and under-resourced towns and rural areas, which may call for different approaches, some of which a fully-developed CLAFET would make suggestions for.

Content of CLAFET in terms of domains and situations

CLAFET focuses especially on the domains that most Latin Americans who need English need most, that is, the educational and occupational domains. Most Latin Americans who really need English need it principally for higher education or occupational training, and later for professional or skilled work and associated activities, all that usually in their own country. Those associated activities may include receiving foreign visitors, looking after them and showing them around, working with them, and corresponding with them, all in the Latin American's own country, and possibly travel, training and work abroad, which takes us into the personal and public domains, useful and unavoidable in beginner and elementary courses, anyway, and essential for children and young teenagers. So, starting in primary school, the personal and public domains naturally dominate, but by upper secondary school the educational and occupational domains should be coming along strongly, and in higher education or occupational training they should dominate, with themes and communicative situations becoming more specific to the degree or other programme of the students. In higher education and occupational training, more English for close relationships with English-speaking people and for living in English-speaking countries should usually be left for individuals to develop from the English they already have if and when they find themselves developing a close relationship or about to spend time living abroad. After all, that's what bilingual people have done, learning more from use of English in their lives than study of English in classrooms.

It's very important to note, and indeed emphasise, that most grammar and much lexis isn't exclusive to one domain or another, but is used in all domains, just on different themes and in different situations, and perhaps with stylistic variations. Levels, which are discussed below, should be seen, not only in terms of can-do and communicative acts, but also in terms of progress from simple language (and, in Latin America, perhaps similarity to Spanish/Portuguese) to more and more complex and alternative language (other ways to express the same idea, synonyms).

Content of CLAFET in terms of can-do, communicative activities and language, and levels

CLAFET roughly follows the CEF levels, but the vast continent-and-a-bit that it's for (South America, Central America, and southern North America) is very different from Europe, so the content of the levels is also different. Most ELT in Latin America should realistically focus on the use of English in the students' own country more than on international travel and living in English-speaking countries, though it shouldn't entirely neglect that possibility either. CLAFET covers the following distinct major ELT scenarios or types of context in Latin America, and suggests variations of content and approach for each:

ELT in primary school: Mainly beginner to A1 level. English for the personal and public domains, in situations including communication and interaction in the classroom with the English teacher and classmates, and in the school at large with English teachers and other English-speaking staff (national English programmes should promote English among non-ELT staff), and in communicative activities such as games, roleplays of interaction with foreigners in the students' country, perhaps including young returnees from the USA, and in places like international airports, vacation centres, and tourist sites, and some in English-speaking countries if students are interested. More reading than usual in A1 classes, with easy illustrated, fairly cognate-rich and/or familiar texts (e.g., about popular films and TV programmes).

Lower and upper secondary school: Beginner (for students who didn't have English, or effective ELT, in primary school) to around

B1 level (for students who did). Some English for the personal and public domains at the lower levels, much as in primary school, but with some English in the educational and occupational domains from the start, and shifting continuously in that direction. That includes more reading than usual at all levels, especially of fairly formal texts, which tend to have a logical structure and many English-L1 cognates. Where courses reach B1 level or higher, most likely in the last year or two of upper secondary school, with 16 to 18-year-old students, they could even shift towards some EAP.

Higher education and occupational training: False beginner or mid-A1 (for students who didn't have effective ELT at school) to around B2 level (for students who did). Some English for the personal and public domains at the lower levels, but with English in the educational and occupational domains from the start, and some EAP, including more reading than usual at all levels, especially of formal texts, which tend to have a logical structure and many English-L1 cognates. Where students receive English courses within their faculty or department, there could be some ESP from the start, with simple, accessible texts even at beginner level. Some courses could be very specialised or focused, for example, academic or technical reading in the students' field, routine information exchanges in the students' field (e.g., travel and hospitality services: information desk, hotel reception, restaurant), listening to talks in the students' field. English courses in companies and institutions could be run on similar lines.

Language centres: Beginner to as high a level as there's a demand, which is likely to be B2 at least. Language centres in institutions of higher education could, and probably should, have educational and occupational domain content from the start, and even EAP. Where the student population is very mixed, more personal and public domain content may be appropriate. Language centres can also offer specialised or focused courses if there's a demand—conversation, reading, writing.

EFL services other than taught courses: An EFL learning website specifically for Latin America on CLAFET lines could be very useful—and popular. Apart from the well-known general tests like TOEFL (which, appropriately for Latin America, is quite EAP) and the Cambridge tests (which are conveniently ranged from CEF A2 level upwards), partial and specialised proficiency tests, could be useful in Latin America, and elsewhere, for example, educational-occupational reading, ESP tests for areas like medicine, business, travel and hospitality. Some international options for such tests already exist.

CLAFET and the CEF

CLAFET naturally reflects its great debt to the CEF, but it also tries to respond to the realities of ELT in Latin America and the needs of Latin Americans. The following figure indicates similarities and differences between CLAFET and the CEF:

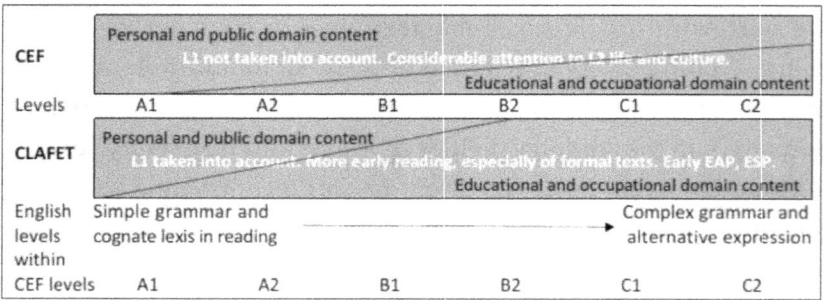

CEF	Personal and public domain content					
	L1 not taken into account. Considerable attention to L2 life and culture.					
				Educational and occupational domain content		
Levels	A1	A2	B1	B2	C1	C2
CLAFET	Personal and public domain content					
	L1 taken into account. More early reading, especially of formal texts. Early EAP, ESP.					
				Educational and occupational domain content		
English levels within	Simple grammar and cognate lexis in reading				Complex grammar and alternative expression	
CEF levels	A1	A2	B1	B2	C1	C2

Figure 7. Similarities and differences between CLAFET and CEF

10

ELT FUTUROLOGY

Back to the future

Let's go back and look forwards from 1965, when I started teaching English in Mexico. I taught in the upper secondary school (Prepara-toria) of the Universidad Autónoma de Puebla, Mexico. Students had a beginner course in the first semester, in spite of having had three years of English classes in lower secondary school. The courses were supposed to go up to what we now call A2 level, but very few students actually got there. Those results were partly because the groups had over 60 students.

That was ELT in public education in those days (not very different from today in many places): curricular English classes in lower and upper secondary school, usually in large groups, and with nobody expecting students to actually learn much English unless they did so through their own noble efforts. In universities, language centres were just beginning to be established—the Departamento de Lenguas of the UAP, where I also taught, in 1965, and the CELE

UNAM at about the same time. There were no common core type English classes for undergraduates until many years later.

Few in 1965 would have predicted that ELT in public education in Mexico half a century later would have expanded exponentially as it has, but it was already clear that English was becoming ever more important for the nation's development, and for many professionals and skilled workers personally.

That realization was reflected in private education before 1965, of course, where most schools had English classes throughout primary as well as secondary. It amused me to see "Inglés obligatorio" on the walls of many kindergartens, conjuring up images of little children being held down and force-fed English and spinach. There were also bilingual schools, with more intensive English and subject classes in English. They were among the few schools, public or private, with good results in ELT.

Much has changed since then, much hasn't. *Plus ça change, plus c'est la même chose.*

Fin de siècle, debut de siècle change

The bits of French above remind me to mention that French, still a vital lingua franca in parts of the world today, was taught in schools in Mexico, including public secondary schools, into the second half of the 20th century. My Mexican wife just missed having French classes at school in the 1950s—they were removed from the curriculum the year before she passed into upper secondary. That should remind us that lingua francas come and go (Greek and Latin) and rise and fall (French and…).

Back to the future in the past of ELT in Mexico. By the end of the last century, the ELT scene had changed considerably and was in a process of more change. Public universities, and many private ones and other institutions of higher education, had language centres with English courses up to advanced levels. They also had common core type English programmes for undergraduates, most starting at beginner level in spite of six years of English in lower and upper secondary school. English was also being taught in some public primary schools in 4 states (Morelos the first to start, in 1992). The teaching of English in selected public primary schools spread to about half of the 32 Mexican states in the first years of the new century, and in 2009, a national programme for English throughout basic education began to be implemented, Programa Nacional de Inglés en Educación Básica, PNIEB.

PNIEB could hardly have been predicted in 1965 because it copied what had been happening in Europe as a result of the formation of the European Union and its language policies (CEFR), and they weren't developed until the 1980s and 90s. Was it appropriate for Mexico to copy Europe?

Well, apart from Mexico being intrinsically different from Europe in many ways, it also had a population explosion, from around 40 million to over 100 million in just 40 years (and to over 120 million today), which severely strained government systems and resources, as well as Mexican society in general. In education, for example, there were just over 6.5 million students in primary schools and just under 400,000 in lower secondary schools in all Mexico in 1965, and by 2005 those figures had risen to just over 12 million and just under 5 million. It should probably also be mentioned that, while the EU has 24 official languages, Mexico has only one, Spanish, itself a major international language. Europe was, and still is, hardly the most appropriate model for Mexico.

2006, "Year of ELT Futurology", part 1

David Graddol's *English Next* came out in 2006. In it, he presented the forces and trends that had made English the world's dominant lingua franca, and those that are likely to reduce that dominance and bring other major languages forwards as alternative lingua francas, as well as connecting more languages to global communication. He referred to languages used on the Internet to show how technology was changing the situation. Here's some of the information given:

	English	Japanese	German	Spanish	Chinese	French	Korean	Portuguese	Other
2000	51.3%	8.1%	5.9%	5.8%	5.4%	3.9%	3.5%	–	16.1%
2005	32%	8%	6%	6%	13%	4%	3%	3%	25%

Figure 8. Languages used on the Internet

Imagine where those languages stand today—certainly English even lower and Chinese even higher. Graddol also wrote that "machine translation of web content is only a mouse-click away".

A major thesis in *English Next* was that "a new orthodoxy [in ELT] appears to have taken root", and Graddol called it the "World English Project" (WEP). He saw ELT shifting from teaching English as a foreign language (EFL), with native speakers (in spite of their confusingly diverse and continually changing English) as the models to be copied, to teaching English as a lingua franca (ELF), with whatever models learners (and their non-native English teachers) have most contact with to be copied (e.g., Indian, Singaporean or Hong Kong English in Asia).

TEFL has traditionally been ELT from secondary school up, with students in higher education continuing to receive English classes, trying to make them fairly proficient by the time they graduate. TELF, on the other hand, is ELT from the beginning of primary school, or before, often through CLIL (Content and Language Integrated Learning), with B2+ or even C1+ level English then required for entry into higher education, where some courses are taught in

English. Obviously, TELF requires much greater investment and many more highly competent English teachers (most with C1+ English) than TEFL.

Thirteen years after Graddol prophesied that TELF-WEP would replace much, if not most, traditional TEFL, it has come true in most of Europe, with excellent results in some places, especially northern Europe, and not very good results in other places. It has been implemented in public education in many other parts of the world also, with very varied results. In Latin America, features of WEP have been implemented (particularly starting English classes in public primary school, as in Mexico's PNIEB), but generally without the investment required for the teaching-learning conditions, ELT quality and CLIL, which are almost essential for successful TELF-WEP. PNIEB (now called PRONI, Programa Nacional de Inglés) has been a general failure, no doubt with a degree of success in some schools.

As mentioned above, something on WEP lines has long existed in bilingual schools and private schools with high quality ELT in Mexico, as in the rest of Latin America and elsewhere. Some bilingual schools still insist on a model of native English, very 'British' or very 'American', but many have broken away from that towards ELF, especially where many students have different backgrounds, for example, parents with more American, British, Indian or other English, or frequent trips to the USA or UK or Australia. You could say that what Graddol predicted was the spread of private bilingual or semi-bilingual school ELT to public primary and secondary schools, and that's what has happened successfully in a few countries.

2006, "Year of ELT Futurology", part 2

The same year that *English Next* was published, 2006, I gave a plenary talk at a congress in Veracruz (FEULE, Foro de Expertos

Universitarios en Lenguas Extranjeras), without having read *English Next* yet. Since it was a congress about foreign languages in general, not just English, I gave the talk in Spanish.

I started by waffling about how English had become so important in higher education and for many professionals and skilled workers, and how ELT had expanded massively, becoming a very large profession. I then veered to the negative: 50 years of expanding ELT in Mexico had been a general failure, with around 75% of students entering higher education still as near beginners in English, and most graduating well below intermediate level. And I rubbished the popular refrain that "Everyone needs English nowadays". I was being provocative, seriously provocative, I hoped.

I was leading towards the grim prediction that, unless educational authorities and ELT professionals got their act together soon and started producing dramatically better results, many English teachers would be out of a job before retirement age. The ELT boom would end. While an important number of Mexicans would continue to need and want English (and the classes and effort usually required to get it), most Mexicans never would need English, and more and more would realize that and would no longer want to slog away at English in classrooms year after year, with much pain and little or no gain.

At that point I showed the slide below, which (unbeknown to me) echoed Graddol: other languages (including Spanish) were rising to stop English being the single dominant lingua franca, technology might dramatically reduce the need for living lingua francas, etc.:

Están cambiando las cosas

- El español cada vez más se usa en el Internet y adquiere mayor importancia internacional
- Los programas de traducción automática son cada vez

mejores (comparados por ejemplo con la comprensión de lectura de una persona con inglés de nivel intermedio bajo)
- Por el gran mercado latinoamericano (y los 40+ millones de hispanoparlantes en EU), cada vez más se publican ediciones en español de revistas profesionales

I cited JAMA, *The Journal of the American Medical Association*, and other journals as examples of the publication of Spanish versions of English language professional and scientific journals and books.

Machine translation has certainly progressed a lot since 2006. In a recent article in my now discontinued online magazine, *ELTinLA*, Jeremy Harmer tells an anecdote of a British teacher in Nanjing, China, who was easily able to get what he wanted in a computer store via machine translation. When will most people who want it have really good, and cheap, machine translation software in their computer devices? Is it already available and I don't know? Machine interpretation of live speech may also be only a quick chip implantation away now. Governments, why invest vast amounts of money, time, sweat and tears in universal school ELT, when quick, cheap chip implants are able to give everyone live conversation in any major language (and the minor language of your choice—Basque, Welsh, Guaraní…)?

Sorry, I'm rambling, perhaps to avoid admitting that ELT jobs are still being created in Mexico 13 years after my prediction. I was wrong. But my conclusion is that the general failure of a profession doesn't necessarily mean the rejection of that profession by its promoters and clients. Consider the medical profession until modern times—matasanos. If ELT were medical treatment, most students of English would be sick or dead today. Perhaps if we let students' blood or applied leeches in every class until they passed a recognized proficiency test at, say, B1+ level, they'd try harder and learn more English.

Dah, dah... different ELT for different contexts?

The current ELT sagas may go on indefinitely, heroic in Scandinavia and some other places, mundane, comic or even tragic in others. But I hope a new... no, not orthodoxy, Graddol's term... a new, but not entirely new, range of realistic, pragmatic approaches to ELT (including deciding not to teach English everywhere, for everyone) will interrupt the Mexican ELT saga and start a better narrative. Naturally, I wish the same for other places where ELT is currently... well, let's say "not working very well".

Yes, a range of approaches, not a dominant orthodoxy. Not just TEFL or TELF-WEP, not this methodology or that methodology, not this national programme or that national programme. A range of different approaches to choose from and develop and customize. Countries and regions with many languages, need a universal second language internally as well as a lingua franca for global use, and English may be good for both: India, Nigeria, the European Union, large parts of Asia and Africa. Countries with national languages little spoken elsewhere need a lingua franca for global use: Finland, Greece, Iran, Thailand, Japan. Countries in a large region where a major international language is spoken already have that language as a fairly global lingua franca, but English may still be needed by some people for some purposes: Latin America, the Arab world, francophone Africa. Rich countries, poor countries, small countries, large countries, may find quite different ELT approaches more appropriate.

Of course, I'm just suggesting the obvious: well-informed, intelligent, realistic, learner-centred and context-based ELT. While that may mean fewer ELT jobs in Mexico and elsewhere (as I predicted in 2006), it could mean more and better learning of English by those who really need it. As for ELT futurology, well, what will be, will be, for better or for worse.

Reference

Graddol, D. (2006). *English Next*. British Council. At https://englishagenda.britishcouncil.org/sites/default/files/attachments/books-english-next.pdf

PART II

SPECIFIC ASPECTS OF ELT
IN LATIN AMERICA

COMMUNICATIVE SKILLS

11

COMMUNICATIVE LISTENING

Listening in real language use and language learning

Babies begin their lives hearing language spoken around them, their native language. They listen to it and begin to recognize common bits of sound, which they explore through babbling. By six months, most babies recognize a significant number of words, psycholinguists believe: they have a small but growing listening lexicon six months or more before they produce any recognizable words or phrases themselves. First language learning and the communicative use of language begin with listening to other people talking around us.

A similar process occurs when people pick up another language through living in a country or community where that other language is spoken and their native language isn't. We all know people—and some of us are among them—who have never taken classes in a foreign language but speak it because they've lived where it's the community language.

Communicative listening is vital not only for communication itself, but also for beginning to learn a language and progressing in it. We've known that for a very long time, and it has been fundamental in some teaching methods, notably Total Physical Response (Larson-Freeman, 2000). However, much ELT still provides beginner and elementary students with very little communicative listening and focuses heavily on getting them to produce sentences, often in mechanical and uncommunicative ways.

Listening in EFL courses

We must recognize, however, that learning English as a foreign language in a classroom, especially as an adolescent or adult, is different from learning a first language, or learning another language through living in a community that speaks it. Students' lives, including their social lives, don't depend on understanding and learning the language in the same way as babies or foreign residents' lives do, and the students have far, far less exposure to English, usually only 3 to 6 hours each week (assuming most of their classes are actually in English, much less if they aren't).

On the other hand, unlike babies, students already know what language is and how it works; they're not beginning from a tabula rasa. Even beginners usually try to recognize common words and phrases in the stream of sound they hear, especially if it's occurring in a familiar context where certain words, phrases and interactions can be expected. Also, in most parts of the world, and certainly in most parts of Latin America, students have heard lots of English— in television, films, songs—even if they've never really tried to understand it much. There are, then, advantages as well as disadvantages in EFL classroom listening compared to babies acquiring English as their first language.

Most modern ELT approaches (in fact, most ELT approaches for over a century now) try to replicate to some extent, within the constraints of classroom courses, the immersion situations of babies learning their native language and foreign residents in an English-speaking country. They include listening in two ways: through English as the main (and sometimes exclusive) classroom language, and through listening comprehension tasks, usually with recorded texts, to develop listening as one of the four basic communicative skills. However, the reality in EFL classrooms around Latin America, and elsewhere, is not so clear and simple. English courses are very different in different places and institutions.

In many commercial language centres, English is the exclusive classroom language, and teachers may even be fired for using the students' native language. In total contrast to that, in many schools, especially those with groups of 40, 50 or more unmotivated students, the students' native language is used in the classroom much more than English. As a Cambridge COTE trainer (before ICELT replaced COTE), I observed a teacher in a Mexican public secondary school where the English teachers had been instructed by the school principal to use Spanish for instructions, explanations etc., and English only in examples and exercises as parents had complained that their children didn't understand the English classes because the teacher spoke English much of the time. In some classrooms, there's a weird mixture of languages (which I also met in COTE and other class observations), with teachers using English but, perhaps unconsciously, immediately translating it into the students' native language: "OK. We're going to do a listening comprehension task—*vamos a hacer un ejercicio de comprensión auditiva*. Open your books on page twenty-seven—*abran sus libros en la página veinte siete*." Somehow the teacher expects the students to understand a recorded conversation or talk that they've never heard before and that may be quite difficult after *not* expecting them to understand the instructions, which are repeated every time they do a listening comprehension task!

Classroom English, for instructions and routine interaction, is communicative by its very nature, while listening comprehension tasks with recorded conversations or talks (mentioned above) may be more communicative or less so. Especially below intermediate level, many courses use listening tasks to consolidate specific "new" grammar and vocabulary (the target grammar and vocabulary of the lesson or unit) rather than to face students with the largely unpredictable and varied language that we meet in real listening outside classrooms (and which we actually want to listen to and understand).

Communicative listening in the classroom: possibilities and strategies

Two contrasting contexts of ELT in Latin America are mentioned above: language centres (typically with groups of 10 to 20 motivated students) and schools with 40, 50 or more unmotivated students. Obviously, establishing English as the main classroom language (and maximizing communicative listening practice) is easy, and usually compulsory, in the first context while it requires an extremely capable, dynamic and creative teacher in the second one. I recommend establishing English as the main classroom language in both contexts but recognize the enormous challenge in the second one. One thing to attempt there (and in all ELT contexts where English as the main classroom language is not established institutional policy) is to agree among all the teachers on English in the classroom. Where all the teachers insist on English as the main classroom language, most students usually collaborate; where some teachers do not, most students are likely to prefer "the easy way", their native language.

Classroom English doesn't usually establish itself magically just because a teacher always stubbornly speaks in English (except perhaps with motivated upper elementary and intermediate students who are still in the habit of using their native language a lot). The teacher usually has to teach it bit by bit, and engage the students in it (Willis, 1981). Essentially, for students in beginner and low elementary courses, learning classroom English can be somewhat like babies and young children learning routine language: they learn to understand and respond to bits of the language through its regular use in context. It is largely a matter of listening routines. Here are three widely used types of routine requiring communicative listening, which may lead into student speaking also.

Routine instructions and indications

The same or very similar classroom instructions and indications are used again and again, lesson after lesson. You can teach and practice them with Total Physical Response (TPR) until students automatically respond to them whenever they're used. Give new or recently introduced instructions, using gestures and demonstration at first if necessary, and have the students do what you say: "Open your books at page 15. Look at the picture. What is it? That's right —a house. Close you books. Stand up. Open your books at page 9. No, don't sit down, stand up! Look at exercise 3. What is it—grammar, vocabulary, listening, speaking, reading or writing? Yes, speaking. OK—now sit down." Established instructions and indications then constitute real communicative listening practice in every class. By upper elementary level, they can consist of more than simple imperatives: "OK. You're going to discuss that proposal now, working in pairs. I want you to consider arguments for and against the idea. Can you…"

Social routines and interactions

Normal life is full of social and transactional routines: we have similar bits of conversation at breakfast every day, arriving at school or work, leaving school or work, meeting people in the street, in cafés, and so on. The same can, and should, be true in most EFL classrooms. Decades ago, good school English classes opened like this, and they still do: "Good morning everyone! [Good morning!] How are you all? [Fine, thank you. And you?] OK, but I don't like this weather. It's too cold for me, and I suspect it's going to rain all day. How many of you like cold, rainy weather? [A few hands are raised.] Well, I..." There can also be routines (incorporating different topics) at the end of classes and at various junctures during classes, for example, after an activity, commenting on it and asking students how they felt about it.

Anecdotes, mini-talks, etc.

Teachers who believe in giving students more listening practice than is normal have always told anecdotes and given mini-talks on topics of interest in class and got students to respond, for example, asking questions afterwards, discussing or summarizing the story or talk. Children's teachers can talk about dolls, puppets and pictures of characters. The anecdotes and talks have to be short, clear and in very simple English for beginners and low elementary students (but the similarities between English and Portuguese or Spanish help in Latin America), and they can increase in challenge in higher levels.

English as the main classroom language (though difficult to establish in some ELT contexts) is by far the largest part of communicative listening practice in most courses. Listening comprehension tasks with recorded material are usually carried out only once or twice a week. They have the advantage of native or strong non-native speakers, of course, while the classroom English is that of the teacher (usually non-native in Latin America) and the students. That's not really a problem, though, because the stronger students speak up most in low level courses, all students get stronger level by level, and much real use of English in Latin America is with non-native speakers from Japan, Germany, France and other countries, not native speakers.

References

Larson-Freeman, D. (2000). *Techniques and Principles in Language Teaching*. Oxford University Press. (Ch. 8, Summary of Total Physical Response)

Willis, J. (1981). *Teaching English through English*. Longman.

12

COMMUNICATIVE READING, AND LANGUAGE LEARNING THROUGH READING

Reading in real language use and language learning

Reading is one of the skills most children begin to develop at school, in their first language, learning the basic system of reading and writing in that language in kindergarten or early primary. After that, reading is a regular school activity, mostly with textbooks, and also a leisure activity for some children and teenagers (note the success of books like the Harry Potter series).

After completing basic education, reading becomes just an occasional or marginal activity for some people (they only read notices, advertisements, bits of newspaper and magazine, and now bits on computer and smartphone screens), but it's a frequent and very important one for others. Many people have to do a lot of reading (especially office workers, professionals and academics), and some people like to do a lot (readers of novels, non-fiction books, etc.).

People who read little tend to have a smaller vocabulary and some difficulty reading long or complex texts, while those who read a lot tend to have larger vocabularies and the ability to handle such texts fairly easily. Reading, then, can assist greatly in first language development, as well as giving access to needed information and ideas or culture and enjoyment. It can do the same in the learning of English as a foreign language, even at beginner level by speakers of European languages that use Latin script, like Latin Americans.

Reading in learning English as a foreign language

Almost all learners of English as a foreign language come to the task already able to read in their first language, and many as very proficient readers. Even so, learning to read in English is a big challenge for native speakers of Russian (русский), Thai (ภาษาไทย), Japanese (日本語), and other languages. For native speakers of Portuguese and Spanish, however, it's a relatively small challenge: not only is the writing system largely the same, but, especially in more formal texts, there are many cognate words, and the grammar operates similarly to some extent. Reading for Latin American students of English can give increased exposure to English and permit the learning or consolidation of grammar and vocabulary from the very beginning, as well as developing reading skills.

Latin American students of English have an advantage in reading even over German students, especially with formal texts, which are what English-using professionals usually need to read most. Consider these three versions of the same United Nations text:

> Darf kein Unterschied gemacht werden auf Grund der politischen, rechtlichen oder internationalen Stellung des Landes oder Gebiets, dem eine Person angehört, gleichgültig ob dieses unabhängig ist, unter Treuhandschaft steht, keine Selbstregierung besitzt oder sonst in seiner Souveränität eingeschränkt ist.

> No distinction shall be made on the basis of the political,

jurisdictional or international status of the country or territory to which a person belongs, whether it be independent, trust, non-self-governing or under any other limitation of sovereignty.

No se hará distinción alguna fundada en la condición política, jurídica o internacional del país o territorio de cuya jurisdicción dependa una persona, tanto si se trata de un país independiente, como de un territorio bajo administración fiduciaria, no autónomo o sometido a cualquier otra limitación de soberanía.

The Spanish version is much more similar to the English version than the German version is. That's generally the case, especially in formal texts. Lots of reading—but not the text above!—can be included even in beginner courses for older teenager and adult students in Latin America.

However, most courses in Latin America use international textbooks (or local textbooks modelled on them) which are designed to be sold around the world, including Germany, Thailand and Japan. Consequently, most beginner textbooks have very little reading in them. I checked five very well-known international beginners' textbooks for young adults sold in Latin America and found that the average number of reading texts/tasks was 1 per 5.4 pages, with 1 per 3.8 pages the highest and 1 per 7.7 pages the lowest. The average to lowest ratio may be fine for Thailand, Japan, etc., where the Latin script used for English has to be taught to beginners, or even for some European countries with languages that share little cognate vocabulary with English, but it isn't appropriate for young adults in Latin America.

Note that classifying material in those five textbooks as reading texts/tasks was not that easy because many that I accepted (and some I rejected) were designed largely to present or consolidate "the new language of the unit/lesson". I accepted those that could be considered texts that beginners in English might possibly want to read for themselves.

Communicative reading

That's really the minimal requirement for communicative reading: readers should at least vaguely want to read and understand something for themselves, even if just to practice their reading in English in a fairly agreeable way. A second requirement (which caused me some trouble with those five textbooks) is that texts should be fairly natural and not be artificially loaded with examples of "the new language of the unit", either to present it or to consolidate it. Given those two basic requirements, it's a matter of the more readers are genuinely interested in reading and understanding the text, the better. And, of course, readers should be able to understand the text. All that presents textbook writers and teachers with a great challenge, especially at beginner and elementary level: finding/adapting/creating texts that interest specific EFL students, that are accessible to those students (with a specific native language), and that are natural written discourse, not peculiar beginner English.

Meeting that challenge fully is virtually impossible for international general purpose textbooks, though some do quite well, for motivated students at least, with simple general interest texts. It requires more focused textbooks, like those for ESP (English for business, medicine, etc.), or complementation of the textbook by the educational institution or the teachers. On that point, after you've read this article, you might want to count and examine the reading in your textbooks (enough of it or too little, appropriate for your students' characteristics and actual or probable needs or not?) and think about the different or additional reading that could help your students more than the textbooks alone do. Sources of reading material are now wider than ever before, with the Internet in addition to traditional printed material, which in itself includes other EFL textbooks and graded readers.

If your students simply read a lot and do whatever they like with it in their heads, that's communicative reading, and very positive. However, you may want or need to give them tasks in order to ensure they do and benefit from reading. There are many types of reading tasks, some just to confirm comprehension, for example, with multiple choice questions, some to develop sub-skills like skimming, scanning and noting logical connections. However, communicative reading is really about thinking about the text, perhaps discussing it with others, and perhaps applying things in it in your life (your studies, work, etc.). The best types of task for communicative reading, then, are answering questions (including questions about the reader's reactions and opinions), discussing the text, and applying the text in other activities (as in Task-Based Learning). That can be difficult in beginners' courses, but even there, you can use simple questions about the text and about the students' reactions and opinions. As the course level rises, the possibilities for communicative reading tasks and related activities become ever greater.

More reading than is usual in beginners' courses for adults can be motivating. For example, many students enter higher education in Latin America (and elsewhere) with little or no English, and they go into a beginner or low elementary English course for the third or fourth time (after two or three "beginnings" at school). If the students do some bits of reading related to their higher education studies, it can make the course more relevant than the beginners' courses they had at school.

Objections to a lot of reading in beginners' courses, and solutions

Lots of reading in beginner and elementary level courses has been frowned upon in the past, and some methodologists and teachers continue to feel that way. Reasons given have included the supposed primacy of spoken language over written language and the effect of early reading on pronunciation. Speaking before writing may be a good, even necessary, principle for teaching young children, but it loses strength as we move to older children, teenagers and adults. In fact, for many older students of English, reading in English is as or more important than speaking it (like many of the students in higher education mentioned above).

The fear of beginner and elementary students falling into "spelling pronunciation" (e.g., students reading: *Lots of ray-adding in begin-air and elemen-tarry co-urses hass bay-en frow-ned...*) has some basis. But with English as the main classroom language, the risk should be much reduced, and more so if you can get your students to do some reading-and-listening outside class, and some reading aloud in class (combined with discussion of what was read). Lots of reading-and-listening material is now available, for example, graded EFL readers with CDs and online material.

The benefits of lots of reading, possible even in beginners' courses for Latin American students, can be really great, and the risks are not great.

EFL reading—beginnings and happy endings

I've asserted that more reading than is usual, even for beginners (and perhaps especially for them), can help Latin American teenagers and adults learn the English language better, as well as developing their ability to read in English. Young children may get fewer benefits and have more problems (I'm no expert on that), but many older children certainly benefit from and enjoy reading. My Mexican (and only!) wife Emma was the librarian in a branch of the Anglo for some years, and she often said how impressed she was by the children. They were an example for the teenagers and adults, she said. Many would take out a children's reader every week, and a few would take out two or three. She used to ask them about the readers they were handing in, and their enthusiasm was infectious, even when they said something like: "Mm… it was OK. I liked the end. The children…". Yes, I know, "the ending" would be better than "the end", but who cares when Mexican children are reading in English and really enjoying it?

13

STARTING AND DEVELOPING COMMUNICATIVE SPEAKING

Communicative speaking versus non-communicative speaking

Strictly speaking, when students repeat something after the teacher, they're speaking. The same applies to substitution drills and 'stating the obvious' using the same structures over and over (e.g., asking and answering present progressive questions about a picture: *What's the man doing? He's playing the piano. What's the woman doing? She's singing. What are the people doing? They're…*). Such non-communicative speaking may help students a bit with grammar, vocabulary and pronunciation, but very little with real communicative speaking.

In real communicative speaking (with the exception of some fairly fixed social and transactional routines), the statements and questions and their grammar and vocabulary are largely unpredictable. You very seldom know exactly what's coming next in a conversation. That's the kind of speaking (usually combined with listening) that I'll be focusing on here. In EFL classrooms, it includes social and phatic communication (greetings, encouragement, etc.), general classroom communication (requests, explanations, etc.), and activities where information is sought and conveyed and the grammar and vocabulary are naturally mixed, not restricted to repeating 'the grammar of the lesson'.

Communicative speaking at different stages of teaching English

Ideally, communicative speaking should start in beginner courses and develop progressively from then on. In intermediate courses students should be using English communicatively virtually all the time, even when they're talking about language items. By that level, they should have virtually all the basic grammar of English and a lot of vocabulary at their disposal, though they may struggle at times to access what they need to express an idea. If students aren't using English communicatively almost all the time, something is wrong. They may not really be at intermediate level, and, even more significantly, English may not have been established as the main classroom language in their earlier courses.

One problem in the earliest courses is that students in beginner courses start with little or no grammar and vocabulary, and those in low elementary courses still have only a limited amount. That restricts the range of topics and activities for communicative speaking. Another problem is that the students often feel insecure and reluctant to speak. Yet another common problem is that they may have no real need to speak English to motivate them. Such problems are normal challenges for teachers of beginner and elementary courses, and good teachers actually relish them: teaching those levels can be very rewarding because the students' progress is usually so much more evident than at higher levels.

Communicative speaking at intermediate levels depends, then, on communicative speaking in beginner and elementary courses, though topics and activities are likely to be rather different.

Communicative speaking in beginner and elementary courses

In some ELT institutions, English is required as the main classroom language even in beginners' courses and the students' first language is restricted to very few situations. The students know that, and the teachers have strategies and techniques for helping students comply from the start (see Willis 1981). However, in many institutions, especially schools, that isn't the case and, while some teachers may try to apply an 'English-(almost)-only' policy, others don't, making it tougher for those that do. The results, in terms of the student's ability to communicate in spoken English, are usually enormously different.

In the article 'Communicative Listening' I wrote quite a lot about establishing English as the main classroom language in beginner and elementary courses, and I refer you to that now (Davies, 2018). What I'll add here is more about students *speaking* classroom English as well as hearing and reacting to it.

I believe that classroom English should be seen as a sub-syllabus to be actively taught in beginner courses, and in following courses if necessary. In some institutions it might even be good to give a printed copy of a prepared classroom English syllabus to all beginner course teachers. By the end of a beginner course, students should, for example, be able to:

- Engage in routine social exchanges, responding as in the second column:

Good morning/afternoon/evening. | Good morning/afternoon/evening.

How are you today? | Fine, thank you. And you?/OK, but a bit tired/cold/etc.
What do you think of the weather? | I like it./I don't like it./I prefer cool weather. What about you?
Goodbye/Goodnight. | Goodbye/Goodnight.
See you tomorrow. | See you.
Have a good weekend. | Thanks. You too.

- Respond to the teacher's instructions, checking questions and explanations, as in the second column:

OK, open your books at page 23. | Sorry. Which page?
(Explanation) | Sorry. I don't understand./Can you repeat that?
Do you understand? | Yes./No./Not completely.
Give me another example of the negative. | (An example of the negative)
Have you finished? | Yes./Almost./No.

- Make requests, apologies, observations, etc.: *Sorry I'm late. Can I come in? / Can I go to the bathroom? / It's hot/cold. Can I open/close the window? / I don't have a pen/book/partner/etc. / I can't hear/see.*

To provide students with such functional classroom English, teachers need to take advantage of moments in lessons when language that will be used again and again is first needed, and teach it through modelling and choral and individual repetition. The next few times that same language is needed it can usually be elicited from the stronger students, but weaker ones may need a little more modelling and drilling. For continuing work on accumulating classroom language, some teachers prepare wallcharts of expressions, to which they add new ones. When an expression is needed and a student can't remember it, the teacher can point to the chart, where the student should recognize it.

When students are understanding the teacher's classroom English and using their own fairly well, they've started on the long march to fluent communicative speaking but, obviously, more is needed. More communicative speaking can be developed through contrived activities. Though restricted at beginner level, there are quite a lot of options. Here are some examples:

Parallel conversations: After listening to a model conversation, pairs (or trios) of students have similar conversations about themselves, their school, city, family, studies, job, etc. The first of these conversations are typically first meetings between people, involving the exchange of names, hometowns/states, occupations, ages, and so on.

General knowledge quizzes: Groups of students prepare general knowledge questions, or the teacher provides groups with cues (Capital of Canada? / Number of states in the USA? / Author of *Harry Potter* novels? / Location of the Ural Mountains? / etc.) and the students write questions based on the cues. The quiz is then a competition between the groups, asking and answering one another's varied questions, and involving other communicative speaking, for example, about turns and the score.

Simulations and role-plays: Similar to parallel conversations, but less modelled/scripted, and with invented information (with the students, or some of them, not as themselves) within a given situation (meeting foreign exchange students at the airport, job interview, congress welcome cocktail, checking in at a hotel, etc.).

Say what you know or imagine about…: Students individually note down what they know or imagine about a topic (a famous person, a football club, a country, a city, a company, an animal, etc.). Then, in groups, they say and talk about what they know, assume or imagine about the topic.

For the above—and any speaking activities—to be really communicative they have to involve the exchange or discussion of information not known to all the speakers (or not agreed upon by them all), and also the use of mixed grammar (not just repetition of 'the grammar of the lesson'). Also, the teacher should accept minor errors and intervene to correct (or elicit correction) only when the errors interfere with communication or when the same errors are being made by several or many students. However, the activities can be monitored and common errors noted for some remedial work next class.

Developing communicative speaking at higher levels

Progressively, the above communicative speaking activities can be extended more freely and added to. In intermediate courses, or earlier with motivated students, the additional activities can include research projects leading to short class presentations, prepared class discussions and debates, and extra-curricular activities (like interviewing and presenting reports on English-speaking people, with online interviews if there are few or no English-speaking people locally). Some institutions also offer conversation courses or a conversation club.

If a course has some, or many, students who have used or regularly use English outside class (in their higher studies, work, travel, social life, etc.), there can be a further focus on communicative speaking: discussion of the student's experiences of real-world communicative speaking and conversation, and attention to any problems or doubts they've had.

Two major issues for communicative speaking in the classroom

I could sign off on the happy note that, even at beginner level, every class should be at least partly a conversation class, no matter what other things are attended to (grammar, vocabulary, pronunciation, spelling, etc.). However, I'll be brutally honest and mention two major issues before I go.

The first issue is the matter of teacher English. Richards (2017) considers this in the light of the fact that around the world the vast majority of EFL teachers are non-native speakers of English. Many, naturally, aren't very fluent or unfailingly accurate, typically because they have little opportunity to practice their spoken English. Many are also limited in their development because they teach only A1-A2 levels. How can English as the main classroom language and an imaginative range of communicative speaking activities thrive when the teachers are uncertain about their own spoken English or have weaknesses?

My answer is, don't worry (or let your teachers worry) too much: if the students seem willing, or even keen, to have a go at communicative speaking, teachers should go for it, even if they make mistakes (like most non-native speakers, even quite fluent ones). Teachers can put their worry to work (so it will be too busy to cause an ulcer) searching online and asking other teachers about their doubts about their classroom English. For example, it's quite common for Latin American teachers to say "Pass to the front/board" (instead of "Come…" or "Go…", depending on where you're standing), "Very well" to congratulate students (instead of "Very good"), "Keep your books" (instead of "Put your books away"), "I want that you work in pairs" (instead of "I want you to…"), and "Make me a question" (instead of "Ask me…"). Where teacher English is a problem, that problem should be worked on, but a communicative approach should not be abandoned unless it's really hopeless (see below).

The second issue is the matter of teaching-learning conditions. I hope you or your teachers are working in favourable or not too unfavourable conditions—groups that aren't very large, courses with time for cumulative work on real communication, students with some motivation to learn English (usually related to need, or probable need, or at least possible need of English). To teachers and institutions with students who are very unlikely to need English, in groups of 40, 50, or more, and with fewer than three hours a week, I suggest, frankly, that you stick to basic classroom English and controlled (not very communicative) speaking activities, making them as much fun as possible, for example, through games and competitions. In the worst cases, I suggest, frankly, that you forget trying to teach English at all—there must be something more relevant and potentially more useful to the students to spend the time and money on.

References

Richards, J.C. (2017). Teaching English through English: Proficiency, Pedagogy and Performance. In *RELC Journal* 1–24, at www.professorjackrichards.com/wp-content/uploads/Teaching-English-through-English.pdf

Willis, J. (1981). *Teaching English through English*. Longman.

14

COMMUNICATIVE WRITING AT BEGINNER-ELEMENTARY LEVEL

This article on communicative writing is the fourth on 'the four skills', which are clearly central to communicative language teaching. In all the previous articles I noted that only certain activities can be considered communicative, and that listening, reading and speaking activities in textbooks and classrooms are often mainly for work on the grammar and vocabulary of the lesson or unit (with the grammar unnaturally repeated) rather than to develop communicative competence. The same applies to writing: when students are required, for example, to write a text using only certain grammatical structures, the task is really grammar work more than communicative writing (which doesn't mean that such writing isn't possibly useful for language learning).

Writing is probably the most difficult of the 'four skills' to handle communicatively in EFL courses at low levels. Since the Direct Method over a century ago, 'professional ELT' has prioritized listening to and speaking English as the main (and sometimes sole) classroom language, even at beginner level, with English used throughout each lesson for real communication (greetings, instructions, requests, explanations, etc.). Many other listening and speaking activities can also be considered communicative if teachers get their students' "willing suspension of disbelief" (a phrase coined by English poet, Samuel Coleridge, which can be applied to activities where we voluntarily accept fiction and make-believe, as in poetry, novels, films, and in simulations and role-plays in EFL courses). Reading can also be communicative and relatively easy to handle at low levels, at least for students with writing systems and languages similar to English, as in Latin America: authentic texts can be accessible for beginners and have genuinely interesting content, including content related to the studies or work of older teenagers and adults.

Writing is a different matter. For a start, until emailing, texting, Facebook, Twitter, and so on, came along, most people seldom wrote much, if anything, even in their native language unless their work involved writing or they were avid letter writers. In most low level EFL courses, communicative writing has been the Cinderella of the four skills, while communicative listening and speaking are essential parts of good ELT, and reading is prominent in most modern textbooks. One well-known EFL textbook series I've just looked at has no communicative writing at all in its Book One.

Writing in textbooks

Below is a brief report on a survey of text writing in eight books that I happen to have on my shelves. Published between 2005 and 2017 by CUP, Macmillan, OUP, Pearson and Richmond, they're all well within the emailing era, which began around 1995. The books include 4 Book Ones (A1 level) and 4 Book Twos (A2 level). I looked at the last 30 pages of the Book Ones and the first 30 pages of the Book Twos (about a quarter of each book) to get a broad picture of text writing tasks in textbooks at the end of A1 and beginning of A2 levels. I invite you to expand my survey by comparing what I found in my survey with the most recent textbooks you have.

Here's what I found:

In the 30-page sections I examined, 1 book (mentioned above) has no text writing tasks, 1 has 2 tasks, 2 have 3 tasks, 2 have 4 tasks, and 2 have 7 tasks. *There's enormous variation in textbooks' attention to writing.*

Three of the 7 books with tasks have both grammar-focused text writing and text writing with no grammar control or guidelines, and 4 have only text writing with no grammar control or guidelines.

Overall, 7 of the text writing tasks have a degree of grammar control or guidelines, and 22 don't. *This, along with the previous observation, suggests a shift towards more communicative or natural text writing compared with older textbooks.*

Three books have tasks described as emails/Facebook posts/blog posts (but only 1 has a task actually involving sending an email to a classmate and that classmate replying). *This suggests little exploitation yet of by far the commonest mode of general writing today, online writing.*

Most of the writing tasks in the books I surveyed are very 'school-like', not anything students are likely to write in real life, typically a brief text describing a person/place/event/etc., either real or imaginary. *This may be because textbook writers/publishers tend to think in terms of what A1-A2 level learners **can** write in English rather than what they actually **may** write in English (usually nothing!).*

Further to that last point, while some students of English may do some real life listening, reading and speaking in English outside the classroom in their early years of studying the language (e.g., in their higher education studies, occasional encounters with foreigners, through TV, films and Internet, travelling abroad, etc.), very few do any real life writing in English at all. In fact, even most of those who later become fluent in English do very little unless their work requires it or they have foreign English-speaking friends. In most English courses, therefore, writing tasks tend to be very contrived, based on the repetition of certain grammatical structures and/or very controlled, especially at beginner-elementary levels (which, I repeat, doesn't mean that such writing isn't possibly useful for language learning). Textbooks can't do much about that, but teachers can in some situations (e.g., in smallish groups, or with very motivated learners), especially with a bit of willing suspension of disbelief.

Beginner-elementary communicative writing ideas

Here are four ideas (two adapted from Hedge, 1988—yes, a very long time ago) for the last part of a beginner's course or in the following elementary courses:

1. Continue in writing a communicative pair or group speaking activity that has gone well and has more potential. This could be started in class in the form of short written notes back and forth or text messages (Teacher: *OK, now continue this activity writing/texting your questions and answers. Don't talk at all—when you don't understand a message, write back "I don't understand"*), and then continued for homework as text messages or emails. Check on the homework in the following class (Teacher: *What interesting/surprising/unusual things did you discover in the homework?*).

2. Send a text/email to all the students in a group—the same short message, individualised with the students' names, asking something about themselves, their family, where they live, etc. When you receive their replies, you need to

reply individually, and after that the correspondence may go anywhere with different students. Obviously, this is better with small groups than with big ones—unless you're prepared to keep up a week or two of correspondence with 30, 40 or more students!

3. Establish a class magazine, with the title chosen by the whole group, and a new topic chosen by them for each issue of the magazine, to be published at the end of each week or fortnight. Get the students to form pairs or trios, who then have to produce a short article on the topic for each issue. Obviously, students are likely to cut and paste from the Internet, but if you insist on a beginning-body-end structure and between a certain number of words (e.g., 30-50, 40-60), they'll have to do some adapting and composing. The topic could sometimes be "The week's news" if you have mature students interested in what's happening in their city or country, or in the world.

4. If you teach in an institution of higher education with a Licenciatura in ELT, each student in the last semesters of that licenciatura could be an email or texting correspondent of students in a Course 2 or 3 of the institution's curricular English courses or Language Centre courses (or in a secondary school English course). Guidelines would have to be established for both the licenciatura students and the English course students, for example, the English course students should begin the correspondence by sending a brief introductory message to their delegated licenciatura student, messages of between 25 and 50 words should be exchanged once a week, etc. The correspondence could be extremely useful, not only for the students in elementary English courses, but also to sensitise Lic. ELT undergraduates to the real but very limited and erratic English and communicative competence of elementary level students of English.

Developing text writing for students' real purposes

There are two main areas where many students of English really do need to develop text writing skills:

- for proficiency tests, which they may have to take or want to take
- for real life use in higher education studies and work, and possibly personal correspondence

The text writing tasks in low level proficiency tests (e.g., Cambridge KET and PET, now A2 Key and B1 Preliminary) are very restricted and guided by specific content instructions and/or input information: responding to a short note or email requiring specific answers or action, writing a short letter or email to a friend about a new house, job, and so forth, making or responding to an email invitation, and so on. Very few students of English at A2 or even B1 level actually do such writing in their lives outside the classroom, but a proficiency test may be important or even vital for some students of English (to graduate from university, get a scholarship or a job, etc.). Proficiency test text writing can therefore be considered a real purpose for them, and ELT that prepares students for it may be important. As people progress in their university studies and professional careers, the development of proficiency test text writing skills may become ever more important for their futures, and the writing tasks in TOEFL, Cambridge FCE (now B2 First), CAE (now C1 Advanced) and IELTS become more and more like real writing for academic and professional purposes.

Writing for real academic, professional and occupational purposes can actually begin to be developed very early on in ESP (English for Specific Purposes). For example, even beginner and low elementary students in English courses for business administration degrees, company courses and similar can begin to work on the composition of simple, basic business emails and letters. The tasks themselves may be rather like traditional beginner/elementary EFL textbook writing tasks and Cambridge A2 Key writing tasks, but they can go through process-writing stages (reading and talking about models, tasks with clear content instructions and/or input, pair writing or revision of drafts, etc.). Some students (e.g., working professionals in company English courses) may actually have to do some such writing already in their work. Another ESP area where this kind of approach can be used in Latin America (where students usually begin with little English) is university degrees in travel and hospitality (e.g., writing brochures and itineraries), and imaginative English teachers can no doubt think of other areas.

Reference

Hedge, T. (1988). *Writing*. Oxford University Press.

THE ENGLISH LANGUAGE

15

ELT AS TEFL OR TELF? OR SOMETHING ELSE?

English language teaching can be teaching English as a Foreign Language on the one hand or teaching English as a Lingua Franca on the other, or it can perhaps be somewhere in between. Here's a representation of ELT with EFL (TEFL) and ELT with ELF (TELF), and other ELT between them:

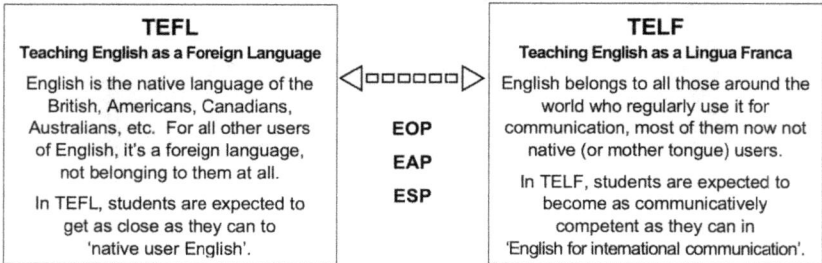

TEFL **Teaching English as a Foreign Language**		TELF **Teaching English as a Lingua Franca**
English is the native language of the British, Americans, Canadians, Australians, etc. For all other users of English, it's a foreign language, not belonging to them at all. In TEFL, students are expected to get as close as they can to 'native user English'.	◁□□□□□□▷ EOP EAP ESP	English belongs to all those around the world who regularly use it for communication, most of them now not native (or mother tongue) users. In TELF, students are expected to become as communicatively competent as they can in 'English for international communication'.

Figure 10: TEFL vs. TELF

Note: The term 'user' covers the four basic communicative skills better than 'speaker'.

Above, I've mentioned the English language, the teaching of the English language, and today's world, so I'll now focus on each in turn, but probably mix them a bit at times.

The English language

In TEFL (teaching English as a foreign language) there are issues with the English language, or at least some teaching decisions to take about it. Is it to be British, American, Australian, or another variety of English? Then, whether British, American or whatever, is it to be more everyday vernacular English or more formal English, or across the spectrum?

Most EFL textbooks (and most textbooks are in fact EFL, not ELF), and many teachers, clearly work on either British or American English. They often slightly falsify or exaggerate features of the chosen variety, for example, suggesting that Brits never say 'Do you have...?' for possession or 'movie' and that Americans never say 'Have you got...?' or 'film'. However, there are indeed typical differences, though they hardly ever interfere at all with communication. Note that the differences tend to be much greater in everyday colloquial speech than in more formal discourse, especially formal writing.

On the vernacular-formal axis, some EFL textbooks, and some teachers, go for a lot of 'Yeah', 'Wow!', 'Cool!', 'I just love...', 'I guess so', and so on (examples taken from actual textbooks) and idiomatic expressions, while others stick mostly to 'Yes', 'I really like...', and so on, and non-figurative language. The textbook writers and teachers inclined towards more formal English may consider that their students are unlikely to often be in very informal everyday situations with native speakers, and if they are, they'll quickly pick up vernacular forms from whoever they're with most —Americans or Britons, hip young friends or serious business associates, etc. I haven't yet met a textbook with 'gonna', 'gotta', 'wanna', 'oughta', 'gimme', or 'G'day!', but there might be some out there, or teachers who dwell on such things (and say their students love it—as a few actually may).

In TELF (teaching English as a lingua franca) there are also issues with the language, or teaching decisions to take about it. For a start, 'English as a Lingua Franca' is not a variety of English like British English or American English. In fact, the English taught can actually *be* British English or American English (for international use), or it can mix both, and other internationally intelligible varieties.

Remember too that there has never been 'pure' British English or 'pure' American English; they both cover regional varieties like those of South England, Wales, North England and Scotland, and North East USA, Deep South, Mid-West and West Coast. Also, like all languages, English is continually changing. In the past, it was changed by Norman French after the conquest of England in 1066, especially in the language of government and law, and by Latin and Greek, especially in religion, philosophy and science, and by the languages of the British Empire, especially those of India, and by Spanish as 'Anglo Saxons' and 'Hispanics' clashed and combined in what is now the south and west of the USA.

The modern use of English as a lingua franca has itself surely influenced native varieties of English too, and will continue to do so. One effect that has been predicted is the continued simplification of English grammar, such as the dropping of the 3rd person 's' ending, which already occurs in 'non-standard' native speech ("It really don't matter"). And native users themselves contribute to change: "If it would happen…" is becoming standard spoken American English instead of "If it happened…", and "He referenced the report" is becoming as common as "He referred to the report".

In short, no 'pure' variety of English need be the target language of TELF, certainly not the obsession of teaching. TEFL has to work with a body of English, of course, but which one or combination doesn't matter that much, though generally 'British English' in Europe and 'American English' in the northern part of Latin American would be logical. TELF is more about *how* you teach English than *what* English you teach, though what you teach is also important. TELF naturally tends towards neutral and formal language rather than the chatty colloquial English in some TEFL textbooks: it's English for effective international communication (including with Americans, Britons, Canadians, Australians and other native users of English, but perhaps more with other non-native users of English), probably largely work-related and not for everyday life in the USA, the UK or wherever.

The teaching of the English language

In TEFL there's a traditional and evolving repertoire of ways to get students to sound, express themselves and even behave like a specific group of native users of English, usually educated Britons or Americans. The word 'educated' is important here because, while these Britons or Americans may say 'Yeah', 'Wow!', 'No kidding' and 'See you' quite a lot, they seem never to mispronounce a word or phrase, never to use a word or phrase in an odd or mistaken way, and never to use deviant grammar (unlike their 'less educated' compatriots who regularly say things like "It don't matter none"). At least that's how it might seem to students of EFL, who are regularly corrected for such things and pushed towards greater 'Britishness' or 'Americanness'. This characterisation of TEFL is an exaggeration, of course, but it gives a sense of where TEFL is directed, even though most teachers around the world are unable to take students there because they themselves haven't got to very native-like English.

The aim of TEFL (often an impossible dream) is to produce native-like users of English, particularly as speakers. The highest praise from a competent EFL teacher might include: "You really sounded like an American all through your presentation! Congratulations!" The rejection of English as a lingua franca by such a teacher may be conveyed in comments like: "What you said was perfectly correct English and perfectly clear, but a British person would never express it that way. They'd say…".

The linguistic aim of native-like English is usually accompanied by a focus on native-like use. Not only are students expected to learn specifically 'American English' or specifically 'British English', but also to use it for all the things Americans or Britons use it for in their daily lives, many of which most students of EFL (especially in regions like Latin America) will never use English for. This is where 'Yeah', 'Wow!', 'Cool!' and 'See you' may come into the EFL course, along with conversations about the students' personal lives, past, present and future, and practice of shopping and other everyday transactions. Of course, that's not necessarily a complete waste of time: most of the grammar and some of the vocabulary can be adapted to what students eventually really use English for, for example, higher education studies, occupational training, work, receiving foreign visitors and showing them around their city. However, it's more logical to go directly for those things, at least from upper secondary school on.

In TELF, that indeed tends to be the communicative focus: less colloquial English for everyday and personal life (or for stays in one's favourite English-speaking country), and more neutral and formal English for international communication. Where groups of students have clear study, work or other practical needs, the TELF can be English for academic purposes (EAP, in higher education), or English for occupational purposes (EOP, in technical institutes or companies) or English for specific purposes (ESP, in any of the above where students are grouped by study or work speciality). TEFL can also eventually go in those directions, after establishing a degree of native-like English, but TELF can do so from beginner level onwards.

Another feature of TELF may be a more relaxed—or pragmatic— attitude towards linguistic accuracy and conventional forms of expression, and a greater emphasis on communicative effective- ness. In TELF, "What you said was perfectly correct English and perfectly clear" would probably be a compliment from the teacher, perhaps followed by "Well done!" That doesn't mean that accuracy and conventional patterns of expression are largely neglected, but models of English users might include Swedish, Indian and Argen- tinian scientists, business people, tourist guides, etc., as well as British, American and Irish ones, and work on accuracy may be more progressive and patient.

Of course, TEFL has also gone in that direction since 'fluency' arose in the 1970s as a consideration to be balanced against linguistic accuracy. In fact, much TEFL has drifted a bit towards TELF, working more on English for international travel and communication, and for study and work, and less on daily life in the USA or UK. EFL textbooks also often now highlight the inclu- sion of different accents of English in their listening material, including non-native users from different countries. However, the non-native users all seem to speak perfect British English or perfect American English, and American and British English are rarely if ever mixed.

ELT in today's world

In today's world (and even yesterday's) American, British, Irish, Indian, Swedish, Nigerian and other English are mixed all the time, of course. A Brazilian or Mexican automotive engineer, parts supplier or machinery supplier (like my son-in-law) may move from an American vehicle manufacturing plant, to a German one, to a Japanese one, to a French one, to a South Korean one, to an Italian one, and now to a Chinese one. Most of the communication will probably be in Portuguese or Spanish (unless it's a trip to the parent company in the USA, Germany, Japan or wherever), but some of it will often be in English. English as a lingua franca.

TEFL was the dominant ELT of the past, and may still be, though drifting towards TELF. Europeans were mostly taught British English, and Mexicans were mostly taught American English. That seemed to be common sense and the obvious thing to do. It still does for some people, especially those teaching or learning English in a specific native user context, like a bilingual school. The hope, if not the reality, used to be that the students would visit Britain or America and 'use' their English there, and also find opportunities to use it for various (mainly 'American' or mainly 'British') purposes in their own country.

However, there are now more than twice as many proficient non-native users of English as native users in the world, and consequently more communication, in speech and writing, between two or more non-native users than between native and non-native users. Many of those non-native users rarely or never use English in an English speaking country, and use it in their own country much more for study, work and professional development than for social or personal purposes. Most have notable non-native features in their English, especially their pronunciation and some idiolectic phrasing, but many may be more articulate in English than many native users, especially in their area of occupational expertise.

Then there's the English teachers. Fifty years ago, especially in private schools, many taught English because they'd learnt the language as children, in a bilingual school or through family members or activities, for example. They usually had no ELT training, but spoke English like or almost like an American or a Briton. Today, without ELT training they'd find it hard to get a decent ELT job, even with excellent English. Most English teachers in Latin America today, certainly in Mexico, have a degree in ELT, but they didn't get beyond beginner level in English until their late teens or after. Their English, though good, is usually noticeably non-native, perhaps noticeably Hispanic or Brazilian. They may try to be good EFL teachers, and succeed to some extent. Or they may see themselves clearly as ELF teachers. As such, they let go of pure EFL and attend more to their students' present or most likely needs, which are more likely to be for ELF than any specific variety of EFL.

So, are you, or the teachers you coordinate, doing, or trying to do, TEFL (perhaps most appropriate in bilingual schools) or TELF (perhaps most appropriate in most of the world, and most of Latin America), or something else? Are you thinking of a shift in your ELT in the near future? Perhaps to EAP, EOP or ESP?

16

SELECTING VOCABULARY

How do you—or does your institution—select the vocabulary you teach in each course?

Some teachers may answer: "We teach the vocabulary in the text-books, of course, and test a selection of the words." Others may answer: "The basis is the vocabulary in the textbooks, but we're a university so we focus particularly on academic vocabulary and add some not in the books". Yet others may answer: "Well... um... what comes in the textbooks, I suppose... and whatever the students ask about". And some may answer just: "Well... um... er...". What would your answer be?

The answer is important because, in each course, teachers (and/or their institutions) can get students to learn only a small selection from the quarter million distinct English words, and it shouldn't be the same selection for all students: young children, teenagers, medical students, business people, and so on, need some different vocabulary, right from their beginner's course.

One logical approach to vocabulary selection is to teach common words first and less common ones later, but that principle isn't at all simple and straightforward in practice, especially when considering the different types of student mentioned above. And many interactions and topics (and their vocabulary) that are common in everyday life and among friends in an English-speaking country (where very few Latin American students of English will ever find themselves) aren't so common in international airports, hotels, manufacturing plants, banks, company offices, congresses, etc., in the students' own countries (where many Latin Americans do or may find themselves), and other different interactions and topics (and their vocabulary) are common in those contexts. Obviously, vocabulary selection shouldn't be taken for granted.

How has ELT vocabulary selection been seen and handled over time?

The answer is, in different ways, generally rather intuitive, arbitrary and random ways. But there have been attempts at more rational and organised approaches.

Michael West's *The General Service List of English Words* (first version 1935, published revised version, 1953), with about 2,000 'most frequently used' words based on a pre-computer corpus of written English, was one of the first serious vocabulary selection projects. It had a notable impact on ELT, or at least on writing and talking *about* ELT. Later came far more words in the 'specific notions' and 'lexical inventories' of the Council of Europe's 1976-7 *Threshold Level English* and *Waystage English*, though these were related to common notions and communicative functions rather than directly to the frequency of occurrence of the words themselves. And then there are 'computer learner corpora', pioneered by the University of Birmingham (funded by Collins publishers), which led to the publication of the first Collins Cobuild Dictionary in 1987.

The implicit assumption, for ELT, in most such selections of words (and massive inventories from which selections can be made) is that all learners of English as a foreign language need essentially the same vocabulary, with the 'commonest' and 'most useful' words to be learnt first. But all learners of English don't need the same words, nor the same 'common' and 'useful' words first. And, to my knowledge, there have been very few, if any, EFL textbooks written carefully checking off the words in a list one by one, with certain words graded for the first book, others for the second, and so on.

In fact, most textbooks since I started using them (over 50 years ago) seem to select vocabulary in three main ways, sometimes all three combined, with frequency of occurrence and general useful-ness left as just something to bear in mind. One way is to select vocabulary required by 'contexts for structures', as in the audio-lingual and structural-situational periods of ELT methodology. To teach, for example, the present progressive, textbook writers, and teachers, would try to come up with 'illustrative contexts', for example, people and animals doing things in a picture (the boy is playing football, the girl is baking a cake, the dog is barking —*forever*) and doing things in the classroom (*right now*, the teacher is walking to the door, and now she's opening the door, and now she's closing the door, and now she's looking at…).

A second way is to select vocabulary for topics that it's hoped will 'engage the students', especially students whose default position is unengaged because they're unmotivated or have juvenile attitudes (however old they may be). To teach, for example, the simple past to 'captive' teenagers (imprisoned in a school curriculum), textbook writers and teachers would try to come up with 'topics that engage the students' attention', for example, gossip about celebrities and things they did recently, and, more recklessly, rap verses (preferably without "That's all of what I done / And now I ain't got no one", etc.).

A third way, is 'whatever comes to mind' (and some strange things sometimes come to textbook writers' minds). That approach to vocabulary selection may have become a partly 'traditional approach', with the same words occurring in generation after generation of EFL textbooks. Let's call it 'the arbitrary-intuitive-traditional approach' to vocabulary selection. Why do so many beginner's books have family members, hair and eye colour, for example? Are they very common and useful in non-native English discourse? The following bizarre scene comes to my mind: *After failing to understand much in an international business meeting, or congress plenary, or training workshop, etc. (too many unfamiliar words), a Latin American professional tries to make conversation with a foreigner in the coffee break, exploiting what he'd practised in an English course*:

Figure 11. Conversation example

You may laugh at that (obviously, *I* find it amusing), but the point is serious.

Apart from the 'contexts for structures' approach, the 'engage the students' approach and the 'arbitrary-intuitive-traditional' approach, there's also learner-centred vocabulary selection. It's particularly notable in English for Specific Purposes textbooks and courses, but it can be applied in any courses where many or most of the students have EFL needs and interests in common. It's really what we should always do whenever and wherever possible. So let's consider…

Who the students are and what they need (or might need) English for

Obviously, young children are very different from older students in their EFL needs, including vocabulary. No matter what young children may need English for in the future when they're teenagers, or the distant future when they're in higher education or working, the English they get in their classes and books needs to be related to what they know and like and other attractive things young children will probably like. West's *General Service List* and other general lexicons would be of virtually no use to young children's textbook writers and teachers: they would require the omission of many, perhaps most, high frequency words in the list other than determiners, pronouns and prepositions.

Older children and teenagers may require vocabulary selection that's much more differentiated according to their socio-economic situation. If they're in a school or language centre for 'the very well-off', all of them with cable TV and Internet, many with parents and others around them who speak some, or even fluent, English, and some with occasional, or even frequent, trips abroad, vocabulary for all such situations would be appropriate (for use in digital media activities, social chat, travel, summer camps, etc.). If they're at the other socio-economic extreme, that would probably not be at all appropriate, and vocabulary selection would be better based on their real-world environment, especially if some English is used in it (vocabulary for living in the capital city, for example, or an industrial area, a beach resort, an international port, a tourist area, etc.) and on their typical interests.

Learner-centred vocabulary selection can be really important and necessary for older teenagers and, especially, adults, but only when groups are fairly homogeneous. In language centres for people of all walks of life, it's usually not possible to go much beyond 'general adult vocabulary' (as in most textbooks). But some vocabulary for the local area (capital city, industrial area, beach resort, etc.) can be added, and whatever other common interests arise in the group (to which the textbook can't respond, but the teacher can). However, in higher education, company classes and private group classes, the vocabulary selection can—and really should—be quite learner-centred: vocabulary for engineering, tourism, medicine, etc., vocabulary for a certain type of company and its activities, vocabulary for a group of acquaintances, perhaps especially for international travel, or even for reading English language novels.

Who does the selecting?

The candidates here are the textbook writers (and editors), the teachers (and their coordinator and institution), the students, and nobody. It may be a combination, each doing some of the selecting (or neglecting). Let's look first at 'nobody'. This means that nobody is doing any conscious selecting of vocabulary at all, and the words in the textbook and the course are unavoidable (determiners, pronouns, prepositions, auxiliary verbs, *name, live,* etc.) and whatever arises randomly out of 'contexts for structures' and/or 'trying to engage the students' (both mentioned above). That usually means that the focus of the textbook and the course is on teaching the grammar, not on providing specific students with the English they really need or might need. Let's move on from there, fast, to...

1 EFL textbook writers

Most EFL textbooks are English for General Purposes (EGP), and the selection of 'general purpose words' (beyond the obvious—determiners, pronouns, prepositions, auxiliary verbs, *name*, *live*, etc.) depends on the writers and their editors. Most seem to consider the CEF on one hand and tradition (what most successful textbooks have done) on the other, but the arbitrary or random inclusion of odd words is often apparent. The words below are in the 'occupations' and 'routine activities' sections of the first books of four well-known series of EFL textbooks produced by four different major publishers. Note that each word is in *only one* of the three books, not in any of the others.

Occupation nouns: *builder, carpenter, chef, cleaner, computer programmer, cook, dentist, graphic designer, journalist, pilot, police officer, politician, researcher, security guard.*

Routine activity verbs: *brush my teeth, get dressed, go to bed, spend money, start work, stay up until midnight, take a shower, take care of patients, walk to work, listen to music, wake up.*

Obviously, other words (e.g., *director, student, teacher*, and *live, study, work*) are in all four books, and other words in two or three of the books. However, the selection of some of the words above, just in one book or another, is definitely *odd*: how many students need to talk, from their first English course, about brushing their teeth, taking a shower, staying up until midnight, and so forth, and how many are, or want to be, cleaners, politicians, security guards, or other occupations? Well, personal hygiene and private habits might engage the students' attention, I suppose, and even lead to some enjoyable extracurricular activities, perhaps ending in a shower, and then breakfast!

I seriously question whether there's a really appropriate selection of vocabulary in most EGP textbooks (including at least some of my own), but I also know that it's extremely difficult to decide on 'general purpose' vocabulary beyond very basic words. I suspect it may be better for writers of EGP textbooks to keep to a fairly limited 'basic' lexicon and let teachers expand it according to the needs and interests of their particular students (see 2 below).

With more learner-centred textbooks, as opposed to EGP ones, it becomes much easier for writers to select appropriate vocabulary. English for Academic Purposes textbooks, for example, should have basic general vocabulary plus a lot of professional study, work and development vocabulary, much of it more formal than EGP vocabulary; English for Occupational Purposes (e.g., for Latin American Automotive Workers) should have basic vocabulary plus technical automotive vocabulary and vocabulary for automotive training workshops; and English for Specific Purposes should have basic vocabulary plus technical and professional vocabulary, for example, medical or business vocabulary.

Unfortunately, international EGP textbooks for adults are a much better commercial proposition, and usually cheaper for users, than different textbooks for every different student population, even substantial ones. With luck, however, new publishing technology and delivery systems (especially electronic ones) should eventually make learner-centred materials more commercially viable and enable materials writers to select vocabulary more appropriately for different student populations.

2 EFL teachers

Some teachers, and coordinators, consider that the grammar and vocabulary to be taught has been selected when a textbook is selected, and their job is to get students to learn it, and then test to check how much they have (and haven't) learnt. They think it's not their job to select vocabulary for the courses, but the textbook writer's. Others, however, consider that it's very much their job.

For the latter, selecting a textbook is trying to find the best option (never perfect) among a limited number of options for their students and their teaching-learning context. Whichever textbook (usually a series) is chosen, it will almost certainly cover most of the basic grammar (though the teachers may not always handle that grammar as proposed in the textbooks), but the vocabulary is likely to require quite a lot of 'learner-centred selection' by teachers (or coordinators), which means both addition to and disregard of some textbook vocabulary. For example, if they happen to come in a selected book, *builder, carpenter, cleaner, politician, security guard, brush your teeth, stay up until midnight* and *wake up* (among other words) may be disregarded (i.e., not focused on or included in tests), and, if they don't come in the textbook, *computer programmer, dentist* and *graphic designer* may be included if those professions are studied where the book is being used (e.g., a university), along with *attend classes, do assignments*, etc. (also university vocabulary).

Teachers using an EGP textbook for teenagers or, especially, for adults should always modify the vocabulary selection in the book, responding to the characteristics and needs of their students and the local context. If there happens to be a cleaner in an international tourist hotel in a course (with the ambition of becoming a doorman and then go higher), the teacher should include *cleaner* and *doorman* in the course vocabulary if the student is open to that. If the course is in a technical high school, some general technical vocabulary should be included (*workshop, factory, machine, device*, etc.).

If a more learner-centred textbook (EAP, EOP, ESP) can be selected, the teachers and coordinators in the institution may have little to do in terms of modifying the vocabulary selection in the book, but they should always be prepared to do so, especially in response to common requests for certain vocabulary from students, for example, because it comes a lot in their native language in their professional studies.

3 EFL students

Coordinators and teachers can select EFL textbooks and, if they consider it necessary, modify the vocabulary selection in the books, thus largely determining what vocabulary is taught and tested in each course. But, in the final analysis, students that eventually reach a good level in English select the vocabulary they actually incorporate into their personal lexicons, whether through conscious learning or sub-conscious acquisition. And after the teaching stops, they continue as learner-acquirers of English, no longer students, usually increasing their fluency and vocabulary more than they did in classrooms.

POSTSCRIPT: *English Vocabulary Profile*

Based on a Council of Europe funded University of Cambridge research project, *The English Vocabulary Profile* indicates what words and phrases (and which specific meanings of each) are known by learners at each level of the CEFR. This pilot resource is available free from Cambridge University Press at http://www.englishprofile.org/wordlists.

I've no doubt that it will be of enormous interest and help to ELT professionals, but as I understand it, the Profile gives the words/phrases/uses known by many different learners at each level, not by all of them, so there's no justification for trying to make all students learn all the words, only the ones they may need. For example, the English lexicons of B1-level secondary school students, medical students and hotel receptionists are likely to be significantly different.

Note that *teeth* (or rather *tooth*), *shower* and *wake up* are included in the A1 level profile in *The English Vocabulary Profile*, but *builder*, *carpenter, cleaner, journalist, pilot, politician, researcher, security guard,* and *brush, get dressed, spend* and *take care of* are not.

References

Cobuild. See "The history of Cobuild" at https://www.collinsdictionary.com/cobuild/

Van Ek, J.A., & Alexander, L.G. (1976). *Threshold Level English*. Pergamon Press for the Council of Europe.

Van Ek, J.A., & Alexander, L.G., & Fitzpatrick, M.A. (1977). *Waystage English*. Pergamon Press for the Council of Europe.

West, M. (1953). *The General Service List of English Words*. Longman, Green, & Co.

17

EXPLOITING COGNATES

We all know about cognates, and false cognates, but we don't necessarily know all we could about them or take advantage of them in Latin American ELT as much and as well as we could.

First of all, it has to be recognized that Latin American learners of English are very lucky compared with most other learners because of the high quantity of English-Portuguese/Spanish cognate vocabulary. They're even luckier if their prime need and use of English is for professional or academic purposes and requires a lot of reading of formal texts since they usually have more Latin and Greek based vocabulary than everyday English, as well as global technical and other neologisms.

Unlike Spanish and Portuguese, many European languages and most non-European ones have few English cognates, which is one reason why international textbooks don't usually work on cognates, or have much reading at beginner levels (where cognates can help a lot, while different scripts—Greek, Russian, Arabic, Chinese, and so forth—can be an obstacle at first). Of course, an abundance of cognates (and the same script) doesn't make texts in

English perfectly intelligible for low level Latin American learners (full and accurate reading comprehension is far more complicated than that), but it helps, especially with formal texts and in topic areas a reader is familiar with, for example, engineering or medicine.

Unfortunately, where there are many cognates between English and a learner's native language, ELT has tended to emphasize the perils of false cognates, not the wealth of exact and near cognates (over 90% of all English-Portuguese/Spanish cognates). I'll start, then, with those, the large majority of cognates.

Exploiting cognates in teaching and learning

New York State's Regional Bilingual Education Resource Network (RBERN), based at the University of the State of New York, has an online publication, *English-Spanish Cognates According to Grammatical Rules Related to the Word Ending*, which shows the extent to which cognates can help Spanish speaking learners of English (and English speaking learners of Spanish). Here's a small sample of the contents of the document (there are many more words in most of the categories, or 'rules'):

1. abdominal - abdominal / impartial - imparcial / vital – vital / etc.
2. accident - accidente / elegant - elegante / urgent - urgente / etc.
3. abandon - abandonar / insist - insistir / represent - representar / etc.
4. angular - angular / popular - popular / vulgar - vulgar / etc.
5. actuary - actuario / necessary - necesario / salary - salario / etc.

6. abbreviate - abreviar / consolidate - consolidar / participate - participar / etc.
7. adjustable - ajustable / favorable - favorable / questionable - cuestionable / etc.
8. act - acto / effect - efecto / product - producto / etc.
9. accuse - acusar / examine - examinar / vote - votar / etc.
10. certify - certificar / simplify - simplificar / unify unificar / etc.
11. adolescence - adolescencia / essence - esencia / science - ciencia / etc.
12. 12 academic - académico / electric - eléctrico / traffic - tráfico / etc.
13. acid - ácido / rapid rápido / valid - válido / etc.
14. agile - ágil / hostile - hostil / textile - textile / etc.
15. astigmatism - astigmatismo / idealism - idealismo / patriotism - patriotismo / etc.
16. artist - artista / list - lista / tourist - turista / etc.
17. active - activo / exclusive - exclusivo / speculative - especulativo / etc.
18. ambulance - ambulancia / independence - independencia / tolerance - tolerancia / etc.
19. author - autor / dictator - dictador / radiator - radiador / etc.
20. ambitious - ambicioso / generous - generoso / odious - odioso / etc.
21. admission - admisión / incision - incisión / version - version / etc.
22. abolition - abolición / exploitation - explotación / vacation - vacación / etc.
23. ability - habilidad / identity - identidad / variety - variedad / etc.
24. accept - aceptar / deport - deportar / protest - protestar / etc.
25. agency - agencia / colony - colonia / victory - victoria / etc.

At this point, some critical thinking or questioning may be going on in your head. Couldn't the categories be better organized? (Possibly —I decided to combine two categories above). Aren't there exceptions to the patterns? (Yes, and some are noted in the document). Isn't the difference in pronunciation a problem? (No more than pronunciation in general, and there are patterns). What about false cognates? (Some are included in the document without being pointed out, but there's a separate RBERN document on false cognates), and so on.

However, the great number of cognates that can be categorized and listed like that, and other cognates that don't fit into those categories, are clearly a goldmine for Latin American learners and teachers of English. There may be some perils in the mine and minor accidents (usually just amusing or slightly embarrassing), but it's still a real goldmine that can be exploited in teaching, and also independently by learner-users. Here are three of the ways to exploit the cognate goldmine.

Early reading (for motivation, consolidation of 'known' English, independent learning, reading skills)

Latin American students of English, especially older adolescents and adults, can understand some texts in English quite well even as almost complete beginners. For example:

> *Comprehension* of *texts* in *English* is *not difficult* when they *contain* many *cognates*, which is *especially common* in *formal* and *technical publications*. These are *precisely* the *texts* that are most *important* for *university students* and *professionals*.

The texts used with beginners have to be carefully selected for intelligibility based partly on cognates, or carefully written, making sure they pass as authentic texts. Formal (and interesting) information texts are among the best (and casual, chatty ones, like ads or promotions—"Come to the sun and zest of Spain! You're bound to fall in love with…"—are among the worst).

More reading of this type than is usual in beginner textbooks and courses can motivate students, especially those who've had beginner courses before and learnt little, and perhaps become rather negative or pessimistic about studying English.

Such reading can also help consolidate the English grammar and non-cognate vocabulary that students have already met and worked on. The more independent students can even begin to learn some English by themselves as they're exposed to it in context and for real communication, and begin to develop as autonomous language learners.

Such early reading, exploiting cognates, also begins the development of strategies and habits that facilitate the comprehension of more 'difficult' texts and more types of text at higher levels. As learner-users of English read more and more, and also more easily, cognates not only help them read in general, but also form and add to the vocabulary they need for higher education and work.

Vocabulary work (on both cognate and non-cognate words)

At all levels but especially beginner and elementary levels, many teachers in Latin America (and elsewhere) do exploit cognates when working on reading comprehension, as suggested above. That comprehension work can be followed by vocabulary work, which can also be done independently of reading work, of course. Here are two techniques:

Formal cognates and informal non-cognates:

Ask students to give you informal or colloquial words that mean roughly the same as formal ones in a text (or a selection on the board): comprehend – understand, frequently – often, edifice – building, fortunate – lucky, converse – talk, commence –

begin/start. If they can't, you can present the informal words and get students to work on them.

Word formation:

Ask students to give you related words, usually different parts of speech: comprehension (noun) – comprehend (verb) – comprehensible (adjective), fortunate (adjective) – fortunately (adverb) – fortune (noun), converse (verb) – conversation (noun), contain (verb) – container (noun). If they can't think of some of the useful related words, you can present them.

A communication strategy (especially in spontaneous speech inside and outside classrooms)

Most people who are ever going to use English for real communication in their lives start doing so long before their English is 'error-free' (which, in most cases, it never will be), and have to struggle to do so. Many simply have to use English for study or work when they're still only at A2 or B1 level. Especially in those cases, cognates can be very useful for getting messages across.

In conversations and spoken transactions (and even in writing if there's no time to search for words online), Latin Americans can often guess cognate words for ideas when they don't know the normal English words for them. For example, if a person doesn't know *worried*, they could try *preoccup...ied*, and they could try *veloci...ty* for *speed*, *recupera...tion* for *recovery*, and so on. This strategy tends to produce peculiar or pedantic sentences like "I'm preoccupied about the velocity of my recuperation", but it usually achieves effective communication, which, apart from its own virtue, facilitates learning: the more people communicate in English, listening, speaking, reading and writing, the more English they learn or consolidate.

The example above, outside the classroom, might get a response like "Don't be worried. Your recovery should be quite fast." and the user-learner would then have the chance to relate *preoccupied* (formal) to *worried* (normal) and *recuperation* (formal) to *recovery* (normal) and learn some more about English. That common formal-normal relationship between 'Greco-Latin' and 'Anglo Saxon' words in English (though, in this case, *recovery* isn't 'Anglo Saxon') is something teachers should point out to students when recommending or encouraging this communication strategy. Teachers should also elicit or provide feedback when students come out with effective and even perfectly correct sentences in class that are peculiar or pedantic, for example, asking the student or class "What's a more common word instead of *preoccupied* / *velocity* / *recuperation*?".

Obviously, teachers should also make students aware of common false cognates and the words that should be used instead: *actual* (*current, present*), *contest* (*answer, respond*), *embarrassed* (*pregnant, expecting*), *library* (*bookshop, bookstore*), *record* (*remind, remember*), etc. Eventually, students should become aware that some words are 'partial cognates', that is, true cognates in some contexts and false ones in others: it's OK when a teacher pretends to be a tourist guide or a bank clerk in class, but not when he or she tells you "I pretend to be a good teacher".

In defence of exploiting cognates in ELT (and EL learning)

There was a time when some ELT experts recommended against encouraging students to exploit cognates. They said it could promote awkward L1-English mental translation instead of working directly in English, so students might never be able to use English like natives, and they might use false cognates wrongly. Some experts and teachers still think that.

First of all, teachers can't determine what learner-users do in their heads. What students do outwardly in class can be controlled to a large extent, but what they do in their heads far less, and what they do actually using English outside class, not at all. Learner-users outside class will do whatever they can to try to understand and be understood, and cognates are usually exploited by native speakers of Spanish and Portuguese when using English.

Second, most non-native learners of English will always be non-native users of English, with some non-native features in their English, but they can still be highly proficient in English, up to C2 level, even with a marked accent, some slightly unusual vocabulary, and so on, just like many totally fluent users of English as a second language, such as Indians, Nigerians, French Canadians and Swedes. After all, what is a native speaker—a Harvard professor from Salem, a Scottish engineer, a Texan beautician, a Jamaican high school teacher, a London girl-band singer…?

Third and last, the benefits of exploiting the cognate goldmine are far, far greater than the risk of injury. Or even embarrassment.

18

TEACHING ENGLISH VERB PATTERNS IN LATIN AMERICA

Verb systems in different languages

All languages have ways of indicating tense (present, past, future, etc.), aspect (simple, progressive, perfect, etc.) and modality (indicative, conditional, hypothetical, imperative, etc.), but they have some different ways of doing it. Even among European languages—not to mention Arabic, Turkish, Thai, Japanese, and so forth—there are some marked differences, as well as many similarities, of course. For example, French and German have no equivalents of the English present progressive patterns (*am/is/are* + present participle), but Portuguese and Spanish do. French relies on adverbials or context—"(*En ce moment,) je fais…*" / "(At the moment) I do…" (= I'm doing) – or uses the phrase *être en train de (be in the process of)* – "*Je suis en train de faire…*".

Also, some similar verb patterns are used for different functions in different languages. For example French is peculiar in using the present perfect patterns for the simple past function in speech (but not in formal writing) – *"Hier j'ai fait..."* / "Yesterday I have done..." (= I did) – and English is peculiar in using the present progressive form for a future function–"Tomorrow I'm doing...". Different languages also have different ways of indicating interrogatives and negatives.

A question, then: Is it the same to teach or learn English verbs (their forms, patterns and functions) in France, Germany, Egypt, Turkey, Thailand, Japan, and any other country or linguistic region?

L1-insensitive and L1-sensitive ELT

Most globalized ELT methodology and international textbooks (precisely because they're international and can't be L1-sensitive) seem to assume it is the same, but teachers with experience or knowledge of teaching in different countries know it isn't. Getting French or German speaking students to grasp the English present progressive patterns and become proficient in using them means getting them to see and handle completely new patterns for a function not formally marked in the grammar of their native language. That's not the case with Portuguese and Spanish speaking students; the words and suffixes are different, of course, but the basic structure is essentially the same in Portuguese, Spanish and English —*estar*/*be* + present participle (*"Estou fazendo"* / *"Estoy hacienda"* / "I'm doing"). The difference between French or German and English, and the similarity between Portuguese or Spanish and English, suggest different teaching treatment of the present progressive.

The similarities and differences between English and other languages are not just in verb systems, of course, but throughout the grammar and vocabulary (and pronunciation, discourse, etc.). Teacher awareness and knowledge of the similarities and differences between English and the students' native language can produce "L1-sensitive ELT". This is an area where English teachers who speak their students' language well, as native speakers or very good foreign speakers, have a significant advantage, to the benefit of their students, over native speaking English teachers who don't.

L1-sensitive ELT is one aspect of learner-centred teaching—not teaching as if your students could be German, Turkish, Japanese or any nationality (and university students, working people, high school students or any type of people), but as the Latin Americans they are (and as primary or secondary or university students). If you know it, you should use their native language in your teaching, not as the classroom language, which should normally be English, but in your planning and handling of lessons. Knowing L1-English cognates, L1-English pronunciation similarities and differences, L1-English grammar similarities and differences, and using that knowledge in your planning and teaching, can make you a better teacher for your specific students than a teacher who doesn't have that knowledge.

Verb patterns that are very different in English and Portuguese and Spanish

In form and structure, the English simple tenses (present and past) are the verb patterns most notably different from their Portuguese and Spanish equivalents. Of course, apart from formal differences and similarities, there are some in usage that also have to be learnt.

The simple present and past are called 'simple' because they don't have progressive or perfect aspect, simply present or past time reference. However, they aren't simple for any foreign learners because the *do/does/did* auxiliary system (and the single inflection, *-s* in the affirmative for the third person singular) is unique to English. In fact, it wasn't fully established until after Shakespeare's time; he used both this 'new' system and the old English simple present and past with inversion for interrogative and *not* after the verb for negative. The following examples are all from *Hamlet*: "Goes it to the main of Poland?", "What think you on't?" and "I heard it not" (the old English forms, meaning "Does it go to Poland itself?", "What do you think of it?" and "I did not hear it."), and "Do you consent?", "What does this mean?" and "You did not love your father." (the new English forms). If the shift to *do/does/did* hadn't happened, today we'd be teaching "Live you in this city?" "No, I live not here." Pity, isn't it?

Since the simple tenses in English are different from all other languages, it's appropriate to teach them in Latin America more or less like anywhere else in the world. That often means some kind of presentation, focus on form, practice, and incorporation into the students' repertoire of English. A consciousness-raising approach can also work in favourable conditions, especially with older teenage and adult false beginners. This early work will take some time, a number of lessons, going through the different patterns, affirmative, negative, interrogative and answers. The focus on form should normally be light or game-like with children, involving a lot of recurrent routine language, but teenagers and adults can be explicitly directed towards the key features (and 'rules') of the patterns. The practice in both cases could include traditional 'meaningful drills', for example:

> A.
> *Teacher:* Tell us something you don't do. I'll start: I don't smoke. Rosario?
> *Rosario:* I don't study much!
> B.
> *Teacher:* Tell us something your father, mother, brother or sister doesn't do and something he or she does do. For example: My mother doesn't play an instrument, but she sings well. Hugo?

C.

Teacher: Ask me questions about what I did last weekend.
Did you...? Yes—Patricia.
Patricia: Did you eat in a restaurant last weekend?
Teacher: Yes, I did. I went to the Maestro Asador with my
family. Another question...

The next stage of 'work' on the simple tenses should include regular use in classroom communication and in genuinely communicative activities—contrived practice should always give way to real use. However, that will probably not be enough. We know from experience that students at the intermediate stage make mistakes in tricky grammar and vocabulary that was focused on at beginner and elementary levels. The simple tenses are no exception. Some remedial work, for the whole group or individualized, may be needed long after the first focus on the simple tenses, and more than once.

The good news is that, though very different in forms and patterns, the simple present tenses in English and in Portuguese and Spanish have the same basic uses, that is, the general present and the fixed future: "The train leaves at 12 (every day / tomorrow)." / "*O trem sai às 12 horas (todos os dias / amanhã).*" / "*El tren sale a las 12 (todos los días / mañana)*".

Verb patterns that are similar in English and Portuguese and Spanish

In form, though not usage, English simple present and simple past are a whole new ball game for Latin American learners, then. In contrast, almost all other affirmative verb patterns—progressive, perfect and with modals—are similar to Portuguese and Spanish, though some of the uses are different.

Most globalized methodology and international textbooks let it be assumed that every verb pattern is as strange and difficult as all the rest and should be handled in exactly the same way. Every new pattern is indeed as strange as the English simple tenses for some learners somewhere in the world, but not in Latin America. This has important implication for teaching—if teachers are fully aware of it.

When teachers in Latin America first focus on the simple present, they can elicit third person -s and then negative and interrogative sentences only from students who already know them, or after carefully designed tasks that get students to notice -s and *do/does* + the simple form in the different patterns. In contrast, the present progressive uses *am/is/are*, which students know already in all the basic patterns (e.g., *It is… / It is not… / Is it…? / What is it?* / etc.), and if the teacher asks students if there's a similar verb structure in Portuguese/Spanish, most students should immediately recognize that there is and feel reassured by that. That recognition and the knowledge of *am/is/are* patterns can enable many students to produce original present progressive interrogative and negative sentences almost immediately. For example, if the teacher says "I'm reading an interesting book. OK? Ask me about it: What book…". with a bit of luck, a bright student will ask "What book are you reading?"—perhaps the first present progressive question asked by a student in that class. And if the teacher says to a bright student "You're thinking about lunch!", with a bit of luck, the student will respond "No, I'm not thinking about lunch. I'm thinking about my boyfriend!"—perhaps the first present progressive negative produced by a student in that class.

Those examples may seem a bit fantastical, and they may be for your particular teaching context, but a good teacher in a good context in Latin America (less likely in France or Germany, and very unlikely in Thailand or Japan) can make them happen. Teaching things that are similar in L1 and English can be like teaching someone to ride a bicycle, needing just an occasional hand on the bike, an occasional push. In Latin America, the basics of the present progressive (but not the present simple) can be well established in a single lesson, though much more practice and use is needed for fluency, of course.

Teaching a sense of how English works

The present progressive, like other verb patterns, exemplifies the basic elements of almost all verb patterns in English. Learners who grasp those elements early on, and develop a sense of how English verbs work, can learn additional tenses and patterns more easily than those who don't. It's the teacher's job to help students develop that sense. Look at these tables (which in some mental way are probably in the brains of good users and learners of English) and complete them:

NEGATIVE	Subject	Auxiliary verb	*not*	Main verb
Present progressive	1ˢᵗ sing / 3ʳᵈ sing / other	*am / is / are*	*not*	verb-ing
Past progressive				
Present simple	3ʳᵈ sing / other	*does / do*	*not*	verb
Past simple				
Present perfect	3ʳᵈ sing / other			verb+ed
Past perfect		*had*		
Ability with *can*	All			verb
Obligation with *must*		*must*		
Etc.				

Figure 12A. English verbs / negative

INTERROGATIVE	Auxiliary verb	Subject	Main verb
Present progressive	*Am / Is / Are*	1ˢᵗ sing / 3ʳᵈ sing / other	verb-ing?
Past progressive			
Present simple	*Does / Do*	3ʳᵈ sing / other	verb?
Past simple			
Present perfect	*Has / Have*		verb+ed?
Past perfect		All	
Ability with *can*	*Can*		
Obligation with *must*		All	
Etc.			

Figure 12B. English verbs / interrogative

When learners have grasped these basic elements and structures, they can easily produce negatives and interrogatives of verb patterns that are supposedly new for them. For example, the passive:

A.
Teacher: I'm going to say some sentences. Correct them if necessary, OK? Volkswagens are made in Mexico. Right or wrong? Yes, right. Coffee is grown in Alaska. Right or wrong?
Student: Wrong. Coffee isn't grown in Alaska. It's grown in Colombia, Brazil, and… and…
Teacher: …here in our country. Right! Japanese is taught in this high school. Right or wrong?
B.
Teacher: Ask me questions with what I mention, OK? Portuguese, Brazil. A question, OK?
Student: Is Portuguese spoken in Brazil?
Teacher: It sure is! Kimonos, China.

The principle of helping students develop a sense of how English works and how specific areas of English work applies not only to verb patterns, of course, but to other phrase and sentence patterns, and even to words. It's extremely important in foreign language teaching because it can help make students more able independent learners, which they need to be. We should recognize that what we teach in our courses is just a part of the English that students who really need or want English will eventually learn, much of it outside the classroom. What's more, they'll learn much of the specific English they really need outside the classroom, one person learning what's needed in the automotive industry, another what's needed in the tourist industry, another what's needed in international trade, and another what's needed for everyday communication with a foreign colleague, friend or spouse.

Further reading

(for those prepared for something a bit tough but very interesting)

Ortega, L. (2013). *Understanding Language Second Language Acquisition* (especially Chapter 3: Crosslinguistic influences). Routledge.

19

WORKING ON THE PRONUNCIATION OF ENGLISH

Back in the 20th century, some EFL textbooks set out to work through almost the whole sound system of English, phoneme by phoneme, typically with a lot of minimal pair/trio practice (heat-hit, fun-full-fool, yet-jet, sip-ship-zip, etc.), but by the end of the century few textbooks continued with that approach. Almost all focused pronunciation work on just a few selected aspects of English sounds (e.g., past tense endings and weak forms) and on stress and intonation. They'd come to the conclusion that work on over 40 phonemes (including diphthongs) was far too much for most ELT contexts and unproductive, and that a more realistic and practical approach was to use model sentences and dialogues to help students with stress and intonation and with the sound of English in general, leaving work on specific problem sounds and sound combinations to teachers.

That made sense since many English sounds, sound contrasts and sound combinations are problematic for learners of English with one native language and not with another. That's often reflected in non-native pronunciation of English, which commonly has typical L1 pronunciation interference—a French, German, Spanish or Chinese accent in English. That means that native speakers of French, German, Spanish, Chinese, etc., usually need some different, specific work on their pronunciation of English.

In this article, I'll focus on Spanish-speaking learners, particularly Mexican ones, leaving pronunciation work for Brazilian learners to those more familiar with them. However, even I have become familiar with some typical features of Brazilian pronunciation, such as /u/ for final /l/ ('Braziu' and 'weu' for 'Brazil' and 'well'), /i/ added after final plosive consonants ('booki' and 'shopi' for 'book' and 'shop'), and /tʃ/ and /dʒ/ for /t/ and /d/ followed by front vowels ('cheam' and 'injex' for 'team' and index').

What matters more and what less

Not all non-native pronunciation features matter equally—unless the learner is training to be a spy who has to pass as a native speaker, for example! A foreign accent that seldom or never interferes with intelligibility can be interesting (conveying something about the speaker beyond their appearance and manner) and even charming. We hear many highly articulate non-native speakers of English on television nowadays (as well as native speakers with notably different accents, and sometimes not as clear and articulate as some non-native speakers with a noticeable accent).

Two particular points should be born in mind when considering pronunciation work. The first is that context usually helps us understand oddly pronounced words and phrases in spoken discourse, and is often definitive: "We transport our products by sheep, not by plane" and "Ship farming, for wool and meat, is very important in my country" are both perfectly clear, especially when 'sheep' and 'ship' are actually pronounced the same by a non-native speaker, as is often the case. Comprehensible expression of information and ideas through vocabulary and grammar is usually more important in spoken interaction than details of pronunciation.

The second point is that consonants convey meaning more than vowels (Arabic and Hebrew are written without vowels, only consonants). The meaning of *W- tr-nsp-rt --r pr-d-cts b- sh-p, n-t b- pl-n-* can be guessed, especially in context, while the meaning of *-e --a---o-- ou- --o-u--- -y --i-, -o- -y --a-e* can't be guessed, at all, even in context.

That second point means that more attention to consonants than to vowels is generally appropriate in ELT, though some attention to vowels is also important, of course. So let's look first at English consonants and typical interference from Spanish, especially Mexican Spanish, which can contribute to a strong non-native accent in English, and perhaps interfere with intelligibility. As an ELT professional in Latin America, you'll probably be familiar with most of what follows on consonants, and later on vowels and other aspects of pronunciation.

Working on English consonants

Many consonant phonemes are similar or almost identical in English and Spanish, and they generally take care of themselves as Spanish speakers learn English, or only contribute to a slight accent. However, some are notably different, at least in allophone (or variant) form, and some English phonemes are unlike any sound in Spanish. The following are some of the main problem areas for Latin American Spanish speaking learners of English.

Problem area 1: /b/ is used for 'b' and 'v' in Spanish (and other aspects of /b/ and other plosives)

The English phoneme /b/ is very similar to /b/ in Spanish, but the letter 'v' is pronounced the same as the letter 'b' in most varieties of

Spanish, and there's no voiced fricative phoneme like English /v/. For example, 'bello' and 'vello' are pronounced the same, and Spanish-speaking learners of English tend to pronounce both 'ban' and van' as /ban/. The contrast between /b/ and /v/ in English must be pointed out to students, then, and worked on. This work can include:

- getting students to position their lips for /f/ and produce /v/ (which is voiced /f/), and then do the same with words: (f)… **v**an; (f)… **v**ery; (f)… **v**ote, etc.
- getting students to distinguish between words with /b/ and /v/ when the teacher says them (ban-van, berry-very, boat-vote, robe-rove, etc.), and then to produce the words themselves.

Apart from the /b-v/ problem, there's also the possible confusion of initial /b/ and /p/, which is generally less plosive and aspirated in Spanish than in English, so 'pill' may sound like 'bill'. To help students, you can *spit out* '**p**et', '**p**ack', '**p**ull', etc., and then get students to do the same. A similar less plosive/aspirated production of /t/ and /k/ may make 'tip' and 'cap' sound like 'dip' and 'gap'.

Voiced plosives (/b/, /d/ and /g/) at the end of words can also sound unlike their allophones (that is, variants) in initial position, becoming fricatives and softer: compare the three 'd's in '**d**uali**d**a**d**' (each tends to be softer than the one before, and the final 'd' may be dropped completely— 'dualida"'). This is, in fact, especially noticeable with final /d/, but sometimes with /b/ and /g/ also: 'pub' may sound rather like 'puv' and 'log' rather like Scottish 'loch', as well as 'bread' rather like 'breath'. You can help students by getting them to repeat phrases with word-final plosives followed by vowels and then, maintaining the same plosive pronunciation, with plosives at the end of a phrase:

'A pub˛ in England / A pub.' 'Some bread˛and butter / Some bread.' 'It's a big˛apple / It's big.'

The affricate /tʃ/ (a phoneme with both plosive and fricative qualities) can also lose its plosive element at the end of a syllable, resulting in some Mexican learners of English washing their TVs instead of watching them!

Problem area 2: /d/, /ð/ and /θ/ are phonemes in English and allophones in Spanish

The automatic production of different /d/ allophones in Spanish according to position in a syllable or word is mentioned above (the three 'd's in 'dualidad'). In English, something like those three Spanish allophones of /d/ are three different phonemes, distinguishing between words like 'breed' and 'breathe' and 'bread' and 'breath', and partially between 'bread', 'breath' and 'breathe'. Spanish speakers don't decide about the allophones of /d/ (they occur automatically according to position in a syllable or word), but in English they have to decide whether to say 'bread', 'breath' or 'breathe' (though context would usually distinguish the first two as nouns and the third as a verb even when pronounced the same or indistinctly). Spanish speakers, then, can produce the three sounds (and most Latin Americans can also imitate the peninsular Spanish /θ/ in 'cena' and 'arroz'), but not at will in any position in a word, at least not until they start becoming fairly fluent in spoken English.

The problem really starts with the base or initial /d/ in Spanish, which is different from the English /d/. Spanish /d/ is dental, like /ð/ in 'they', but more plosive than the fricative in 'they'. English /d/, in contrast, is alveolar (tongue tip against the palatal ridge behind the teeth, like /l/) as in 'day'. So, while English distinguishes clearly between 'they' and 'day', a Spanish-speaking learner of English may pronounce them the same.

Work on this area can include:

- getting students to produce initial alveolar English /d/ (as opposed to dental Spanish /ð/) by positioning their tongue for /l/ and producing /d/, or saying the letters 'l' and 'd' together (el-dee, el-dee, el-dee), and after that, getting them to say words: **d**ay, **d**esk, **d**ifferent, **d**oor, etc.
- getting students to produce /d/ in final position by repeating phrases with word-final /d/ followed by a vowel and then, maintaining the same plosive pronunciation, with /d/ at the end of a phrase: 'Some brea**d** and butter / Some brea**d**.' 'It's a ba**d** apple / It's ba **d**.' 'A be**d** of roses / A be **d**.' 'There's mu**d** on your boots / There's mu**d**.'
- getting students to produce /ð/ by preparing for Spanish /d/ and trying to make it a continuous voiced fricative (d-d-d…, d-d-d…), and after that, getting them to say words: **th**ey, **th**en, **th**is, **th**at, etc.
- getting students to produce /θ/ by imitating peninsular Spanish 'c-z', and applying that to English words: cinco-**th**ink, zanco-**th**ank, paz-pa**th**, bocina-bo**th**, etc.
- getting students to distinguish between words with /d/, /ð/ and /θ/ when the teacher says them (**d**ough-**th**ough-**th**ought, ba**d**-ba**th**e-ba**th**, o**d**our-o**th**er-au**th**or, etc.), and then produce the words themselves.
- pointing out that /ð/ is common in 'grammatical words', among others (**th**e, **th**ey, **th**em, **th**is, **th**at, **th**ese, **th**ose, **th**en, **th**ough, o**th**er, etc.) and /θ/ is common in number words (**th**ree, **th**irteen, **th**irty, **th**ousand, **th**ird) and some other very common words (**th**ank, **th**ing, **th**ink, **th**in, **th**ought, etc.).

Problem area 3: in addition to /s/ and /tʃ/, English has /z/, /ʃ/, /ʒ/, and /dʒ/

These six phonemes produce different but similar sounding words like these: **sue-zoo-shoe-(zhu)-chew-Jew**. To complicate matters, the phonemes can be represented in writing by different letters: **face-phase-potion-usual-picture-lodge**. These phonemes in English may require similar work to that suggested above for /b/-/v/ and /d/-/ð/-/θ/. It would take several pages to go into all major aspects of this area, so I'll keep it to a few observations and suggestions and leave you to apply them in the classroom if and when you consider it when appropriate.

- Something like /z/ occurs automatically in Spanish as the allophone of /s/ before /b/, /d/, /g/ and /m/: **esbelta, desde, esgrima, mismo**. This may help students note the sound and its production.
- Something very like /ʃ/ occurs in Mexican indigenous names, like Xola and Xel-Há.
- Something very like /ʒ/ occurs in Argentinian Spanish in words like 'caballo' and 'sello', and other Latin Americans can usually imitate that pronunciation.
- Spanish /tʃ/ (always spelt 'ch') can turn into the allophone /ʃ/, especially after a vowel as in 'muchacho', leading sometimes to sentences like 'I wash a lot of television' (dirty television?).
- In Spanish something between /dʒ/ and /y/ (or /j/ in IPA) can occur in words like 'hielo' and 'hierba', leading sometimes to the same pronunciation for 'jet' and 'yet', 'jail' and 'Yale'.

Obviously, you shouldn't work on all that at the same time, but bit by bit, and as the need or opportunity arises. The same applies to all pronunciation work, of course— gradually, as needed, not too much at once.

Problem area 4: intrusive /e/ before initial s+consonant

eSpanish doesn't have words estarting with s+consonant, so eSpanish espeakers tend to put /e/ in front of those words in English. Enough said? You can help students by getting them to repeat a list of words, stretching the initial /s/ of each word (Ssspanish, ssspeak, ssschool, ssstudy, etc.), and phrases or sentences with vowel-s linking ('They study Spanish in many schools in the States'—avoiding word by word production, which may produce intrusive /e/: 'They estudy eSpanish in...').

One other common problem: intrusive /g/ before initial /w/ in some words

In Spanish (or Mexican Spanish, anyway) some words may be pronounced with a slight /g/ sound with an initial /w/ (some people are unsure whether it's 'haurache' or 'guarache'). This can lead to the very similar pronunciation of 'good' and 'wood' (/g/ with rounded lips), and the pronunciation of 'woman' rather like 'gwooman'. However, the problem doesn't seem to arise with 'women' (/wimin/), and it may be that back vowels (like /u/ in 'woman') draw the tongue back and produce a slight /g/, whereas front vowels (like /i/ in 'women) don't. Some practice with /g/-/w/ minimal pairs may help (good-wood, one-gun, etc.), and with front-back vowel minimal pairs (women-woman, well-wool, etc.).

Working on English vowels

As mentioned towards the beginning of this article, vowels generally convey meaning less than consonants, but they can be important, even with a fairly clear context: "It's time to live now" and "Here's the full story" are very different from "It's time to leave now" and "Here's the fool's story".

Work on vowels should be similar to work on consonants, with listening-repeating and distinguishing between words with similar sounds as key tools. The similar sounds to work on are where English has two vowel phonemes (mostly long/strong vs. short/weak) where Spanish has only one (/i:/-/i/, /a:/-/a/, /o:/-/o/, /u:/-/u/), and some cases where English has three or four phonemes where Spanish has just one or two (e.g., /a:/-/a/-/ʌ/-/3:/). That calls for some comparative work on pairs of words like seat-sit, hat-heart, caught-cot and fool-full, and on groups of words like cart-cat-cut-curt.

Apart from the large number of English vowel phonemes (about twenty, including diphthongs, depending on the variety of English), another problem is that, unlike the five vowel phonemes of Spanish that match the five vowel letters, English vowels can be represented by different letters and combinations of letters, for example, 'woman' and 'women' (/wumən/ and /wimin/). This can lead students into 'spelling pronunciation', with some beginners producing things like 'tay-a-chair' for 'teacher' at first (though I suspect that specific example is rare). Vowels can also be omitted in pronunciation in English and, for example, students have to learn that 'called' is /ko:ld/, not /ko:led/.

In spite of the apparent chaos of English spelling and pronunciation, there are, in fact, patterns, and most British and American children eventually learn them. We shouldn't expect more of non-native learners of English: we should expect a long, slow process in which most students *eventually* master the most important aspects of pronunciation, spelling, and spelling-pronunciation correspondences. That process requires not just time, but a lot of exposure to good models of pronunciation and to written-spoken versions of texts (e.g., through printed and recorded versions of texts and reading aloud), along with help from teachers.

Few students of EFL, or even learners through immersion in an English-speaking community, acquire completely native-like pronunciation, but many become consistently easy to understand as well as able to understand good speakers of English with different accents, native and non-native. Pronunciation work should be primarily about comprehension and intelligibility. Remember that if a student pronounces 'cup' and 'bus' as /kup/ and /bus/ (instead of /kʌp/ and /bʌs/), they sound a bit like a Beatle (or Liverpudlian), and if they pronounce 'drain' as /drrein/ (with a trilled '/r/'), they sound a bit Scottish. Unless you work in a spy training programme, don't be obsessed with absolutely native-like pronunciation. Help students to achieve consistent comprehension and intelligibility, and be thankful for students with 'a really good ear for languages' who get close to native pronunciation, or even get there completely.

Stress (and weak syllables and weak forms) and intonation

As mentioned in the first paragraph of this article, most textbooks today work on just a few selected aspects of English sounds (e.g., past tense endings and weak forms) and on stress and intonation. I won't go into that area here, but I hope the following observations will interest you.

The standard view of English sentence stress is that key information words are stressed strongly and the least important words (especially 'grammatical words like pronouns and prepositions) tend to become weak forms or contractions (unless they have special importance in the sentence), for example, "The **President**'s in **Buenos Aires**, and he'll be **attend**ing the **G20 summit**" (the essential information is "President – Buenos Aires – attending – G20 summit"). However, on international news programmes (BBC, CNN, etc.) such sentences are now usually pronounced rather like this: "The President **is in** Buenos Aires, and he **will** be attending the G20 summit." The prominence of 'is', 'in' and 'will' here are not because there were reports that he was considering not going there for the summit and that's being denied or corrected here: he was always going, and there he is (which might account for some stressed auxiliary verbs and positions, as mentioned above).

My guess is that international news programme readers and reporters have been instructed (perhaps even trained) to enunciate extra clearly and avoid 'sloppy' native speech in order to facilitate understanding by an international audience, including many non-native users of English. I haven't been able to confirm that guess on the Internet, but I'm sure something like that is going on. If I'm right, and it continues, it's likely to have an impact on non-native speaker English, seeming to confirm to them that syllable-timed English is OK and information word stress + weak forms and contractions are not compulsory. It could have an impact on native English.

The standard view on English intonation is that, normally, statements and Wh questions have falling intonation, while Yes-No questions have rising intonation, for example: "I'm certain about that.↘" "Where do you live?↘" "Do you work here?↗↗↗" However, rising intonation for statements seems to me (and others) to be becoming more common, for example, "I'm certain about that.↗ I've read the report.↗" This rising intonation in statements was imitated and commented on by a comedian I saw on TV as 'the-not-sure-if-I'm-certain-Australian-accent'. That's not fair on Australians, of course, and if they do express uncertainty in their intonation, that uncertainty seems to be spreading to the intonation of other native speakers of English around the world. Well, the world is certainly changing radically and becoming more and more uncertain.↗ I mean "uncertain".↘ Well, you decide for yourself, and, as you think about it, if your thoughts and mumblings don't have very orthodox English stress and intonation, don't worry much while native and non-native users of English show they understand you when you speak to them.

20

WHICH ENGLISH TO FOCUS ON?

The English in EFL textbooks and the English students need

Most ELT in Latin America, as elsewhere, is carried out working with a textbook, usually related to the Common European Framework nowadays, and perhaps also to an official syllabus. The textbook usually determines to a large extent which English, or combination of varieties of English, is focused on. For example:

- British English, or American English, or international English (different varieties of English of fluent users, non-native as well as native).
- English for everyday life in an English-speaking country, or English for international travel and work, or English mainly for study, work and professional development in the student's own country.
- More colloquial English, or more formal English (or both, perhaps contrasted at times).
- English for general purposes (social, transactional, etc.), or

English for specific purposes (academic, business, medicine, engineering, etc.).

Textbooks are usually selected—and always should be—with the teaching-learning context and the students in mind. However, there's little choice in EFL textbooks that are readily available and accessibly priced in Latin America. Almost all are either American or British English, and English for general purposes (or, as has often been said, for no particular purpose).

That isn't an issue with ELT for children. Textbooks for children, especially young ones, should be visually attractive and the activities should be easy and fun for the children, but the specific variety and uses of English don't really matter much, except in certain schools or language institutes. American and British bilingual schools and language institutes obviously select American and British textbooks respectively, and they tend to focus on visits to and stays in the United States, Britain and other countries, which some students may already have experienced and a few may experience every year.

The problems with EFL textbooks and varieties of English arise especially with older teenagers and adults, when probable or actual specific uses of English become predictable or completely defined. For example, high school students planning to continue into higher education are likely to need English for general academic purposes and later for professional or skilled work, and undergraduates in medicine or nursing clearly need English for health sciences.

British, American and internationally intelligible English

Overwhelmingly, most English courses for teenagers and adults in Latin America are based on either American or British English textbooks. American English textbooks dominate from Mexico to central South America, with British English ones used more going south towards Argentina and Chile. Does the textbook distinction between British and American English really matter?

As a British co-author of both British English and American English textbooks (with a Canadian co-author for some British English textbooks) and a teacher-director in a British language institute with some American, Australian and Canadian colleagues, my answer is "No, it doesn't". As I've just suggested, those of us familiar with major dialects of English can produce their main stereotypical features (as teachers and as materials writers), and, anyway, learners of English usually shift to the variety they eventually have most contact with, not necessarily the variety in their school English classes. A Mexican working in a German car factory is likely to pick up German-British English, and an Argentinian working in an American-owned bank is likely to pick-up American English. The English-speaking workers in the car factory in Mexico and the English-speaking workers in the bank in Argentina can communicate with one another in their different varieties of English because all major varieties of English are internationally intelligible, like all major varieties of Spanish.

What did I mean by "stereotypical features" above? Well, for example, in EFL textbooks, British English uses "have got" for possession and American English "(do) have", but that's simply not borne out in Britain and the United States or in British and American songs, TV and films. Of course, there are typical British and American forms and words, but so are there typical regional forms and words in Britain and the United States. Among reasonably educated people, they're almost always intelligible.

What most learners of English as a foreign language definitely do need is internationally intelligible English, whatever its minor peculiarities (American or British or Latin American) and comprehension of good non-native English as well the main varieties of native English. The English most Latin American students hear in the classroom isn't either real British or real American English, but the English of their Latin American teachers (good, it is to be hoped, and probably with notable British or American features, but non-native English). The English they read in their textbooks, supposedly British or American, may be stereotypically British or America in dialogues, but in texts, especially formal ones, there's often little or no difference, just the occasional difference in spelling: note that there are no British-American spelling differences in this article so far, and only one word that's standard in British English and not in American English, though it is also used in the United States—film.

All the above said, it's perfectly logical and appropriate that most textbooks used in Latin America should have so-called American English. But other variations in English may matter much more.

English for different people and purposes

In the first section of this article I listed several varieties of English apart from British and American English (which themselves include, respectively, London, Liverpool, Welsh and Scottish English, and New York, New Orleans, Mid-Western and Californian English). I'll consider now four of those other varieties or types of use:

1. English for everyday life in an English-speaking country or community (fairly colloquial English).
2. English for international travel and work (standard international English).
3. English for use in the student's own country, especially for study and work (fairly formal English).
4. English for a specific field of work, for example, business, medicine or engineering (mainly formal English).

Obviously, more than one variety can be taught and studied, and actually learned, given adequate conditions and time.

Most international EFL textbooks work mainly on a combination of 1 and 2, with topics and situations related to English-speaking countries (particularly the US in American English books and the UK in British English books) and international topics and situations. That's logical for international books, which don't 'know' the nationality or needs of the different students using them, and it provides contexts and content for the practice of basic grammar (noun phrases, verb tenses and phrases, sentence structures, etc.) and vocabulary (especially structural words, like pronouns, prepositions and determiners). It can work fairly well, at least up to upper elementary level. Those two varieties may also make English seem glamorous for some students, even if everyday life in the US or UK and international travel are not in the present or the future of most Latin American students of English and varieties 3 and 4 might be much more useful for them. To make English seem more useful for their students, some teachers shift away from the textbook's focus on 1 and 2 towards the topics, situations and specific language in varieties 3 and 4 that their students really need or might need.

Here are some examples of English of varieties 1 and 2, typical of many international textbooks:

Hi there. How are you? / OK, I guess. / And your wife? / She's kind of stressed. / And the kids? / Great.

Is your sister that tall girl with blond hair? / Yeah, but that's not her natural hair color. She has brown hair. / Oh! What's she like? / A good pal, but a bit crazy sometimes.

Where are you going this vacation? / Bangkok. / Sounds cool. And you? / I'm staying home this year.

Hi. What can I do for you? / Uh, I'm looking for a laptop. / How much do you want to spend? / Well,…

Ambrose Hotel. How can I help you? / I want to make a reservation for next month. / Yes, sir. When…

This beautiful hotel is in the heart of downtown Prague. While you can step out of the lobby into a medieval and renaissance wonderland, the hotel has all modern conveniences. Every room has a…

And here are some examples of English of varieties 3 and 4, rare in international textbooks:

Excuse me. Are you Susan Hill, the exchange student from Dallas for Prepa Hidalgo? / Yes, I am. / Welcome to Mexico! I'm Laura Ortega and this is José Téllez. We're students in Prepa Hidalgo, and we'll be looking after you. / Nice to meet you, Laura, José. I'm really looking forward to this! / Let's…

Good morning, Mr Tanaka. Is your hotel satisfactory? / Yes, thank you. / The Technical Director, Mr. Ferreira, will be here at 10 o'clock, so we have half an hour. Would you like to look at the latest sales figures while we wait? / Yes, that's a good idea. / Fine. This way, please. Would you like a coffee or…

Normal values for an adult human are approximately 120 mmHg systolic and 80 mmHg diastolic pressure, but there are large variations from person to person. There is also variation in an individual, from heartbeat to heartbeat and in the course of a day (the circadian rhythm).

Obviously, there's overlap between varieties and types of use of English, with basic grammar and structural words common to most. Note also that varieties (or types of use) 3 and 4 in particular are two sides of one coin: Latin Americans abroad (not so many of them) and Latin Americans dealing with visitors from abroad (many of them, working in travel, hospitality and tourism, and in international industry and business). However, the above examples for 1, 2, 3 and 4 should illustrate that there can be significant differences, and should raise the question of which variety or varieties/uses are or may be most needed by specific students. That question becomes increasingly important from upper elementary level on, when basic grammar has been covered and styles, registers and lexicons of English become more significant for learner-users.

But remember, finally, that teachers can only prepare learners so far. If they become real users, most learners acquire the variety or varieties of English they need, more British or American or international, more colloquial for everyday life, or more formal for work in their own country, or technical and mainly for reading, or several of those. If you're a non-native speaker of English, or another additional language, you've probably experienced that in your own development in the language: what you learned in the classroom became something rather different as you actually used the language in your life.

AIDS AND RESOURCES

21

SOME PERSPECTIVES ON EFL TEXTBOOKS

EFL textbooks are seen in very different ways by teachers, by teaching institutions (or their ELT coordinators), by publishers, and by authors. They are also seen in very different ways by different teachers and different teaching institutions; for example, some evaluate textbooks in general terms, just "as textbooks", while others do so more in terms of how appropriate they are for their specific students and context. And different publishers and authors also see textbooks in different ways. Below, I consider in turn some typical perspectives of teachers, teaching institutions, publishers, and authors.

EFL teachers' perspectives on textbooks

Except where EFL textbooks aren't available or are beyond students' means, most teachers of English use them and seem content to do so. Certainly, for inexperienced teachers and those with many classes to teach it would be hard without them. They help teachers work through the English language bit by bit, and, perhaps more importantly, they provide graded listening and reading material that it would be difficult to gather otherwise.

Different teachers have significantly different views of the textbooks they use, and of textbooks in general, of course. Most teachers (and ELT institutions) seem to see textbooks as almost indispensable. They find some better suited than others to their beliefs about language teaching and learning, of course, and some better than others for their teaching situation, but they can hardly imagine teaching without a textbook. However, some teachers, especially very learner-centred ones, don't see textbooks so positively. They consider international textbooks to be almost always largely unsatisfactory because they're for worldwide consumption and therefore can't possibly be really appropriate for specific students, in specific teaching-learning contexts, in specific countries. Most local textbooks (e.g., those provided by ministries of education) are probably little better because they tend to imitate international textbooks, some being adaptations by agreement with an international publisher.

When learner-centred teachers are obliged to use textbooks, they tend to do so critically and creatively, omitting or adapting a lot of material, and substituting or adding material and activities they consider more appropriate for their students. These teachers have often gathered, evaluated and modified a considerable body of such material over their years of teaching, and some make a point of trying to keep a lot of their material updated and relevant for each new group they teach.

Most of the adaption and substitution of textbook material by these teachers doesn't affect the grammar covered, which tends to be more or less as in the textbook, but rather the topics, situations, styles of English, types of text, and the vocabulary that goes with them. Appropriate topics and situations for Latin American students are often not the same as for the French, German, Turkish, Indonesian, Japanese and other students using the same international textbooks. Unlike French and German students, for example, very few Latin American students of English ever visit or live in English-speaking countries or need the colloquial English and everyday topics and situations in many international textbooks. And unlike Indonesian and Japanese students, for example, Latin American students have an enormous amount of cognate vocabulary to facilitate early reading, especially of the formal texts they're most likely to need in higher education and professional work.

Teachers who do little adaptation and supplementation and work almost entirely with the material in their textbooks (probably most teachers) may still use them in very different ways. Teachers who "love" a certain textbook or who have an extremely heavy teaching load may work through the textbook material mostly section by section, page by page: the textbook provides their syllabus, methodology, lesson plans, and often their tests. Other teachers, however, may stand the textbook on its head. This can happen when a teacher is obliged to use a textbook but strongly disagrees with its methodological approach and the sequence of material reflecting it. For example, teachers who believe in a language-focused approach (PPP—present, practice, and get production of target language items and only then include them in skills tasks) may turn a strongly communicative textbook into a language-focused book. For example, if each unit in the book has two pages of genuine communicative skills tasks first, not focused on any specific language items but containing some of the language to be focused on later, followed by some language-focused and other skills work, the dissenting teacher uses the language-focused material first (and probably not using the book's inductive approach) and, after that, goes back to the communicative skills tasks on the previous pages. Of course, the students are now very aware of the target language in the communicative skills tasks and are distracted from communication and worried about making language mistakes. The tasks are no longer genuinely communicative.

Much, much more could be said about teachers' views on textbooks and their use of them, but I'll leave that for you to think about, considering yourself and your colleagues, past and present.

ELT institutions' perspectives on textbooks

Most institutions select textbooks for their courses and require all teachers to use them (again, except where they aren't available or are beyond students' means). The use of the same textbooks by all teachers helps institutions to make all teachers give roughly the same courses (though, as mentioned above, teachers can do very different things with the same textbook, so coordination and class observation are also needed to keep them in line).

Like teachers, institutions can handle textbooks in different ways. Some virtually make the textbooks the courses: their syllabuses, methodology guides, sequence of lesson plans, and tests. Other institutions, however, encourage teacher creativity and learner-centredness, indicating to teachers that the textbook should be the course guide and the main source of materials and activities, but it should be adapted to teachers' specific students' needs and wants, with alternative and additional material and activities where appropriate. Yet other institutions leave the use of the textbook, and, in effect, the "creation of the course" (including the tests) up to each individual teacher. I've known cases where those institutions have had to ask teachers to use the textbook more because students (or their parents) have complained about the cost of buying books that are then used very little, and they may also shift to institutional book-based tests instead of allowing different teachers to use different tests.

Apart from having all teachers giving roughly the same courses year after year, textbooks can be a crucial element when an institution wants to change its methodology or syllabuses. That was the case in the 1980s when most institutions began to move from audio-lingual or structural-situational syllabuses and methodology to notional-functional ones. By 2000 ELT institutions had little choice because almost all the textbooks were, at least nominally, CLT (communicative language teaching)! Then came the PPP (presentation-practice-production, or similar) vs TBL (task-based learning, or similar) choice in so-called CLT textbooks. Even now, many still focus on "new language" at the beginning of each unit or lesson, with language presentation dialogues or texts followed by practice exercises, and put communicative skills work afterwards (often largely to consolidate the "new language"), while others put genuine communicative activities first. Institutions that want to move from language-focused to communication-focused teaching usually start by finding an appropriate communicative textbook to replace the language-focused one they've been using.

Much, much more could be said ELT institutions' policies on textbooks and their use of them, but I'll leave that for you to think about, considering the institutions you've worked in or know about.

ELT publishers' perspectives on textbooks

First and foremost, of course, publishers are in business. To make money and survive, they have to sell sufficient books, and to do that, they have to satisfy sufficient customers and keep them satisfied. That means producing textbooks and supplementary components that stand up to teacher scrutiny and to actual use in courses (or that satisfy ministries of education). Apart from that business motivation, most people actually contributing to the production of books for publishing companies (publishing managers, editors, authors, etc.) are seeking professional satisfaction, trying to do their best for the ELT world. Competition from other publishers also pushes them to produce the best textbooks they can.

Publishers see the enormous EFL textbook market in terms of sub-markets, and they publish books (or decide not to publish books) for different ones: textbooks for young children, older children, teenagers and adults, textbooks for public primary schools and public secondary schools, textbooks for ESP areas, like business, medicine and engineering, and so on. Most sub-markets are freely competitive, but state school markets are often controlled, with, according to the country, textbooks under contract to ministries of education or requiring approval from them; if that means captive markets and very low prices, it can affect the quality of the text-books. Some sub-markets are too small to interest many publishers, for example, textbooks for ESP areas like business, medicine and engineering. So far, Latin America seems to have been too small a sub-market for almost all international publishers of young adult and adult textbooks, and they only offer books for worldwide use (see geographical areas below).

Publishers also see methodological sub-markets, with, for example, old-fashioned teachers and institutions wanting old-fashioned text-books, and very progressive ones wanting state-of-the-art text-books. Some books first published 30 or 40 years ago still sell quite well in the old-fashioned sub-market and new ones on the same lines are still launched from time to time. However, the EFL teachers and centres that tend to get the best results, including good international proficiency test results, generally demand progressive textbooks. Apart from the knowledge, experience and beliefs of those teachers and institutions, reputable modern profi-ciency tests (Cambridge, TOEFL, Trinity, etc.) may have an influ-ence: they now focus on communicative competence, and test language indirectly through communicative skills tasks, and don't employ old-fashioned language-focused tasks.

One natural division of the international EFL textbook market that's generally ignored by international publishers is geographical areas with distinct linguistic, socio-economic and cultural features (except, that is, where it's demanded, as in parts of the Moslem world). Latin America is one such area, with its speakers of Spanish (a very important international language) and Portuguese, few ever travelling to an English-speaking country, but many needing fairly formal English for higher education studies and professional or skilled work. Clearly, textbooks sold in France, Germany, Turkey, Indonesia, Japan and elsewhere can't be really appropriate for most students in Latin America, but they're all that most publishers offer. After all, why go to the expense of producing textbooks specifically for Latin America (apart from state school books) when they can sell the same ones as in the rest of the world? Fortunately for some lucky Latin American students, their conscientious and capable teachers put in an extra effort and do what publishers rarely do: they adapt international textbooks to their country, their context and, above all, their students.

Much, much more could be said about ELT publishers' provision of textbooks in general, and to the Latin American market in particular, but I'll leave that for you to think about, considering your experience with textbooks, and perhaps your dreams of ideal ones.

An ELT author's perspective on textbooks

That means *me*. The first opportunity I had to co-author a series of textbooks was in 1969, for use in the Anglo Mexican Institute (now The Anglo Mexican Foundation). They were eventually published by Macmillan, as *Active Context English: ACE*, in 1971, and were quite successful in Mexico, Latin America, and as far away as Japan (a weird fact that relates to my comment above about international textbooks sold everywhere—we authors of *ACE* in Mexico knew virtually nothing about ELT in Japan, but the publisher found a market there!). *ACE* gave me my first glimpse of ELT in Latin America outside Mexico, with promotional visits to universities, other institutions of higher education and language centres in Brazil in 1972, from Fortaleza in the north to Curitiba in the south and João Pessoa, Recife, Juiz de Fora, Niteroi and Río de Janeiro in between. It was all very exciting, interesting and satisfying for the young—well, youngish—man I was then!

Since then, I've co-authored 6 more series of textbooks (or 8, counting new editions), 28 books in total (or 36 counting new editions, and not counting workbooks and teachers' guides). They've including two series for Mexican state secondary schools. I've been back to Brazil as an ELT author 5 more times (plus a great stop-over for pleasure) and to 7 other Latin American countries.

ACE and the following two series were, naturally, structural-situational books, before the notional-functional or CLT revolution. After that, they were all CLT, and the most recent ones quite progressive CLT. *Skyline/Sky High* (Macmillan, 2001/2006) put communicative skills development before language focus, which itself was strongly inductive (though, no doubt, some teachers reversed all that!). *Make It Real!* (Universidad Autónoma del Estado de Hidalgo: UAEH, 2017) does the same, but even more so, as well as working on the English language communication situations and types of text Latin America students in higher education are most likely to face. And now I'm an old man, and I see ELT textbook writing (and publication) a bit differently!

My interest in ELT won't stop for some time, if ever (well, you know…), but I won't be writing and profiting from any more textbooks (I don't receive royalties from *Make It Real!*), so I'll be frank. For a start, I firmly believe there's too much ELT in Latin America (and too little good ELT in good conditions that gets most students receiving it really learning English). What I see as the excessive ELT (largely mandated by governments that have little or no understanding of ELT or of realistic and useful goals in national bilingualism) is of poor quality, in poor conditions, not needed by most of the recipients, and not effective. However, it's a market for textbooks. The authors and publishers of these textbooks are—or should be—fully aware that very few students will learn English in these school courses, but they write and publish the textbooks anyway. Who can really blame them? Business opportunities are business opportunities. The best that can be said of most such Latin American National English Programme school textbooks is that they give the poor teachers something to lean on, and a few gifted children, especially those with gifted teachers, may actually learn a little from them.

Above that bottom end of the market for ELT in generally unfavourable conditions, EFL textbooks generally get better and there are more to choose from, and towards the top end, the textbooks are generally good, in different ways. However, let me repeat what I said above: there should be more textbooks written specifically for Latin America, and for specific sectors within it. Even then, capable and conscientious teachers can make them even better for their specific students by adapting and supplementing them a bit.

Finally, I (and, I believe, many if not most EFL teachers, ELT institutions and ELT publishers) see textbooks for many contexts (or submarkets) no longer as just printed books. Online platforms can offer things printed books can't. Back in 2000, my best publishing manager at Macmillan (if she reads this, she'll know I mean her) thought textbooks would largely have gone from print to screen by now. She was wrong in timing, but I think it can't be very far in the future now. Of course, online ELT materials and resources still need authors, editors, publishers and users (teachers or tutors, I believe, as well as students).

P.S. Courses without textbooks can be very effective with teachers that have the time, resources and ability to put good lesson plans and material together. But that's another story, and one that most Latin American teachers, with 30 or more hours a week in the classroom, can only listen to and dream about.

EFL Teaching-Learning Platforms

A 21st century and post-pandemic AIDS AND MATERIALS section would be ridiculous without something on IT in ELT. Although it is outside my area of expertise, I was involved in the development of ELT platforms in my last employment as the leader of an ELT development project at the Universidad Autónoma del Estado de Hidalgo, Mexico, between 2013 and 2018. The head of the IT side of the project was **Jorge Hernández**, of the UAEH, and he contributed an article to my website, *ELTinLA*, titled 'Developing an ELT platform for Latin American students in higher education'. Jorge is an IT professional who was not in ELT at all until the UAEH project but pulled into it and now quite knowledgeable about ELT (more than me about IT). His article briefly presents the ELT reform project that led to UAEH ELT textbooks and platforms, the main version of which now serves an international edition of *Make It Real! Professional* called *Make It Real! English for Higher Education in Latin America*. As Jorge wrote in his article, "*that title explicitly conveys the learner-centred and context-centred nature of the material in the books and on the platform.*" As Jorge wrote, platforms have a clear advantage over textbooks for some things: "*ESP would have been virtually impossible without the platform (too costly and complicated through printed material), and* Make It Real! *would have been distinctly less learner-centred and context-centred.*" Platforms also provide out-of-class study and practice, of course, and Jorge sees many more advantages: "*When you put together the technology and the content of* mironline *you get things like 3D models of the human body to help students in Health Sciences grasp and learn the relevant vocabulary, and 360° visits to different biomes for students in agriculture and environment (a student favourite in the ESP section). As mentioned above, it would* *have been impossible to offer students that, and much more, without a platform."* Among the lessons he and his colleagues learnt, Jorge included: *"Developing and running a good ELT platform is extremely demanding, and keeping up with a plan and timetable is likely to be difficult unless conditions are very favourable and resources abundant. The team needs lots of energy and determination"* and *"Everything we develop on a pedagogical platform should be centred on the needs of the users, no matter what our field of expertise is. If you are a software developer, the applications and systems should be specifically for your target users. If you are an ELT materials writer, the same (for example, ESP was a must in our case)."*

TEACHER DEVELOPMENT

22

ACTUAL ELT IN LICENCIATURAS IN ELT

The first university Licenciaturas in ELT in Mexico (and probably the rest of Latin America) started in the 1980s, over 30 years ago. They were generally modelled on existing licenciaturas in social sciences and humanities, following university guidelines, with elements based on Normal Superior specializations in ELT and on shorter ELT training courses like those of RSA/Cambridge at that time. A lot has changed in ELT since then, both globally and in Mexico and Latin America, and many licenciaturas in ELT have not changed accordingly. In this article I'll focus on a specific component of licenciaturas in ELT—explicit attention to actual classroom teaching. Currently, this doesn't start until the third or fourth (last) year in most licenciaturas in ELT, with components like "Class observation" and "Teaching practice".

For most students, licenciaturas in ELT are pre-service programmes: the students have never taught English, and most won't until the last of four years, or even after graduating. However, they've had a lot of experience of ELT—at school. As students entering a licenciatura in ELT, they're products of Mexican school English teaching. That's where I'm going to begin here, and then I'll continue with three other focuses on actual ELT possible in most licenciaturas. The four I'll consider are:

1. The students' experience of ELT while at school, especially just before entering the licenciatura
2. The English courses in the licenciatura, usually starting between A2 and B1 level
3. The observation of ELT in the licenciatura, through video and in live classes.
4. The teaching component that's normal during the last semester or two of a licenciatura

Apart from those four focuses on actual ELT (with the licenciatura students as receivers, observers and doers of the teaching), there's usually also simulated teaching (peer-teaching, micro-teaching), which is useful but isn't the real thing, lacking the reality of real students in real time and over time.

1. Focusing on the students' experience of ELT while at school

Most students now entering a licenciatura in ELT in Mexico (and probably most of Latin America) have between A2 and B1 level English. Less is accepted in a few universities (where Inglés I in the Licenciatura programme is a false beginner course), and more is required in a few, but A2 or B1 are the entry levels in most. That's where most young Mexicans who want to be English teachers are after between 6 and 12 years of school ELT, some with extra classes outside school. It's not where they should be after all those years of English classes, and it begs questions about school ELT, but A2 or B1 is something, and it's worth asking how they got there.

However, those questions—why not a higher level after so many years, and what actually got them to A2 or B1 level?—are not formally asked at the beginning of most licenciaturas in ELT. I´m suggesting here that they should be, in the very first semester of the licenciatura. There are two places where that could be done—in the first English language course (Inglés I, especially if it's at B1+ level), or in a course called something like 'Introduction to ELT'. In either case, the exploration of the students' experience of ELT as school students prior to entering the licenciatura could start with a questionnaire. It could include questions about the extent, contexts and conditions of their English classes at school (and outside school where that applies), for example:

- When did you start studying English—in pre-school, primary or secondary?
- In each type of school, how large were the groups—under 20, 21-30, 31-40, 41-50, over 50?
- In each school, did all, some or none of the teachers make English the main classroom language?
- Did you study English outside the school? If so, were the classes notably more effective than at school?
- Where you went to school and lived, do many people speak English or very few?

Discussion of the students' answers to the questionnaire, in groups and in the whole class, should raise general awareness of some of the issues in actual ELT, and what tends to produce better results.

The next step could be to ask students to recall the best English courses and teachers they had, and reflect on why they were better than the other courses and teachers. The emphasis could be on the English classes they had immediately before entering the licenciatura (upper secondary), but if courses and teachers before that stand out in their memory, they should also be mentioned. This could be left as homework so that students have time to recall and reflect, with the reports presented from notes in the next class, first in groups and then some in the whole class. There could be a further step: getting students to recall one of the very best classes (i.e., lessons) or sequence of classes they had while at school (either in school or in a language centre) and describe it in as much detail as they can. Again this could be left for homework, with presentations given in the next class, in groups and in the whole class.

For all this work on the students' experience of ELT prior to entering the licenciatura, it's important to remember two key things, and it may be useful to point them out to the students. First, the students are just beginning the licenciatura and are quite uninformed about what might, in general, be 'good' or 'bad' in English language teaching in the classroom; by the end of the licenciatura they should be much better informed. Second, their ideas about what might be appropriate and inappropriate in different contexts —e.g., in a group of twenty 10-11 year old children versus a group of forty 15-17 year old teenagers beginning English again for the second or third time in upper secondary school—are also quite uninformed; this should also change by the end of the licenciatura.

2. Focusing on the English courses in the licenciatura

How to focus on the actual ELT in the English courses most students receive during a licenciatura will depend on the nature of those courses, especially whether they start at A1 (false beginner) level, A2, B1 or above. In any case, the English courses in a licenciatura in ELT should obviously be a model of high quality ELT, which means very careful course design and selection of course teachers.

Whatever the level of the first course, all courses should be designed specifically for young adult Latin Americans (native speakers of Portuguese or Spanish) who have had many years of English classes prior to entering the licenciatura. The group size should be taken into account, with between 20 and 30 probably most appropriate, given that it's in the range of what most graduates are likely to teach (some perhaps will teach groups of under 20 in private institutions, but many with groups of 30 or above). If the licenciatura courses start at false beginner or little above, that should be given great consideration in the course design: young adults still at such a low level after 6 or more years of English classes are likely to have uncertain motivation and expectations and they need English classes that are distinctly different from (and better than) those they had at school.

To exploit the new experience of actual ELT (the courses in the licenciatura, after many years of school ELT), I suggest the following:

1. Give the new licenciatura in ELT students a semester of English course without comment or analysis.
2. At the end of the semester have one or more sessions (within the English course or in 'Introduction to ELT') focusing on that semester of English course, looking at what the teacher and students did in it, what the students liked and didn't like, comparing it to their previous English courses, etc.
3. Have short sessions of analysis at the end of every month of the English course from then on.

Those sessions should raise the licenciatura students' awareness of what tends to work and what doesn't, at least for students like themselves, from the points of view of themselves as individual students, the group in general, and the teacher.

3. The observation of ELT in the licenciatura

Most, if not all, licenciaturas in ELT in Mexico include observation of actual teaching in their programmes, often not much, if any, until the third or fourth year. They generally use videos of actual classroom teaching, and have licenciatura students observe live classes.

Videos have the advantage of being able to go into ELT contexts the university itself doesn't have (e.g., children and teenagers). It also has the advantage of allowing replays to examine specific bits of teaching in detail. I suspect that most licenciaturas in ELT have a very limited stock of videos and should try to expand and diversify it, covering the main contexts in which graduates are likely to teach.

Live observation has the advantage of 'the real, full experience' (not fixed camera angles and editing as in videos). However, it may be limited to the university's classes for adults and not include ELT for children and teenagers, which most graduates may eventually teach. That can be remedied if the university has a language centre with classes for children and teenagers, or by making arrangements with schools. The live observation that students do, individually or in pairs (with strict instructions not to talk during class observations), can be done with different observation forms and can be reported and discussed in a 'Class observation' course, or in methodology-related courses.

4. *Teaching practice*

In most licenciaturas in ELT in Mexico, actual teaching practice with groups of real students comes in the last year, as is logical. However, it takes different forms in different licenciaturas, from extensive and partly supervised teaching to very little individual teaching at all and no feedback. One plan is described as follows:

> At the Universidad de Quintana Roo (UQROO) in Chetumal, Mexico, students in the course Práctica Docente II (Teaching Practice II), have the unique opportunity to be 'immersed' in a classroom as part of their teaching practice. ...each student works with one teacher trainer in her classroom for eight hours over the course of four days, first observing, then assisting, and ultimately teaching part, or even all, of a lesson. (Mackler, 2008)

Ten years ago that may have been progressive, but today it should be considered close to the acceptable minimum. Most universities should be able to place students as assistant teachers with solid university English teachers for a whole semester, or even two semesters with different teachers. They can also be placed with experienced graduates of the licenciatura working in schools and other institutions. At least some Mexican universities have, in fact, been doing something on those lines for a long time now, even if it's not specified in their current curriculum.

Conclusion: Licenciaturas in ELT, and their focus on actual ELT

I confess that I haven't surveyed all licenciaturas in ELT in Mexico for their focuses on actual ELT with groups of real students in the four ways I've considered: recall of and reflection on school ELT, focus on Licenciatura English courses, observation of ELT (preferably in a range of contexts, through video and live), and teaching practice. However, I have the strong impression that few, if any, use the first two focuses, and that some use observation and teaching practice in a limited and weakly organized way. Where that assessment applies, change is urgently needed, and even where it doesn't apply, or not fully, improvement may be possible.

New licenciatura in ELT students are the product of school ELT, and many of them will become English teachers in schools, whether pre-school, primary, lower secondary or upper secondary. Strong evidence suggests that current results of school ELT in Mexico and most of Latin America are generally extremely poor: see *A review of two surveys of ELT in Latin America* in this book, and, assuming you're engaged in some way with a university (or normal superior) licenciatura in ELT, check the level of English of students entering your licenciatura in ELT, and of those entering other licenciaturas and specializations.

The circle of students coming from schools to be students in licenciaturas in ELT and, after four years, returning to schools as English teachers can be largely virtuous or vicious, or something in between. By spreading the focus on actual ELT with groups of real students across the whole four years, and by focusing on the students' own experience of ELT, at school and then in the licenciatura, the circle could become distinctly more virtuous.

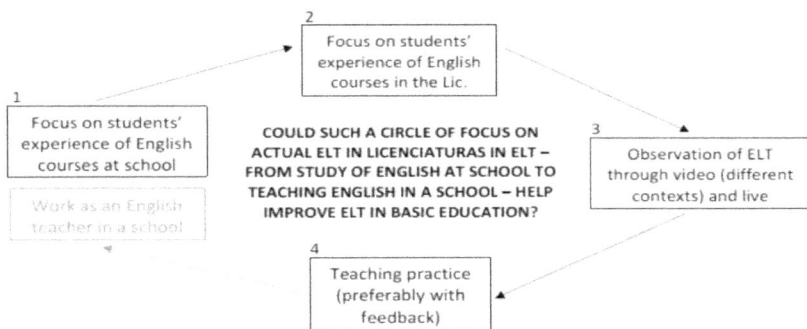

Figure 13. A circle of focus

Reference

Mackler, J. (2008). EFL practice teaching immersions: The whys and wherefores. In *MEXTESOL Journal*, vol. 32, no. 2.

23

CONTEXT AND LEARNER-CENTRED ELT TRAINING

This article arose from a talk I gave at IICIFEL at the Benemérita Universidad de Puebla, Mexico, in March, 2019. It focuses on training in Latin American university licenciaturas in ELT, but considers other types of training too. Courses vary greatly in their approaches and practices, but there's a general and probably natural tendency to focus on "the teaching of the English language (to anyone, anywhere)" and neglect "the teaching of appropriate English to specific types of student in specific types of context", sometimes almost completely. Obviously, principles and practices for teaching English grammar, vocabulary, functions and discourse patterns are fundamental to ELT, but they (the principles and practices, and the grammar, vocabulary, functions and discourse patterns) should obviously be rather different for young children, older children, teenagers and adults in different contexts, for example, public school, bilingual school, higher education, company courses, beginner courses, intermediate courses. This article kicks off from there.

Types of ELT training course and their focus

There are many types of ELT training course in Latin America. In Mexico, they range from short courses (100-200 hours) requiring B2+ English (e.g., the Anglo TTC), to 4-year licenciaturas, some requiring almost no English on entry. They all deal with 'ELT basics', and a few focus on a specific type of student and context (e.g., normal superior licenciaturas for teaching in lower secondary school), but most deal with 'general ELT'. Some ELT is indeed very general with diverse learner needs and wants, for example, in commercial language centres, where groups may include older teenagers still at school, higher education students in different degree programmes, people working in different jobs, and well-off people who frequently holiday abroad. However, most ELT in Latin America is in basic and higher education and it has fairly defined types of student in fairly specific contexts. A 4-year degree programme really should prepare graduates for some of that.

Even some shorter general ELT courses pay some attention to ELT for certain types of student in certain types of context. In 2003, I designed a new version of the Anglo's TTC. The plan included the usual 'ELT basics' (the English language, teaching language items, teaching listening skills, teaching speaking skills, teaching reading skills, teaching writing skills, lesson planning, etc.), but the very first 'topic area' was 'TEFL contexts, programmes and environments'. The first 2 of the 5 modules of that topic area are on general aspects of ELT contexts and programmes (+/− factors in TEFL, teaching objectives and stages/cycles, establishing and developing classroom English—as part of a 'positive learning environment'), but the last 3 are on specific contexts and types of student: different types of TEFL contexts and responses to them, adolescent vs. adult learners and groups (the Anglo has a separate training course for teaching children), different levels (beginner / false beginner / elementary / intermediate), analysis of real TEFL situations and responses to them (situations and responses the trainees in a given group are interested in).

Some 4-year university ELT degree programmes in Mexico include one or more context and learner related courses. I found the following in different university programmes: English-Spanish comparative linguistics (learner-centred because most Mexican students of English are native speakers of Spanish, not German, Turkish, Arabic Indonesian or Japanese), teaching children, teaching adolescents, teaching adults, teaching in basic education, English for specific purposes. However, many licenciaturas don't have any such courses at all, even as options. Graduates go out into the world and suddenly find themselves facing groups of 5-6 year old children in a school, or groups of 50+ teenagers in a school, or groups of university undergraduates in 'general English' beginners' courses for the third or fourth time, or groups of medical students or business students in A2-level ESP courses, or groups of over-worked business people in company classes, or...

Incorporating context and learner centred ELT into a licenciatura in ELT

One way to attend to context and learner centred ELT in a licenciatura is to have a course specifically on that—'Context and learner centred ELT'—probably best given in the last half of the licenciatura. Another, or additional, way is to have courses on common context and learner centred situations—'Teaching children', 'Teaching adolescents', 'Teaching adults', 'Teaching in basic education' (i.e., English as a compulsory school subject), 'English for specific purposes' (which should be the commonest ELT in higher education, though it isn't yet). Yet another way in certain cases is to integrate some attention to context and learner centredness into other courses.

Every licenciatura in ELT focuses quite a lot on the English language: English grammar, how it works and how to teach grammatical items (as such, or as exponents of notions and functions), English vocabulary, how it works and how to teach lexical items, the English language in discourse, how it works and how to teach it. But the fact that ELT for young children, for older children, for teenagers, for business people, for medical students and doctors, for globe-trotting playboys and girls, etc., should involve some different grammar, vocabulary and discourse is usually neglected. Perhaps it's simply not even considered as something to pay attention to in ELT training. I disagree: see my articles in this book on:

- English for different types of student and in different contexts—everyday colloquial, more formal spoken English, academic and technical written English, etc.
- Teaching verb patterns specifically to our Latin American students, taking their native language into account
- Selecting vocabulary for different types of students in different contexts, for example in different university degree programmes

Let's take vocabulary as an example. Should a 4-year licenciatura in ELT leave graduates with the impression that it's only *how* to teach it that matters, not *what* to teach because the textbook of a course determines that? Well, here's some of the vocabulary in the Book 1 of a widely used textbook: *aunt, beard, blouse, bracelet, carpenter, cashier, chef, cook (verb), dance, cousin, disco, furniture, game, guess, hate, jeans, lawyer, necklace, mustache, pants, ring (noun), shopping, singer, shower, supervisor, toy, wear*. Suppose that was the textbook for a beginners' course for medical students that you were giving. How many of those words would you *not* actively teach or put in a course test? What other words *would* you actively teach the medical students?

As a teacher trainer, how would you deal with this issue of English for general purposes vocabulary and groups of students who have vocabulary for specific purposes needs?

Some aspects of context and learner centred ELT that aren't related to the English language and English in discourse can be integrated into a methodology course if enough time is given to it or if it's divided into two parts, Methodology I and Methodology II, or into a Syllabus Design course that some university licenciaturas in ELT have. That may apply to teaching different age groups (children, adolescents, adults), teaching different levels (beginners, false beginners, elementary, intermediate and upper intermediate/advanced), and English for Specific Purposes. It may however, be better to attend to them in separate courses.

ESP, for example, involves many things: some kind of needs analysis and selection of appropriate English discourse types and vocabulary (which can be drawn to some extent from ESP textbooks and websites). For different ESP areas, it may be appropriate to pay more attention to some skills than to others, for example, spoken discourse (listening and speaking) for business and tourism, but not so much for medicine and chemistry, where reading is perhaps more important. Appropriate ELT In higher education contexts should mostly be ESP (Davies 2008).

A definition of "appropriate ELT"

Appropriate ELT =

- teaching selected English language: selected for specific types of student in specific types of context (see below)
- to specific types of student: young children, older children and teenagers, adults who will never travel outside their own country (the vast majority of Latin Americans, who may be sub-divided into present or future non-professional

and low-skilled workers, doctors, engineers, business
people, etc.), adults who will frequently travel outside their
country for work and pleasure and perhaps live abroad (a
minority of Latin Americans), etc.
- in specific types of study context: English as a compulsory
subject in primary school, lower secondary school, upper
secondary school, higher education, bilingual school, etc.),
and voluntary study of English in a language centre,
private class, company course, etc., and study of English in
Latin America (as opposed to the Netherlands, Germany,
Turkey, Thailand or China)

4-year degrees in ELT should work on appropriate ELT, not just
what's covered by a traditional concept of ELT, which tends to
focus on teaching "the English language" and neglect teaching
specific types of student, in specific types of context, what they
need or most likely will need.

References

Davies, P. (2008). ELT in Mexican Higher Education should be
mainly ESP, not EGP. In *MEXTESOL Journal,* vol. 32, no. 1. At
www.mextesol.net/journal/index.php?page=journal&
id_issue=28#ee90365d8f4dc8fb456f232ae5f1c966
Davies, P. (2018). Which English to focus on, Teaching English verb
patterns in Latin America, Selecting vocabulary. All in *ELTinLA* and
this book.
Davies, P. (2020). What do we know, not know and need to know
about ELT in Mexico? In *Revista Lengua y Cultura,* vol. 1, no. 2,
Universidad Autónoma del Estado de Hidalgo. At https://
repository.uaeh.edu.mx/revistas/index.php/lc/issue/archive

ELT MANAGEMENT

24

ELT COORDINATION: WHY AND HOW

Solo and collaborative ELT

When we teach English, we normally teach it alone, that is, alone in a classroom with our students. However, only teachers of private classes and those who are the only English teacher in a school really teach alone, without colleagues to turn to for ideas and support, or to offer them ideas and support. The vast majority of English teachers work with some other English teachers, often many of them.

Unavoidable solo teaching (private classes or as the only English teacher in a school) can be satisfying and worthwhile for teacher and students, but it tends to be professionally isolated unless an effort is made to read about ELT a lot (now facilitated by the Internet) or attend ELT association events, and can be a struggle for inexperienced teachers and be unfavourable for their development.

Solo teaching in schools or institutions with colleagues is unnecessary, unprofessional and bad, but it happens a lot. In extreme cases, where all or most of the teachers, perhaps 5, 10, 20 or even more, are solo teaching, typically behind closed classroom doors, it can be very disconcerting and discouraging for students and severely impede their progress in English. It can mean that some teachers use only English in class while others use the students' native language a lot, some teachers insist on correct English all the time while others accept errors in communicative activities, different teachers use different textbooks (or no textbook), different teachers give their own different tests, and so on.

Working as a novice teacher in a school or institution without coordination, or with scant or poor coordination, can also be discouraging and severely impede a teacher's progress in ELT, though some do manage to develop fairly well anyway. Two and a half of my first four and a half years in ELT were in such institutions (6 months in 1960 in an English institute in Zaragoza, Spain, while I was still at university, and 1965-6 in the Universidad Autónoma de Puebla's Prepa or high school—now much improved). Fortunately, before my two years in Puebla I'd had two years in two well-coordinated institutions in Madrid (particularly the British Council institute), so I had ideas and criteria to work with. Also, while teaching in Puebla, I attended several teachers' seminars at the Instituto Anglo Mexicano de Cultura (now The Anglo Mexican Foundation) in Mexico City, another very well-coordinated institution, which gave me more grist for my mill.

In 1967, I began work at the Anglo as director of its branch in the south of the city, required, like all branch directors, to give a number of classes as well as run the branch. I was suddenly in ELT management and coordination as well as teaching, but with guidance and support from head office and the main institute. After a year or two there, on top of my previous experience, I was very aware of the enormous benefit of coordinated ELT within an institution, both for the teachers and the students. The teachers benefit from the consistent approach, the carefully selected materials, the teachers' meetings, the feedback on class observations, the common tests, and the teamwork in general. The students benefit from the fruit of all that, the consistency and quality control of the courses in general.

Obviously, to be really good for teachers and students, the coordination should promote current best practice in ELT, taking the specific students and contexts into account (which may sometimes mean quite conservative methodology and unambitious goals, for example, with groups of 40+ unmotivated students).

How coordinators actually coordinate

As a past EFL teacher (without and with coordination), ELT coordinator (and general manager, in a good English institute) and EFL teacher trainer and ELT consultant (seeing all sorts of schools, universities and other institutions, without coordination and with good and bad coordination) I've seen a broad panorama of ELT coordination, in Mexico at least. And I've seen many different specific scenes or situations, from different perspectives. Here are four scenes, painted for me again and again by trainees on teacher's courses, particularly Cambridge COTE (which, if you didn't know, preceded ICELT):

A. *My coordinator won't listen to our ideas and suggestions. It's her way or the highway. That wouldn't matter if her way were good, but she's really old-fashioned. Most of the things we've seen in this COTE course are anathema to her. She sometimes visits our classes and tells us to stop doing those things! And the tests, which she writes...*

B. *My coordinator doesn't really coordinate at all apart from doing the timetable and allocating teachers to courses. Well, we do all use the same textbooks, but in different ways. It's chaos, except for a couple of teachers and me. We get on well and exchange ideas. But that's just three out of nineteen teachers. The teachers write their own tests. Except the three of us, who share our tests.*

C. *My coordinator's really good. She has a nice manner for a start, very friendly and open, but professional and, when it comes to it, clear and decisive. I'm really happy at my school, and proud of the results we get— all of us together, the school, the coordinator, the teachers, the students. Oh, I must rush—we've got a teachers' meeting this afternoon!*

D. *I'm the coordinator, since last month. And, frankly, I'm lost. The one before me was terrible, and he was so conflictive. The atmosphere among the teachers is very bad still. That may be the first thing for me to work on. But how? Two teachers were his friends—the last coordinator's—and the rest weren't, to put it mildly. At least he's left the Language Centre. If he'd stayed as a teacher!*

As a teacher or a coordinator, or both, you may recognize those scenes and recall others. They can make you nod approvingly, smile, laugh, groan, or cry.

The good news is that C is quite common nowadays, as more and more trained teachers enter ELT and fewer untrained ones. But it depends on character, of course, not just professional training: "She has a nice manner… very friendly and open… when it comes to it, clear and decisive". Also good news, and partly for the same reason (more and more trained teachers), is that bad coordination or absence of coordination in institutions can often be corrected fast if there's the will, either from above (owners, management) or below (teachers, even students).

The bad news is that there's still a lot of bad coordination and absence of coordination around, for all sorts of reasons, some of them contextual and difficult to overcome (e.g., a poorly funded school in a marginalized area—though amazing things sometimes happen in marginalized communities) and some of them political, in the broadest sense.

Any institution that wants the improved ELT results that can come from good coordination should aim to make it a part of the culture of the institution: once an institution (and the people in it) has enjoyed good ELT coordination and the results from it, any fall in the quality of the ELT coordination begins to sound alarm bells. It also means that the next coordinator can be apprenticed to the present one.

What to coordinate and work on

Institutions with English classes, and those dedicated to teaching English, vary in many ways, and what some can insist on is beyond others, for example, just a few institutions in Latin America have the luxury of employing only educated native speakers of English and non-native speakers with C1+ level certification in English. However, good ELT coordination should try to push the English courses in any institution to the highest level possible for that institution. The following guidelines and suggestions, based on current best ELT theory and practice, should be interpreted in that light, more completely in favourable ELT contexts and more modestly in less favourable ones. My recommendations and suggestions are:

1. *Teachers' English.* Most Latin American English teachers need to work at maintaining and improving their command of English. Coordinators can promote that by having regular teachers' meetings and workshops in English—and even conversation and book club sessions over drinks and snacks! This can be especially useful where English is rarely spoken, outside EFL classrooms, in your town or area.
2. *English as the main classroom language.* Coordinators should establish this as strict policy, and help teachers achieve it, with techniques and ideas. There may be exceptions for some circumstances or aims, for example, technical reading courses for higher education students with little or no English (or time).
3. *Selection and use of textbooks.* Coordinators should involve

teachers in the selection of textbooks, and get agreement on how to use them, especially giving importance to the communicative work in the books and not putting excessive time and emphasis into the language work and consequently neglecting communicative work. Again there may be exceptions for some circumstances or aims.

4. *Learner-centredness*. Coordinators should help teachers see clearly who they're teaching English and why (often there's no good reason, so classes must at least be interesting or fun), and therefore the appropriate methodology (e.g., very game-like for children, and inductive in higher education), and the appropriate adaptation and supplementation of the textbook, for example, local and national examples and references for general English, and medical reading texts for medical students.

5. *Class observation and feedback*. Coordinators should, if possible, periodically observe teachers' classes, discreetly and empathetically, and talk about the class with (not just *to*) the teacher afterwards, focusing a lot on how students responded and participated (or didn't). If teachers can be persuaded to visit one another, it's a positive thing; a start to that can be made if the coordinator invites teachers to visit (by arrangement) his or her classes.

6. *Tests*. Coordinators should ensure all teachers give the same tests, or key ones. The teacher's guide or website of the textbook may provide them, or the coordinator can adapt them from some other source; if proficiency tests are a goal, for example, Cambridge KET, PET and FCE, parts of them can be used.

The actual teaching in an institution can be coordinated, moulded and developed by all six elements above.

Self-coordination

The post of paid ELT coordinator doesn't exist in many institutions and is unlikely to be created, but English teachers without a coordinator can get together and coordinate themselves. When two or more English teachers are working together, collaboration and coordination are always possible.

25

GENERAL CONSIDERATIONS FOR ELT MANAGEMENT

Introduction

There are many different types of ELT management situations, and roles within them, each with its own features and challenges, and different possible responses to them. By trying to cover virtually the whole of ELT management in this series of 4 articles, I'm taking on a lot and may end up being too general and superficial for many readers. However, for two reasons, I am going to take a broad, general approach, but dealing with *aspects* of ELT management, not very specific management situations and roles.

My first reason for taking such an approach is that most ELT management situations and roles don't stand alone but are connected with and dependent on others. In most cases, other situations and roles, above or below, should be taken into account. For example, in Mexico and other Latin America countries, public basic education ELT syllabuses, guidelines and sometimes textbooks, are produced at national level; norms for the employment and supervision of English teachers are established at national or state level;

those norms are ignored by some school principals, who may also take key ELT decisions even though they can't speak English; in some schools there's ELT coordination, but in others teachers use different methodology (in spite of the national syllabuses) and give different tests. Imagine the challenge facing a teacher in a newly created ELT coordination post in a school with the worst combination of the above who wants to improve ELT for the specific students in the school and the local context. Perhaps you don't have to imagine!

My second reason for taking a broad, general approach is that almost every ELT management situation is unique in some ways and continually changing, so fixed formulas and prescriptions, even for a specific type of ELT operation, are seldom enough in practice. Good ELT management requires astute observation and analysis of the specific situation, followed when necessary by adjustments or changes. These may require considerable creativity and agility on occasions, as well as steadiness in general. For example, setting up and running a branch of an ELT institute is likely to be significantly different right now in São Paulo and in Porto Alegre in 2030. In the public sector, ELT programmes in Mexican secondary schools should be different (but aren't), or be implemented differently, in Mexicali (state capital on the US border), León (industrial and commercial city in central Mexico), Cancún (international beach resort, with tourist sites nearby), and Comitán (small town near the Guatemalan border). ELT managers have to deal with quite different situations in those different places, and at different moments in time.

Apart from those two reasons for taking on virtually the whole panorama of ELT management (or aspects of it, and focusing on Latin America) rather than focusing on one or two specific ELT management situations or roles, I'm emboldened by the wide range of ELT management work I was involved in, directly and indirectly, over some 50 years.

What is ELT management?

"The organisation and coordination of the activities of an ELT enterprise or operation". We could argue out a more detailed definition, but I'll take the one above as my starting point. What can organising and coordinating the activities of an ELT operation involve? Well, in the private or independent sector for example, when setting up a new ELT enterprise or trying to radically change and improve one that's working very poorly, it can include all the following, while with an ELT operation that seems to be working quite well it would probably start at number 5:

1. Researching and analysing the context of the proposed ELT enterprise (with the target students at its heart) and the resources available, and establishing objectives
2. Developing a plan for the ELT enterprise, including types and design of the EFL courses to be offered, as well as other services, like certification through proficiency tests, and premises, promotion, etc.
3. Finding and organising the requirements and resources for implementing the plan
4. Promoting and launching the ELT enterprise
5. On-going organisation and coordination of the ELT operation, partly routine and cyclical (periods or dates for promotion, timetabling, enrolment, course starts/tests/results, proficiency tests, teacher workshops, etc.), and partly reactional, trouble-shooting and developmental (teacher substitutions, students' complaints, staff problems-firing-hiring, on-going teacher development, change of textbooks, etc.)
6. Evaluation of the ELT operation, which might lead to modifications, or even to radical change, perhaps meaning a return to 1 above

The different aspects or components of ELT management above can include many sub-components.

Initial and fundamental questions in ELT management

Researching and analysing the context of a proposed ELT enterprise or operation and the resources available, and establishing objectives (1 above) can mean very different things in different ELT cases. For example, if two or three English teachers, either with their own resources or with a business sponsor, are considering setting up an ELT centre or school, they should answer questions like these:

1. Where are we going to aim our offer of courses—at adults, teenagers, children, all those, other?
2. Is there room in our city/area for such a commercial ELT centre or is the market already saturated?
3. If there is room, where would a good location be, are premises available there, and what might start-up costs be, and then running costs?
4. How much should/can we charge for courses (checking existing language centres' fees), how much income might that generate (compare that with estimate of running costs)?

After answering such questions and more, the teachers might abandon the project, or they might move on to detailed and costed planning (2 above).

If, however, a new private primary-secondary school is being set up, some of the above questions would apply to the school as a whole, but ELT of some kind would be predetermined—you simply can't run a private school today without English classes throughout the curriculum. The first question that should be asked specifically about ELT might be: Should we aim at 'ordinary school ELT' or should we make 'high quality school ELT' a feature of the school? In other words, who are we aiming at—parents mostly only just able to pay for a private school or those able to pay, within reason and market norms, "whatever it takes to get the best"? According to the answer to that question, other questions follow.

ELT management in basic public education is a very different matter from the two examples above. In contrast to those examples of ELT operations, ELT in national public education is non-profit and, from the evidence, distinctly loss-making in Latin America in terms of 'profit-in-kind from investment'. That profit-in-kind, or benefits arising from the ELT, includes:

- Satisfied parents and school-leavers. (Currently, most parents and children in Latin America recognise that little English is learnt in public schools—or in many private ones.)
- Satisfied 'requirers' of English speakers. (Currently, institutions of higher education, employers in areas where English is needed, and so on, find that most students from public schools—and from many private ones—start higher education, vocational training or work with little or no English).
- Improved national or regional economy. (All Latin American countries have foreign trade, investment and tourism, but they could be increased with more good English speakers, as could the quality of a country's scientists and other professionals.)

Also, in public education in Latin America ELT is never now a completely new operation (like a new language centre or private school) because there has been ELT in secondary schools for many decades. ELT In public education could, however, be radically changed (even virtually re-started). The most fundamental question then would be: How can we significantly improve on the results of our current ELT in public schools (which most honest ELT managers in public basic education in Latin America would recognise to be, not only unsatisfactory, but very poor)? That question, and different answers to it, is the topic of the next article, Management of ELT in Basic Education.

Management of up-and-running ELT operations

Setting up or radically modifying an ELT operation is an occasional or one-off project or challenge, while keeping an ELT operation running well is the continuous challenge of ELT management. Again it will be significantly different for different ELT situations, with some roles existing within certain situations and not others. Just consider the ELT in all the different schools, public and private, in the different cities and regions of your country; add the different institutions of higher education; add the different language centres, commercial and non-profit, individual or part of a chain of language centres; add the ELT management decisions taken by educational authorities in your city, state or nation. What can I say about up-and-running ELT management that applies to most of those—and in just half a page or so?

Well, let's go to point 6 in the section above sub-headed 'What is ELT Management?': "Evaluation of the ELT operation, which might lead to modifications, or even to radical change, perhaps meaning a return to 1 above." Too many ELT operations do little or no evaluation of how they're working and, obviously, the management of the on-going ELT operation is usually weak or worse as a consequence.

Some ELT operations do have built-in evaluation instruments or systems (from occasional questionnaires for students and other stakeholders to boards or committees that meet regularly and consider results), or even pay for periodic external evaluations. However, some don't pay much or any attention to what's revealed. The consequences can be fatal for some ELT operations and chronically unhealthy for others.

Without continual evaluation and effective responses to it, ELT operations that depend on their clients' voluntary support (the income, recommendations to other potential clients, etc., that they provide) usually soon go into decline and eventually have to be terminated. In commercial and non-profit but self-supporting ELT centres or institutes and private bilingual schools, there are powerful incentives for good ELT management: profit/sustainability vs. loss/closure, employment vs. unemployment from the staff's perspective. Poor or conflictive ELT managers are usually soon 'let go' by such ELT operations or, if they're owner-managers, their ELT enterprise sickens and dies under them.

In contrast, ELT operations not dependent on the students' and other stakeholders' support and the vital financing they provide can continue endlessly with poor (or worse) results and unhappy or indifferent students and stakeholders. Such is the case in many 'ordinary' private schools, where English is just one of many subjects and one in which parents are used to pass (and even high) grades in English even when their children clearly remain far from being able to communicate in the language. It's also the case in the massive ELT operations in public education.

To maintain or improve the quality of their ELT management, operations dependent for their survival on student/stakeholder satisfaction must answer questions like the following two, and operations not dependent on student/stakeholder satisfaction (nor learning results) *should* answer such questions:

1. Are our English courses and related services good enough to make the time students invest in them worthwhile? For example, Cambridge Assessment estimates up to 200 hours of guided study (in-class and required out-of-class study

time) for each CEF level, so courses should generally achieve something not too far from that.

2. If our 'customers' (students, parents, institutions of higher education, employers requiring speakers of English, etc.) are not satisfied with our courses and services (irrespective of number 1 above), what can we do, within our budget, to satisfy them?

26

MANAGEMENT OF ELT IN BASIC EDUCATION

Almost all children and teenagers now study English at school, and that's where they're supposed to get a good start at learning the language. In countries where a considerable percentage of people speak English as a foreign or second language, like in northern Europe, most do indeed reach a functional level in English at school, mostly public school. However, in countries where only a small percentage of people speak English, like in Latin America, most of those learn it in private schools, higher education or language centres, not in public schools. In both types of country, ELT in schools is by far the largest area of ELT, for better or worse (better in northern Europe and worse in Latin America, for example).

Good models for ELT in basic education, that is, in schools

Naturally, we'd like ELT in basic education in our particular Latin American country, and in Latin America in general, to become significantly better and more effective than it is. Models of effective ELT and ELT management in schools may help us achieve that more than theory and grand plans, and there are good models in Latin America as well as in Europe and elsewhere. Most of the best models in Europe are public schools, but in Latin America most are private schools, though far from all of them. In some Latin American countries there are also public schools that are good models, but very few of them.

What makes certain Latin American private schools good models of ELT and ELT management? Among other things:

- The ELT is well planned and coordinated from pre-primary or primary through to upper secondary.
- The ELT is well coordinated across all teachers, who are expected to work as a team.
- Teachers that don't live up to expectations are 'worked on' and, if they don't respond, 'let go'.
- From their first year at the school, students see older students above them improving in English level by level and, expecting to improve in the same way, they do.
- Groups have a maximum of 30 students in them, usually less, and the conditions are generally good.
- Each school is independent and responsive to its local context, not locked into an enormous regional or national system, with its bureaucracy and political vagaries.

As I said above, only certain schools are good models, and most (almost all public schools and many private ones) don't get anywhere close. In the case of public schools, the first and the last points above are highly consequential. There is no good planning and coordination of ELT across all the school levels (ELT usually starts at beginner level in lower secondary, even after English in primary, and again in upper secondary), and external bureaucracy and politics can impact negatively on ELT in different schools all around the country (in the case of Mexico, that means from Tijuana on the border with the USA to Tapachula near the border with Guatemala, almost 4,000 km away).

That's almost all I'll say about ELT management in individual Latin American schools. I'll just add that, apart from the development of coordinated courses (with materials, tests, etc.), and the team leadership and management of teachers referred to above, many other things are usually part of ELT coordination in a school: timetabling and allocation of classes to teachers, substitution of absent teachers, records of students' results, etc. To learn more about good ELT management in a school, if you need to, you could identify one or more private schools (not bilingual) in your city or area with a reputation for good ELT and try to find out what they do. Perhaps your school is one of them!

Ministry of education management of ELT in Latin American public basic education

I'll now move on from effective ELT management in individual schools, which is vital for ambitious private schools, but often difficult or almost impossible in public schools, precisely because of what I'm moving on to: ministry of education management of ELT in public basic education.

One typical element in that management in many countries in Latin America is the imposition of the same syllabuses and course guidelines on all public schools across the country (e.g., as mentioned above, from Tijuana to Tapachula in Mexico, where ELT programmes and materials should really be 'rather different'). Another is increasingly strict enforcement of the requirement that English teachers in public schools should have an ELT-related degree (from an Escuela Normal or one of the many universities that now have Licenciaturas in ELT). That's very positive, but the continued imposition of the same syllabuses and course guidelines across the country, inappropriate in itself, indicates that the central authorities don't trust the increasingly professional body of English teachers with key ELT decisions. They may be recognising that many teachers are still not professional and some are crudely improvised (especially in public primary ELT), but imposed syllabuses and guidelines won't help much, if at all, in those cases.

Key tasks in ministry of education management of ELT in public basic education are to evaluate results and, if necessary, make changes in order to improve them. In Mexico (and other Latin American countries) results seem to have been informally evaluated over a decade ago and found to be extremely poor, an assessment that matched research on the level of English of students entering higher education (most with beginner English) and estimates of the percentage of adult Mexicans with a functional command of English (perhaps 10-15%). The response, attempting to improve results, was to start moving towards what has produced excellent results in northern Europe and good results further south: starting ELT in public primary schools. But Mexico (and the rest of Latin America) isn't Europe.

That approach was probably taken not only because of the example of Europe, but also because, "as everyone knows, young children learn languages better than older ones, adolescents and adults". Well, that's popular wisdom anyway, but the facts (as far as they're ascertainable) aren't so simple. Research and observation suggest that after late childhood it becomes more difficult to acquire an almost native command of a language (especially pronunciation), but that is acquired only in immersion-type contexts such as living in an English speaking community or attending a bilingual or semi-bilingual school. In other words, not only will it not be acquired in Mexican public primary schools as they are today, but little more than a bit of 'parrot English' will be learnt in most. And it's important to set against that the observable fact that teenagers and adults can learn a foreign language well (perhaps you're an example of that—I am). In fact, I'd bet that most English teachers in Latin

America, certainly those in public schools, didn't get much beyond A1 level until their late teens or as young adults in higher education. I certainly know many English teachers with excellent English for whom that's the case.

So starting ELT at the beginning of primary school isn't the only way, or necessarily the best way, to improve results, and it doesn't work at all unless the ELT is high quality, as in northern European public schools. Also, centralised imposition of the same syllabuses and course guidelines (one size and style for all) on public schools across a country, especially a large and varied one, may not be a good idea even though it's hard to break from that 'tradition'. In the case of Mexico, it would perhaps have been much better some 10 years ago to explore and evaluate different options in different parts of the country or the educational system.

A very negative assessment of the results of current ELT should take ELT managers in ministries of education back to the first of the six ELT management steps in the first article in this series: "Researching and analysing the context of the ELT enterprise and the resources available, and establishing objectives". A comparison of a European and a Latin American context and its resources is revealing:

———

THE NETHERLANDS

Almost all Dutch people need or want English because Dutch is hardly used outside their country and little used on the Internet, in business, science and technology. English is widely used in work in the Netherlands. Most Dutch people are well-off and frequently travel outside their tiny country.

The Netherlands is a rich country that can afford very high quality public education. There's no shortage of English teachers with excellent English and high quality ELT training.

Appropriate objectives for ELT in public basic education in Netherlands: 100% of students should leave school (aged 17-18) with B1+ level English, many of them with B2+.

————

MEXICO

Mexico is a 'middle-income country', still struggling to eradicate poverty, provide quality public education, etc. Even for the current ELT in public basic education there's a shortage of competent English teachers.

Most Mexicans don't need English or want to put in the work to learn it because Spanish is a major international language, used in many countries (including USA), on the Internet, etc. Most available work in Mexico doesn't require English. Few Mexicans have the money for frequent (or any) foreign travel.

Appropriate objectives for ELT in public basic education in Mexico: Around 25% of students should leave school (aged 17-18) with A2+ level English, some of them with B1+.

————

If you accept that "around 25% of school leavers with A2+ level English, some of them with B1+" is a realistic and appropriate target for a country like Mexico, these questions, among others, arise:

1. *Shouldn't having around 25% of schools leavers with A2+ level*

English as the target for ELT in basic public education lead to a different approach from having 100% with B1+ level English as the target? My answer is most definitely yes, it definitely does call for a very different approach (or approaches).

2. *Who are the 25% that really need English?* Obviously, they include most school students who continue to higher education, and others who go into certain types of vocational training in upper secondary education. They can't be identified in public primary schools, but in lower secondary schools students begin to show the academic and technical abilities they'll carry into their adult lives, and in upper secondary school career ambitious begin to become clear. There's strong logic (considering all the above, including early-age language learning), for keeping ELT only in lower and upper secondary public schools, though in some places (US border, international vacation centres, major commercial-industrial cities) ELT in primary school may be a good investment and really benefit many students if ELT of satisfactory quality is affordable.

3. *How can we make sure those specific people do reach A2+ level in English (some with B1+ level) by the end of upper secondary (aged 17-18)?* Well, the best option (perhaps different ones in different places) isn't known until different options are actually tried out and evaluated. However, one thing is clear: the students must obviously receive good quality ELT, close to that offered in private schools with good ELT, or in commercial and university language centres, or the very best ELT currently offered in public schools—not the junk ELT or ELT in almost impossible conditions (pity the English teachers!) that most school students in Latin America get at present, with the results we know well.

Options for trying to make sure those who need English can actually get it

This is the next step for ELT managers, Step 2 of the six ELT management steps in the in the previous article, General Considerations for ELT Management: "Developing a plan for the ELT enterprise, including types and design of the EFL courses to be offered, as well as other services, like certification through proficiency tests". In the case of ELT in public basic education, I've suggested that different options should be explored first. Here are some possibilities:

A. Extend ELT down into public primary school, or even pre-primary.

[This is the option currently in progress in Mexico, with 'political' and other interruptions and modifications. It seems to be a costly general failure so far, because of lack of financial and human resources, and a lack of integration of primary, lower secondary and upper secondary ELT, among other things.]

B. Work hard on improving the quality of ELT in lower and upper secondary schools (stopping **A** completely), for example, eliminate any remaining unqualified English teachers (with some qualified teachers from primary schools probably available to replace them), split groups for English classes where they're over 30 students, encourage English teachers to adapt courses to local contexts (US border vs. international vacation centre vs. industrial city vs. rural area), make A2 the starting point of upper secondary ELT with students entering below that level put into an intensive remedial English programme, pay bonuses to school staff other than English teachers (especially school principals) with certified B1+ English and involve them in English classes and extra-curricular activities in English.

C. Shift ELT to a 3 year curricular + language centre model (Davies 2009). The 3 years of curricular (compulsory) English could be at the end of primary school and/or the beginning of lower secondary school. After those 3 years of curricular English for all public school students, English courses would be free for anyone under the age of 18, 19 or 20 in ministry of education language centres in schools after regular classes, and with ministry of education vouchers in university language and commercial language centres (where they might be able to study French, German, Chinese, etc., instead of English). That's what actually happens in most of Latin American now, except that the language centre classes aren't free: many students and parents give up on the English classes in public school, or want to go beyond it, and register in a university or commercial language centre. The cost (and hassle) for the ministry of education would probably be less than extending ELT to the beginning of primary up, and the results would be much better (evidence suggests that voluntary and motivated study of a language tends to produce much better results than compulsory study).

D. De-centralise almost completely, letting local educational authorities and/or individual schools (i.e., the English teachers in a school) do whatever they want, just providing them with very general guidelines and options, and with an ELT support website. It couldn't be much worse than at present in general, and some local educational authorities and/or individual schools would almost certainly start standing out with much better than average results, examples for the rest.

All four of those options could be tried out in different places: **A** continuing where it's currently working best, **B**, **C** and **D** where a state, a city, a group of schools or individual school volunteers to run a project for a period of several years. Then results of **A**, **B**, **C** and **D** (and possibly **E**) should be compared and new decisions taken, perhaps dropping one or two of the options and continuing with 2 or 3, where they're wanted or considered best for the local context. Why bet everything on a single plan for the whole country? So far, most, if not all, such big bets have resulted in losses, many of them enormous.

Reference

Davies, P. (2009). Strategic management of ELT in public educational systems. In *TESL-EJ*, vol. 13, no. 3. At http://www.tesl-ej.org/wordpress/issues/volume13/ej51/ej51a2/

27

MANAGEMENT OF ELT IN HIGHER EDUCATION

In some countries, English at B1+ level is taken for granted in students entering higher education. In Mexico and other Latin American countries, however, even prestigious private universities receive 10%, 15%, 20% or more of their new students with little or no English, and in other private universities and almost all public institutions of higher education (IHEs) from around 50% to over 90% of the new students enter with little or no English. That's in spite of up to 12 years of English classes at school.

Most IHEs in Mexico have responded to this situation by requiring undergraduates to take compulsory English courses, but generally only up to A2 level. Most students entering IHEs, often almost all, are placed at beginner level in these courses, and have to study all the general English they covered at school again, for the third or fourth time. In most IHEs this approach has worked very poorly, with many, and often most, students graduating still with little English. Some reasons for this general failure are fairly obvious; for example, the groups in the compulsory English courses generally range from 40 students up to 60 or more (I won't name the specific university I know that has groups of 80 students). There are clearly better ways to manage ELT in higher education than that.

There are, of course, IHEs in Mexico that receive most of their students with substantial English, like the prestigious private universities mentioned in the first paragraph above, and even some public ones like the Colegio de México. There are also a few that do notably better than most at getting their students from beginner or low elementary level up to a certified intermediate level by the time they graduate. The focus of this article is on the majority of IHEs in Mexico and other Latin American countries, most of whose new students enter with little or no English.

Evaluation, and back to the drawing board

In a previous article, General Considerations for ELT Management, I presented a 6-step approach to ELT management, and I'll apply some of it now to ELT in Mexican and other Latin American IHEs. Since almost all already have ELT operations, the first thing to do is to evaluate that current ELT and its results, which is actually Step 6: *Evaluation of the ELT operation*.

My assessment of ELT in most Mexican IHEs, based on observation, information and comments from ELT staff, and published studies, is that most students enter with little or no English, and many, if not most, graduate still with little English, even after compulsory English courses. Some IHEs achieve better results, particularly in university language centres, where students can take classes voluntarily and up to higher levels, but my general assessment suggests that something is radically wrong with the compulsory ELT in most Mexican IHEs, and it calls for radical change, based on a return to Step 1.

Step 1: Researching and analysing the context of the ELT operation

The full specification of this step in Part 1 of this series of articles is: *Researching and analysing the context of the proposed ELT enterprise (with the target students at its heart) and the resources available, and establishing objectives.* In this case, an ELT operation (compulsory, or common core, English courses for undergraduates) is already running in most IHEs, but generally failing. A significant investment is being made in these courses, but most students graduate still with little English. The ELT operation needs to be radically changed, or replaced with something quite different and much more effective.

One factor that may contribute to the failure was mentioned above: large groups, sometimes with 50, 60 or more students. The IHEs appear to be making a gesture towards "the importance of English in today's world", but a largely empty gesture, with a largely wasted investment. Another factor might be the repetition of essentially the same general English syllabuses as in lower and upper secondary school (not very motivating for the students), and there must be more factors. An analysis of the context, with particular attention to the students, should suggest better ways to achieve what the IHEs would like, which is to have most, if not all, students graduate with a functional level in English (B1+, say, which is a good springboard for autonomous learning through actual use of English).

Here are some typical aspects of the ELT context in Latin American IHEs:

A. ELT in IHEs is preceded by 6 to 12 or more years of ELT in school education that leaves most students still at beginner level (in some cases, courses from pre-school to upper secondary school).

B. The impact of that failure on students entering an IHE may include a dislike of English as a subject of study, low expectations of ever learning English, and poor motivation for the compulsory IHE English courses.

C. IHE students are all among the segment of the general population of the country that's most likely to need English (especially for professional study, work, and continuous up-dating and development).

D. IHE students are grouped by areas of study such as health sciences, business studies, engineering, and hospitality and tourism.

E. IHE English courses have professionally trained and coordinated teachers (most public universities in Mexico have degrees in ELT and the teachers of their compulsory English courses are graduates).

F. Other ELT staff in IHEs have high levels of professional development, especially in universities, including MAs and PhDs in ELT or related areas.

I invite you to think about the above points in relation to your IHE and/or others that you know about, considering the possible implications for the ELT that should be offered to undergraduates in future.

Whatever those course are to be, they should take into account the resources available and the objectives of the courses. The resources start with E and F above, human resources. Is the current ELT staff adequate and adequately organized or does it need to be improved? If so, that may mean extra cost, as might other aspects of resources, like classroom space/time, materials and aids. The resources an IHE has and would like for ELT eventually comes down largely to cost: can the current budget for ELT be better deployed, and can it even be increased as an investment in notably better ELT results?

The objectives of the courses might be essentially the same as at present (though, at present, they're presumably not being achieved), for example, to get all students to a certain level in English by the time they graduate, such as A2+ or B1+. However, they might also include objectives related to points A-D above: to motivate students after their generally bad school experiences of ELT, to provide students with the English they're most likely to need (for higher studies, professional work and continuous development).

All that takes us to the next step in ELT management, as presented in the in the article referred to previously, General Considerations for ELT Management.

Step 2: Developing a plan for the ELT operation

It's impossible, of course, to develop a specific plan without a specific IHE context and some key decisions on objectives, resources and budget. However, considering points A-F above, the general approach, within the allotted budget, should try to:

Make beginner and elementary English courses notably different from those students had at school. Students should not feel that they're virtually repeating what they studied (and failed to learn) at school, but that English is now more necessary or potentially useful for their professional studies and future lives, and that the IHE teachers are making the courses not only different but better for them.

From the start, incorporate a strong element of EAP in the courses, and where possible actual ESP. This in itself (in contrast to EGP—'English for no particular purpose') will make the courses different from school English courses, and better for the students, that is, more appropriate for their professional studies and future working lives (Davies 2008).

Ensure reasonably good conditions for the English courses in terms of real class time, teaching-learning materials and aids, maximum group size, etc. English courses with few real classroom hours, without modern materials and aids, and in very large groups generally achieve very poor results, and are a largely wasted investment. They convey to students the IHE's lack of real seriousness about the teaching and learning of English, with a negative impact on students' attitudes.

There are different ways in which English courses for undergraduate students can be planned and offered in an IHE, but they should all take the above points into account and relate to the objectives of teaching English and any requirement that students reach a certain level in English to graduate. The general objective is, presumably, to enable students and graduates to be the best professionals they can be in the modern world. Any minimum target level set within an IHE should be realistic (otherwise few students will graduate simply because they haven't reached the level of English required), and should vary from degree programme to degree programme, for example, higher for Tourism and Hospitality, International Trade, International Relations, etc., and lower for Accountancy, Architecture, Social Work, etc. The level required for students in the latter category to graduate might be just A2 at first (as it is now in many IHEs in Mexico), but it can be raised if more and more students begin to enter higher education with better English than now (see the previous article, Management of ELT in Basic Education).

Here are some of the ways in which English courses can be offered to undergraduates, taking into account the general considerations above:

Curricular English courses within a degree programme, such as Tourism and Hospitality, International Trade or International Relations. Here, English is considered an essential component of training in the professional field. A great advantage is that the ELT can and should be partly ESP, which, apart from serving the students better than EGP, can be motivating and interesting for students still at or near beginner level, and also for those with a higher level of general English but unfamiliar with vocabulary and texts of the professional field. The target level for such degree-related English courses should be at least B1+, and B2+ if possible.

Common core English courses within a faculty or school, such as Business and Economics, Engineering or Health Sciences. Here, English is considered useful for all students in the faculty or school but not so essential as to justify the cost of ESP for each separate degree programme. The ELT can and should be partly EAP, leaning towards the professional fields within the faculty or school. The target level for such English courses should be at least B1+, but budget limitations or IHE policy may set it at A2+ only.

Optional English courses in the IHE Language Centre. This option is possible only where an IHE actually has a language centre, and the courses are likely to be EGP only where the general public is admitted as well as IHE students and staff. This option has several advantages:

- placement of students by level (as opposed to Inglés I, II, etc., for all students in semester I, II, etc.)
- probably better conditions and context (smaller groups, courses at genuine B1 and B2 levels, teachers working as a team, language centre atmosphere, etc.)
- probably greater student motivation (voluntary study, and the points immediately above)

This option needs to be combined with strict application of the requirement of a certified level of English for graduation, of course, with students deciding how to reach that level if they don't already have it (with this IHE language centre option probably their best option).

Common core English courses for all undergraduates in the IHE, irrespective of their degree programme. The courses should be at least partly EAP.

The last option above may be the 'cheapest and simplest' one for many IHEs, but it's unlikely to be the best one. In fact, many IHEs in Mexico currently have something like it, but spoilt by being EGP, not EAP, thus virtually repeating what students had at school, and not motivating or serving them well.

The different options above can be combined within an IHE, of course, for example, with curricular ESP where English is an essential component of a degree program, and common core EAP where it isn't. ESP can also be provided in a self-access centre or online to complement common core EAP in classroom courses.

Next steps, and summing up

Steps 3, 4 and 5 in the article referred to previously, General Considerations for ELT Management, are: *Finding and organising the requirements and resources for implementing the plan, Promoting and launching the ELT enterprise,* and *Ongoing organisation and coordination of the ELT operation.* They're all important in ELT in an IHE, including the promotion of the new or radically modified courses and complementary resources, and the orientation of students about them. Each step involves a host of details, as any of you who've worked on ELT in an IHE will know. For example, Step 5 (which is really an on-going stage) includes work that's "partly routine and cyclical (periods/dates for promotion, timetabling, enrolment, course starts/tests/results, proficiency tests, teacher workshops, etc.), and partly reactional, trouble-shooting and developmental (dealing with teacher substitutions, students' complaints, staff problems-firing-hiring, on-going teacher development, change of textbooks, etc.)".

And that, after some years of the new ELT set-up, leads back to Step 6, *Evaluation of the ELT operation, which might lead [again] to modifications, or even to radical change.* Hopefully, it will in fact lead only to minor adjustments. However, even if the IHE ELT operation seems to be working well, the world around it is continually changing, and one day one of those changes should include a significant improvement in the results of school ELT. That particular outside change would call for a radical modification of ELT within IHEs. They, especially universities with ELT degree programmes, could—and, I believe, should—contribute to that outside change by promoting and sponsoring much more research into school ELT and experimentation with better options than at present. That could be enormously positive for school ELT, and for IHE ELT, shifting it up to where it should be, A2-B2 level, mostly EAP and ESP, instead of the A0-A2/B1 EGP that most IHEs offer at present.

Reference

Davies, P. (2008). ELT in Mexican Higher Education should be mainly ESP, not EG'. In *MEXTESOL* Journal, vol. 32, no. 1. At http://www.mextesol.net/journal/index.php?page=journal&id_article=992

28

MANAGEMENT OF ELT CENTRES

This is my main area of ELT management experience and expertise. For 20 years, I was a branch director at the Instituto Anglo Mexicano de Cultura (now The Anglo, part of the Anglo Mexican Foundation), including being the founder director of one of its provincial branches; for 2 years I was the central director of studies there; for 6 months I was acting director general; for 2 years I was director of operations, setting up several 'new-style' branches to compete with the many commercial English institutes that arose over the 1980s; and I did consultancy work for several university language centres, through the British Council and free-lance, up to 2012. All that should make this article of at least some use to ELT centre management staff today still, or it might make it a bunch of old man's anecdotes, or a bit of both. I'll start with a bit of anecdotal history.

Why and how ELT centres started and spread in Latin America

There were private class teachers of English in Mexico and some small ELT schools or institutes before the Instituto Anglo Mexicano de Cultura was set up in 1943, run largely by The British Council at first, and then the Instituto Mexicano Norteamericano de Relaciones Culturales in 1947. And after that, more small ELT schools opened up, but 'the Anglo' and 'Relaciones Culturales' overwhelmingly dominated the Mexican ELT centre scene in Mexico City up to the 1980s, with as many as 60,000 or 70,000 students between them, plus branches or affiliated institutes in some major cities around the country.

Then as now, the private class teachers were in ELT to make a living, and the 'commercial' schools or institutes to make a profit. The Anglo and Relaciones Culturales, on the other hand, were in ELT as part of a 'diplomatic' and 'inter-cultural' mission, directly related to the Second World War in the case of the Anglo and The British Council (promoting pro-British sentiment in a region where there might be pro-German, and pro-Italian sentiment). For that mission, they had regular cultural and social events as well as English courses. However, they were—or became—largely self-funding, so the successful 'marketing' of English courses was almost as vital for their survival as for that of private class teachers and commercial institutes. Surviving, or prospering, in the ELT marketplace is fundamental to the management of most ELT centres (except, perhaps, in those with a captive market, as in some institutions of higher education).

In the last half of the 20th century, even as more and more teenagers, and then children, received English classes at school, the adult ELT market grew extremely fast. When I started my first ELT management job, as Director of the Sucursal Sur of the Anglo in 1967, the queue of people wanting to enrol in our courses stretched around the block for two or three weeks and most courses were full before they started. Those were the days! Well, perhaps not: an Anglo branch director's job in those days included teaching several courses, coordinating and developing teachers, often substituting absent teachers, timetabling, hiring-managing-firing staff (from teachers to cleaners), trouble-shooting with staff and students, assisting with enrolments (at the reception desk through to counting the takings at the end of the day, getting home at 10pm or after), and budgeting. Advertising and promotion of courses and events was handled by the Head Office and Main Institute in Mexico City, but later, as a provincial branch director in Puebla from 1976, that was part of the job also, as well as getting the permits for it to open. Few would do that job today, and it would very likely be some kind of disaster, anyway.

Note that almost all English courses in ELT centres were for adults only until the 1980s, due, no doubt, to the increasing demand for proficiency in English in professional and skilled work and in higher professional studies, along with the general failure of school ELT. From the 1980s, the Mexican ELT centre scene—and market—began to change fast, probably as a consequence of increasing demand for English classes after regular school (for adults) and outside regular school (for teenagers and children, still with ELT generally failing in schools), the economic crisis of 1982, which shook up thinking about commercial enterprises of all kinds, and the success (and search for new markets) of commercial ELT schools and chains of schools in English-speaking countries. In Mexico, they now include the Instituto Anglo Americano, Berlitz, Harmon Hall, Interlingua, International House and Quick Learning, among others.

The arrival and growth of such commercial ELT centres hit the not-for-profit Anglo and Relaciones Culturales like an ice bucket challenge that wasn't going to stop unless they radically changed their management and organizational style and structure. The Anglo had already started courses for teenagers as well as adults, and they later started courses for children, and those became its new growth areas (not touched by many commercial ELT centres). But note that teenagers and children require new arrangements for security and care, among other considerations, which has its costs. Much more had to be changed if the old bi-cultural centres were to survive, let alone thrive. In fact, Relaciones Culturales closed down in 1993, mainly over a labour dispute, but also considering the Mexican ELT centre situation described above. The Anglo has survived very well, but is radically different now from what it was 50 years ago, or even 25, along with commercial ELT centres like those mentioned above, and the ELT (or language) centres that major universities and institutions of higher education have set up, mostly since the 1980s, many open to the general public, and with courses for teenagers and children. The Mexican ELT centre scene—and market—is rather crowded now and very competitive.

The changing styles or models of ELT centre

I'd guess that the factotum-director model of ELT centre described above is quite rare nowadays, though it probably still exists, especially in small centres with an owner-manager-teacher at the helm. Of course, a good ELT centre has really always been the product of team work and not mainly the 'heroics', acrobatics and perhaps hysterics of one person, and has also usually had some kind of shared linguistic-cultural-social life bonding many of the people, in different posts and jobs, that help make the centre run well. ELT centre teams are generally much more structured and compartmentalized now.

There's often a dedicated administrative side of the team (sometimes the dominant side now, especially in commercial language centres) and an ELT side. It's important that the administrative side should have a good understanding and appreciation of the ELT side, and that at least the top people on the ELT side should have a fair understanding of administration systems and issues too. A lack of understanding or actual misunderstanding can be highly prejudicial or fatal for an ELT centre. It helps enormously if the key people on the administrative side speak English well and continually consult and involve people on the ELT side in plans and key decisions. In fact, some of these can only be sensibly made jointly between the administrative and the ELT sides, for example, the types of course and other services to be launched as new ventures (such as courses for young children or a proficiency test) or, on the other hand, to be dropped or radically changed because of low uptake or other problems.

The administrative side of the team often has to report to a board of directors, or higher authorities in an institution of higher education, and get approval for new projects, changes of strategy and other key decisions, which may put constraints on the operation of the centre that purely ELT people don't like or even resent, calling for explanation and discussion with the ELT people. The administrative side also has to take care of things that ELT operations within regular schools don't: business (or enterprise) planning; acquiring, adapting and maintaining premises and facilities; getting permits and registrations; preparing budgets and managing finances; doing marketing and promotion; designing and developing enrolment and other customer-handling systems; and so on. All that is vital for the smooth running and success of the ELT centre, whether commercial, not-for-profit or a service provider within an institution of higher education or other community.

Within the environment created and maintained by the administrative side (a favourable one for ELT, it is to be hoped), and in collaboration with the administrative side, the ELT side has to do its best for the students and customers (who may include the parents of children and teenagers).

The English language teaching in ELT centres (or language centres)

Here are some of the basic questions and considerations for ELT courses and services in centres dedicated to the teaching of English (or English and other languages):

What courses and other services to offer?

Unless this is largely pre-determined (e.g., in a university language centre, most courses will be for undergraduate students, and in a large company's language centre, for staff), decisions on the courses to offer should initially be based on market research or assessment, which might lead to courses for adults only, for children and teenagers only, or for both, and perhaps for preparation courses for a specific set of proficiency tests. After a centre has been running for some years, initial decisions may be revised based on how the operation has been going and on requests from students and would-be students (e.g., by request, courses for children and teenagers might be added to the original ones for adults only, and more intermediate and advanced courses and fewer beginner courses might be offered as students progress upwards).

Some chains of ELT centres specialize in a limited range of 'products and services' (like fast-food chains and other businesses), but even they should be open to change and innovation as demanded by the market and as opportunity offers.

Most ELT centres have a very mixed student population, which usually calls for general purpose English courses (EGP), but some have a more defined population, which may allow (and actually demand) some kind of ESP (e.g., Business English in ELT centres in business areas of metropolitan cities, and English for Hospitality and Tourist Services in ELT centres in holiday resort areas).

What ELT approach, or approaches, to take?

Long gone are the days when the choice seemed to be among a few defined methods or approaches (Audio-Lingual or Structural-Situational or early CLT or even Natural Approach). But some ELT centres still have a 'proprietary approach/method', perhaps embodied in textbooks produced in-house by a chain of ELT centres, or consisting of strict guidelines for the use of a series of textbooks selected from those available on the open market. Such approaches usually have a brief training course or programme for new teachers (even those with a degree in ELT and considerable experience), and regular supervision through class observations to ensure that teachers stick to "our approach".

Certainly, it's very important for all teachers in an ELT centre to take essentially the same approach in their ELT, and common textbooks, teachers' meetings and class observations (among teachers as well as by supervisors) are usually fundamental for that. However, I believe it's usually best when teachers add something of themselves to their ELT, and—very importantly—try to attend to the needs and wants of specific groups and of students within each group. Also, it's not rational or professional to be using the same approach with the same materials year after year and decade after decade: not only is ELT likely to have evolved significantly over a decade, but the market also.

The best ELT centres I've known have depended on their ELT coordination and teaching staff to maintain high quality ELT and to develop and modify it when appropriate, and have tried not only to *get* good ELT people but to *keep* them. ELT staff should be capable of moving with the times, as well as responding to their customers' needs and wants.

These needs and wants may be quite homogeneous (e.g., adults only, wanting/needing English for a variety of purposes, which means EGP methodology and materials) or they may be clearly differentiated (e.g., young children, teenagers, adults, perhaps some of the last wanting preparation courses for fairly academic or professional proficiency tests like TOEFL or IELTS). In that latter case, significantly different approaches and materials are required for the different types of student in different courses, and large language centres can benefit from dedicated coordinators, for example, for children's courses, for teenagers' courses, for general adults' courses, for proficiency test courses. There may even be specific purposes courses for adults (e.g., English for Academic Purposes courses in a higher education language centre, and the courses in Business English and English for Hospitality and Tourist Services mentioned above). These may call for notably different approaches to ELT, for example, much more reading of formal texts than usual for EAP, and more work on prepared spoken presentations of information in Business English.

How to create a favourable language learning environment in an ELT centre (and attract and hold customers)?

Most ELT is done in environments and in classrooms not set up specifically for ELT. Schools (with the exception of bilingual ones) usually treat English as just another subject, along with maths, geography, biology and the rest, and classes for all subjects (except laboratory and workshop ones) take place in the same classrooms and school environment. In many schools, one notable aspect of that environment is that English teachers are the only members of staff who speak English (sometimes not very well), and in almost all schools very few other members of staff do. In Latin America, most public schools (which serve around 90% of the population) have beginner-elementary English courses in lower secondary school (not to mention primary school), and again in upper secondary school, and yet again in higher education for students who continue to that level. Most school students never see, or become, intermediate or advanced level learners of English because nobody progresses beyond A2, and few get even that far. Some of them, or their parents, turn to ELT or language centres, where the environment is, or should be, the opposite.

English (perhaps along with other languages) is the *raison d'être*. The whole centre is, or should be, themed for the learning of English, with posters (some with substantial texts to read), notices and other things in English on the walls and doors. All the teachers are ELT (or other language) specialists, and other members of staff also speak English. Perhaps even more important, there are students at intermediate and advanced level, who speak English outside the classroom with teachers, and perhaps among themselves.

Some of that, especially the students at higher levels, may not exist in a brand new ELT centre, but it should be built over the years as students progress upwards in the centre: in year 3, 4, or 5, some of the students who entered as beginners in the first year or two should be in upper intermediate and advanced courses, and there may eventually be more of those courses than courses for beginners.

Almost all aspects of a good and developing ELT centre can be exploited to attract and hold customers. They should all contribute to its strongest element—its reputation, which can only be built on good ELT and results. Most people first visit or call an ELT centre because they've heard good things about it (as they say, the best marketing is done by satisfied customers). When they enter the centre, prospective customers should be favourably impressed (posters and notices in English, people speaking English, helpful and efficient staff). After some weeks of their first course there, and again and again after, they should feel that they're really learning English at last, or that they're progressing better than before. Then they may mention the centre positively to relatives, friends and colleagues, and a virtuous circle has begun to turn, or an existing one is kept turning.

That virtuous circle has to be oiled and maintained, of course. Any significant decline or blip in the quality of ELT, other ELT services, and customer attention services can affect its motion, and even reverse it into a vicious circle. And don't think everything can be controlled. What can be called 'fortune' can affect even the best ELT centre negatively—things like an economic recession, another and more 'aggressive' centre opening nearby, a shift of potential customers away from the area of the centre, and perhaps, one day, a miraculous improvement in public school ELT. Then you'll need all your ingenuity, pragmatism, and, perhaps, stoicism.

APPENDIX

Other articles published in *ELTinLA online magazine*

The CEFR and other matters. Interview of Richard Rossner, former Editor of the *ELT Journal*, CEO of the Bell Educational Trust and Director of Eaquals, and currently a member of the Council of Europe's coordinating group on the linguistic integration of adult migrants. October, 2018.

ELT realities in Latin America, and… um… a modest proposal. Jeremy Harmer, ELT writer and presenter. November, 2018.

Reengineering ELT in a Mexican state university. Edward Amador, Verónica Espino, Claudia Hernández and Laura López, Universidad Autónoma del Estado de Hidalgo, Mexico. December, 2018.

ELT in a Mexican university's language centres. Interview of Celso Pérez, Director, Facultad de Lenguas, Benemérita Universidad Autónoma de Puebla, Mexico. February, 2019.

Developing an ELT platform for Latin American students in higher education. Jorge Hernández, Universidad Autónoma del Estado de Hidalgo, Mexico. March, 2019.

Reading is fun for young children. Angela Llanas, ELT writer and presenter. April, 2019.

Teaching English in Mexican indigenous, multicultural and multilingual contexts. Rebeca Tapia, Benemérita Universidad Autónoma de Puebla, Mexico. June, 2019.

Food for thought on government English programmes for children and teenagers. Paul Davies. August, 2019.

Confessions of an EFL textbook writer. Paul Davies. September, 2019.

Teaching English in Mexican public primary schools. Angela Llanas, ELT writer and presenter. October, 2019.

Team teaching in a BA in ELT course, and in general. Martha Lengeling and Amanda Wilson, Universidad de Guanajuato, Mexico. November, 2019.

ELT and… un cuento navideño. Paul Davies. December, 2019.

Teachers' perceptions of ELT in public secondary schools in the State of Guanajuato. Martha Lengeling and Amanda Wilson, Universidad de Guanajuato, Mexico. February, 2020.

Inductive, deductive… or seductive?. Paul Seligson, ELT writer and presenter. March, 2020.

———

NOTE: All the above people have extensive experience of ELT in Latin America, especially Mexico, including those not currently based there.

ABOUT THE AUTHOR

Paul Davies retired in 2018 after 55 years in English Language Teaching, based mostly in Mexico. His main places of work were the Instituto Anglo Mexicano de Cultura (now The Anglo Mexican Foundation), The British Council Mexico, and several Mexican universities.

In the Universidad Autónoma de Puebla, in 1965 and 66, he taught in the Preparatoria Benito Juárez (High School) and the Departamento de Lenguas. In the Anglo, between 1967 and 1991, he was Branch Director, Director of Studies and Director of Operations.

In The British Council, between 1992 and 2012, he was an EFL teacher trainer and Senior ELT Consultant. In the Universidad Autónoma del Estado de Hidalgo, between 2013 and 2018, he was the team leader and main author of the *Make It Real!* ELT materials project. He also taught in public secondary school for 2 years, and did teacher training in that sector, organized by The British Council and the Mexican Secretaría de Educación Pública. In 1973 he was a Founder Member of MEXTESOL and its first Parliamentarian, and later President of the Puebla Chapter and National MEXTESOL President.

He co-authored EFL textbooks for Mexican public secondary schools published by Macmillan and by Oxford University Press. Apart from *Make It Real!*, his 21st century publications include *Success in English Language Teaching* (Oxford University Press, 2000),

Skyline and *Sky High* (Macmillan, 2001 and 2006). He also had many ELT articles published, in *MEXTESOL Journal, ELT Journal, Modern English Teacher, English Teaching Professional, TESL-EJ,* and *Revista Lengua y Cultura (UAEH).*

Between August 2018 and July 2020, he published, edited and wrote articles for the 24 monthly numbers of an open access online magazine, *English Language Teaching in Latin America.* This book contains most of his articles in that magazine and citation of articles by other contributors.